Japanese in Plain English

HELLO
my name is

キャサリン

Ms. Kathleen Johnson-Cosrnus

Japanese
in
Plain English

Boye De Mente

PASSPORT BOOKS
a division of *NTC Publishing Group*
Lincolnwood, Illinois USA

1991 Printing

Published by Passport Books, a division of NTC Publishing Group,
4255 West Touhy Avenue, Lincolnwood (Chicago), Illinois 60646-1975 U.S.A.
© 1987 by Boye de Mente.
Manufactured in the United States of America.
Library of Congress Catalog Card Number: 86-60033.

1 2 3 4 5 6 7 8 9 ML 9 8 7 6

Contents

Part Two: Glossary of Useful Vocabulary 51-237

(An English-Japanese wordlist of more than 1,200 words and expressions, arranged alphabetically, with sample sentences in English and Japanese)

Preface

With *Japanese in Plain English*, you can actually learn to understand and speak Japanese in a very short time. You will quickly learn to pronounce more than 1,200 high-frequency words and expressions, and be able to use them in practical sentences that will enable you to *communicate* in Japanese.

Keep in mind that most of us, in going about our routine activities, use only 600 to 800 words a day. Thus, if you master the words and expressions in this book, you should be able to get by in most everyday situations in Japanese.

Of course, we are not saying that you will know the Japanese language in great depth. But you can learn some very important—and useful—Japanese in just a few minutes; and what you learn you can use immediately.

The words and example sentences included in *Japanese in Plain English* were chosen to be of immediate, practical use to anyone who comes in contact with Japanese people traveling or living abroad, and to anyone who is going to Japan for business or pleasure. The words and expressions in this book will be of particular interest to people whose jobs bring them in frequent contact with

Preface

the Japanese: airline pilots, flight attendants, Customs officials, taxi and bus drivers, hotel employees, restaurant personnel, bartenders, tour guides, and shop clerks.

The organization of *Japanese in Plain English* follows a natural progression from pronunciation, dealing with numbers, time, days, weeks, months, and dates to handling practical situations that arise in everyday life. These words and expressions are presented in the first part of the book.

The second part features an extensive bilingual glossary. Designed to be totally functional, the glossary provides one or more sample sentences for each entry, allowing the first-time user to actually engage in a conversation in Japanese. The list is organized alphabetically according to the English word, with the Japanese equivalent and its pronunciation next to each entry. Sample sentences are provided in English and Japanese, with the pronunciation of the entire sentence spelled out in an easy-to-use phonetic system designed especially for this book.

Japanese in Plain English is the fastest and surest way to communicate in Japanese . . . so away with your inhibitions! Learning *and* using Japanese can be both valuable and fun.

Boye De Mente
Tokyo, Japan

Part One: Demystifying the Great Barrier!

*T*his handbook is designed to serve as a simplified guide for English-speaking people who have had little or no experience with the Japanese language. It can be used immediately, without prior preparation or study if you so desire, because learning how to speak some Japanese is not nearly as difficult as it has been made out to be. Every Japanese word in this book has been phoneticized in English, so all you have to do is read or say the phonetics in their standard English pronunciation and what you say will come out as Japanese!

Language and Pronunciation Hints

The Japanese language is made up of syllables that are based on only six key sounds—five vowel sounds, *a* (ah), *i* (ee), *u* (uu), *e* (eh), *o* (oh), and *n* (pronounced like the *n* in the word "bond"). Prior to the 1860s, Japanese was written only in the very complicated Chinese ideograms called *kanji* (kahn-jee) and two simplified script forms called *hiragana* (he-rah-gah-nah) and *katakana* (kah-tah-kah-nah).

Dr. Charles Hepburn, one of the first American missionaries to enter Japan after the country was opened to the West in 1854, worked out a system of writing Japanese with the familiar ABCs.

This system of spelling out Japanese words in Roman letters, called *roma-ji* (roe-mah-jee), which means "Roman letters," made it possible to study and learn the language without having to master the tremendously complicated Chinese ideographs the Japanese have used to write their language for well over 1,000 years.

A person who has never heard Japanese spoken can learn how to pronounce it correctly in just a few minutes. That's right! Just a few minutes. People who claim the language is difficult to pronounce are mistaken. They confuse the difficulty of getting several unfamiliar words out in a smooth flow with pronunciation, which is simply making the sounds of individual words.

By following very simple directions explained in this book, you can teach yourself to pronounce Japanese properly in just 20 to 30 minutes. This will allow you to begin communicating in the language immediately.

If you do not have the time or patience to memorize the pronunciation charts provided, go directly to the text of the book. Every Japanese word and sentence in this book is spelled out phonetically.

All you have to do is read or pronounce the phonetically spelled version as if it were English!

Once again, all but one of the syllables in the Japanese language are based on the five vowel sounds *a, i, u, e, o,* which are pronounced ah, ee, uu, eh, oh. The one exception is represented in our alphabet by the letter *n,* and is pronounced like the *n* in the word "bond" or "ring."

Remember, all Japanese words are combinations of the following syllables. Learn how to pronounce the syllables and you can pronounce any Japanese word!

Japanese Pronunciation Chart #1
(In Japanese and Phonetically)

A	**I**	**U**	**E**	**O**
ah	ee	uu	eh	oh
KA	**KI**	**KU**	**KE**	**KO**
kah	kee	kuu	kay	koe
SA	**SHI**	**SU**	**SE**	**SO**
sah	she	sue	say	soe
TA	**CHI**	**TSU**	**TE**	**TO**
tah	chee	t'sue	tay	toe
NA	**NI**	**NU**	**NE**	**NO**
nah	nee	nuu	nay	no
HA	**HI**	**HU**	**HE**	**HO**
hah	he	who	hay	hoe
MA	**MI**	**MU**	**ME**	**MO**
mah	me	moo	may	moe
YA	**I**	**U**	**E**	**YO**
yah	ee	uu	eh	yoe
RA	**RI**	**RU**	**RE**	**RO**
rah	ree	rue	ray	roe
	(Trill the *R's* a bit if you can)			
GA	**GI**	**GU**	**GE**	**GO**
gah	gee	goo	gay	go
	(As in "geese")			
ZA	**JI**	**ZU**	**ZE**	**ZO**
zah	jee	zoo	zay	zoe

DA	JI	ZU	DE	DO
dah	jee	zoo	day	doe

BA	BI	BU	BE	BO
bah	bee	boo	bay	boe

PA	PI	PU	PE	PO
pah	pee	puu	pay	poe

Pronunciation Chart #2

(The following 33 syllables are combinations of some of those appearing above. Pronounce the two-part phonetic aids rather rapidly, "binding" the parts together. Pronounce other combinations as one syllable.)

RYA	**RYU**	**RYO**
re-yah	re-yuu	re-yoe
	(Trill the *R's* a bit)	

MYA	**MYU**	**MYO**
me-yah	me-yuu	me-yoe

NYA	**NYU**	**NYO**
ne-yah	ne-yuu	ne-yoe

HYA	**HYU**	**HYO**
he-yah	he-yuu	he-yoe

CHA	**CHU**	**CHO**
chah	chuu	choe

SHA	**SHU**	**SHO**
shah	shuu	show

KYA	**KYU**	**KYO**
q'yah	que	q-yoe

PYA	**PYU**	**PYO**
p'yah	p'yuu	p'yoe

BYA	**BYU**	**BYO**
b'yah	b'yuu	b'yoe
JA	**JU**	**JO**
jah	juu	joe
GYA	**GYU**	**GYO**
g'yah	g'yuu	g'yoe

Again, the secret of pronouncing Japanese words correctly is simply to enunciate the above phonetics at normal speaking speed, so that p'yuu comes out as one word instead of P—yuu. Also note that unlike English and some other languages, Japanese is not intonated. In other words, each syllable is given equal stress.

With a little practice you will be able to recognize the individual syllables in any Romanized Japanese word you see (and many of those that you hear). With a few exceptions the syllables are always pronounced the same way. (The exceptions are slight changes that make the pronunciation easier.)

For example, the pronunciation of the Japanese word for "lawyer" is *bengoshi* (bane-go-she), which consists of four syllables: *be-n-go-shi.* The word for "goodbye," *sayonara* (sah-yoe-nah-rah), also has four syllables: *sa-yo-na-ra.* By the way, the literal meaning of *sayonara* is "If it must be so!"—a very poetic way of expressing this sentiment. The word for "trip," *ryoko* (rio-koe), has two syllables: *ryo-ko.*

In fact, the Japanese are so conditioned to pronouncing words in syllables, that all of the thousands of foreign words (with English now in the majority) that have been absorbed into the Japanese language are automatically broken up into approximations of the familiar Japanese syllables and pronounced as if they were Japanese!

For example, "blue" becomes *bu-ru* (buu-rue). "Baseball" becomes *be-su-bo-ru* (bay-sue-boe-rue). "Strike" becomes *su-to-ra-i-ku* (sue-toe-rye-kuu), and so on.

It is now virtually impossible (or at least almost unheard of) for a Japanese to talk for more than a few minutes without peppering his or her conversation with Japanized foreign words.

Interestingly enough, there are perfectly good Japanese words for some of the English, French, and other foreign terms the Japanese have adopted, but they prefer the exotic flavor or nuance imparted by the foreign words.

On occasion the combination of two or more Japanese syllables forms the sound of a common English word. For example, the syllables *ko* and *n* when joined are pronounced exactly like the word "cone." In Japanese, *kon* is a shade of blue.

The pronunciation of the syllable *shu* (also a word), is just like "shoe." *Ju* is pronounced like "jew," and so on. In some instances I have used such words as substitutes for other phonetic spellings just to show there is nothing at all mysterious about pronouncing Japanese.

After you have read a Japanese word or phrase slowly a few times, practice saying it at ordinary speaking speed to get away from the bookish or slowed-down tape-recorder sound. In any event, don't be afraid to speak with an accent.

There are two other very important points I would like to make about learning and using a foreign language, specifically where Americans are concerned. Americans who speak only English have an irrational tendency to automatically compare whatever foreign language they encounter with English, and say such things as: "That's backwards! That doesn't make any sense! Why do they say it that way?"

This automatic comparison and criticism sets up a block in their minds, because they can't or won't accept the foreign language for what it is—a language that may be just as good as English, if not better (at least for expressing some things).

The result, of course, is they almost never learn more than a smattering of the language (while continuously complaining about how complex and how hard or how "dumb" it is).

In English we say, "I'm going shopping." In Japanese one says, *"Watakushi wa kaimono ni ikimasu"* (Wah-tock-she wah kie-moe-no nee ee-kee-mahss). Or, "I shopping am going."

The Japanese sentence says exactly the same thing the English sentence says. It is grammatically correct. It is perfectly fluent. It makes sense. It is not backwards. It is different from English, but that doesn't make it weird or wrong.

The Japanese do not distinguish between singular and plural. The meaning is clear from the context or it is explained.

If you are even half-way serious about learning enough Japanese to communicate on just a basic level, do *not* question the grammatical construction of the language! Don't even think about it! You will be much better off if you totally ignore the grammar of the language until you have become so familiar with the patterns of sentences that the right usage comes to you automatically. You do this by memorizing whole sentences; and by repeating them aloud (ALOUD!) many times, they and their construction become permanently imprinted on your brain.

This brings up a second vital point. The only way to learn to speak a foreign language is to *speak* it. That means you must commit to memory not only words but sentences as well.

The way to memorize sentences and words in a

foreign language is to repeat them over and over, particularly in the "right" or "living" context.

The primary difficulty in learning to speak a new language is not memorizing the vocabulary and grammar, but in mechanically saying sounds!

Our mouths have to be mechanically conditioned to make the new sounds smoothly and clearly—and this can be achieved only through repetition, by saying the word or sentence over and over until it becomes automatic and requires virtually no effort at all.

So there you have the secret of effective language learning. Forget about grammar in the early stages. Speak the language as it is spoken, without questioning its construction or without being embarrassed by how you sound; and always study and practice OUT LOUD to give your mouth and ears the necessary conditioning.

Other Pronunciation Hints

In Japanese *g* is always pronounced hard as in "go." The consonants *b, d, j, k, m, n, p, s, t,* and *y* are pronounced just as they are in English. *H* is always hard as in "hey" or "hoe."

There is no true *l* sound in Japanese, and the Japanese usually substitute the *r* sound when Japanizing words that have *l*s. For example, "leisure" becomes *reja* (ray-jah). And the Japanese *r* sound is slightly trilled, as it is in Spanish. If you know Spanish pronunciation, you are way ahead of the game, since Japanese vowels and most of the consonants are pronounced just like they are in Spanish.

There is also no *v* sound in Japanese, so the *b* sound is used instead. "Vacation" becomes *ba-kan-su* (bah-kahn-sue); "volume" becomes *bo-ryu-mu* (boe-ryuu-muu).

Japanese has a fairly large number of words with double consonants, which require stressing or "holding" for the meaning to be clear. For example, *kekko* (wonderful) is pronounced *keck-koe*, with both of the adjoining *ks* clearly enunciated. *Sekken* (soap) is *sake-kane*.

The five vowels in Japanese (a, i, u, e, o) may be pronounced long or short, depending on the word. A long vowel may be represented (in printing) by a line over the letter (ō) or by doubling the vowel as in *ii* (ee) or *oo* (oh).

Another technique to indicate a long vowel is to add an additional letter. The long *e* may be written *ei;* the long *o* as *oh.*

There are also many Japanese words in which the *u* and *i* vowels are virtually silent when pronounced in ordinary speech. These will be obvious from the phonetic spellings used in this handbook.

Those Very Important Numbers

Knowing how to count and use numbers is essential in developing the ability to communicate in Japanese.

For one through 10, there are two sets of words for each number. One set, which goes only from one through 10, is native Japanese. The other set, which goes from one to as far as you want to add zeros, is Chinese in origin.

The native Japanese number words are a bit complicated, but very important to learn:

one **hitotsu** (he-tote-sue)
two **futatsu** (fuu-tot-sue)

three **mittsu** (meet-sue)
four **yotsu** (yote-sue)
five **itsutsu** (eet-soot-sue)
six **muttsu** (moot-sue)
seven **nanatsu** (nah-not-sue)
eight **yattsu** (yaht-sue)
nine **kokonotsu** (koe-koe-note-sue)
ten **to** (toe)

The second set, borrowed from the Chinese ages ago, has 10 basic numbers (just as we have in our Arabic system of 1, 2, 3, etc.) that are then combined to produce higher numbers:

one **ichi** (ee-chee)
two **ni** (nee)
three **san** (sahn)
four **shi** (she); also **yon** (yoan)
five **go** (go)
six **roku** (roe-kuu)
seven **shichi** (she-chee); also **nana** (nah-nah)
eight **hachi** (hah-chee)
nine **ku** (kuu)
ten **ju** (juu)

In Japanese, 11 is 10 plus one, or *ju-ichi* (juu-ee-chee); 12 is 10 plus two, or *ju-ni* (juu-nee); and so on: *ju-san* (13); *ju-yon* (14); *ju-go* (15); *ju-roku* (16); *ju-nana* or *ju-shichi* (17); *ju-hachi* (18); and *ju-ku* (19).

Twenty is two 10s, or *ni-ji*. Twenty-one is two 10s plus one, or *ni-ju-ichi*; 22 is *ni-ju-ni*; 23 is *ni-ju-san*, and so on.

Thirty is three 10s, or *san-ju*; 40 is *yon-ju*; 50 is *go-ju*; 60 is *roku-ju*; 70 is *nana-ju*; 80 is *hachi-ju*; 90 is *kyu-ju* (note the change from *ku* to *kyu* for ease in pronunciation).

There is a new, specific word for 100: *hyaku* (he-yah-kuu), and then the above pattern is repeated:

101 is *hyaku-ichi;* 102 is *hyaku-ni;* 103 is *hyaku-san;* etc.

One hundred and fifteen is *hyaku-ju-go* (100 + 10 + 5); 120 is *hyaku-ni-ju* (or 100 plus two 10s); 121 is *hyaku-ni-ju-ichi;* 130 is *hyaku-san-ju;* 140 is *hyaku-yon-ju;* 145 is *hyaku-yon-ju-go* (or 100 + four 10s plus 5).

Two hundred is (you guessed it) *ni-hyaku;* 300 is *sam-byaku* (euphonic change for ease in pronunciation again); 400 is *yon-hyaku,* etc.

One thousand is *sen* (sin), and the same pattern continues: 1,235 is *sen-ni-hyaku-san-ju-go.* Five thousand is *go-sen* and eight thousand is *ha'sen* (the *chi* is dropped from *hachi* to make it easier to say).

There is also a new word for 10,000: *man* (mahn). So 10,000 is *ichi-man* and 20,000 is *ni-man;* 30,000 is *san-man.*

Forty-three thousand six hundred seventy-eight is *yon-man-san-sen-roppyaku-nana-ju-hachi.*

One million is *hyaku-man,* or 100 ten-thousands. Two million is *ni-hyaku-man;* three million is *sam-byaku-man.*

Other examples:
1,200 yen = **sen-ni-hyaku en** (inn)
2,150 yen = **ni-sen-hyaku-go-ju en**
$20.00 = **ni ju doru** (doe-rue); **doru** means "dollars"
$35.00 = **san-ju-go doru**
$47.00 = **yon-ju-nana doru ju-sinto**

The Ordinal Numbers

The ordinal numbers are made by combining the cardinal number with the suffix *bamme* (bom-may). First (1st) is *ichi-bamme;* second (2nd) is *ni-bamme;* third (3rd) is *san-bamme,* and so on. The 23rd is, of course, *ni-ju-san-bamme*. (This is the 23rd thing or person. There is another way of expressing the days of the month, which is introduced later.)

Telling Time

After you learn the Japanese for "second," "minute," "hour" and the duration of time, telling time in Japanese is simple (it follows the same pattern as English, in fact).

The concept of time in the sense of hours of the day and the passing of time is expressed in Japanese by the term *ji-kan* (jee-kahn). In other words, *ji-kahn* means "time past."

The word for *"second"* is *byo* (be-yoe) and one second is *ichi-byo*; two seconds, *ni-byo*, etc.

Japanese for "minute" is *pun* (poon), *hun* (hoon) or *fun* (fune), depending on the euphonic demands. One minute is *ip-pun* (note the change from *ichi* to *ip*); two minutes is *ni-hun*; three minutes is *sam-pun*; four minutes, *yom-pun*; five minutes, *go-hun*; six minutes, *rop-pun*; seven minutes, *nana-hun*; eight minutes, *hap-pun*; nine minutes, *kyu-hun*, and ten minutes, *jip-pun*.

One hour in Japanese is *ichi-jikan*; two hours, *ni-ji-kan*; three hours, *san-jikan*; four hours, *yo-jikan*.

One o'clock is *ichi-ji* (without the *kan*). Two o'clock is *ni-ji*; three o'clock is *san-ji*, etc.

"After," as in "after the hour," is *sugi* (sue-ghee). After one o'clock: *ichi-ji sugi*. Fifteen minutes past two is *ni-ji go-jip-pun sugi*.

"Before the hour" is expressed by *mae* (my), as in "ten minutes before ten": *ju-ji jip-pun mai*.

"A.M." in Japanese is *gozen* (go-zane). "P.M." is *gogo* (go-go). "Eleven o'clock A.M." is *gozen ju-ichi-ji*. "Eleven o'clock P.M." is *gogo ju-ichi-ji*.

Time Chart

1 o'clock	**ichi-ji** (ee-chee-jee)
2 o'clock	**ni-ji** (nee-jee)
3 o'clock	**san-ji** (sahn-jee)
4 o'clock	**yo-ji** (yoe-jee)
5 o'clock	**go-ji** (go-jee)
6 o'clock	**roku-ji** (roe-kuu-jee)
7 o'clock	**shichi-ji** (she-chee-jee)
8 o'clock	**hachi-ji** (hah-chee-jee)
9 o'clock	**ku-ji** (kuu-jee)
10 o'clock	**ju-ji** (juu-jee)
11 o'clock	**ju-ichi-ji** (juu-e-chee-jee)
12 o'clock	**ju-ni-ji** (juu-nee-jee)

To express the half-hour, just add *han* (hahn) to the hour: 1:30/**ichi-ji-han**; 2:30/**ni-ji-han**. Remember *han* is not used except in the sense of the half hour. 2:35 would be *ni-ji san-ju-go-hun*.

Other examples: 2:20/*ni-ji ni-jip-pun sugi;* 15 minutes before 5/*go-ji ju-go-hun mae.*

Example Sentences

What time is it?
Nan-ji desu ka?
(Nahn-jee dess-kah?)

It is one o'clock.
Ichi-ji desu.
(Ee-chee-jee dess.)

It is five thirty.
Go-ji-han desu.
(Go-jee-hahn dess.)

What time do you leave (depart by airplane, etc.)?
Nan-ji ni demasu ka?
(Nahn-jee nee day-mahss-kah?)

Is it time to leave/depart?
Deru ji-kan desu ka?
(Day-rue jee-khan dess kah?)

I have no more time.
Moh ji-kan ga nai desu.
(Moe jee-khan gah nie dess.)

Do we still have time?
Mada ji-kan ga arimasu ka?
(Mah-dah jee-khan gah ah-ree-mahss-kah?)

Counting things

It is important to know several of the special numeratives used in Japanese to count things. One of the most important of these is *nin* (neen), used when counting people. *Ichi-nin* is "one person"; *ni-nin*, "two people"; *san-nin*, "three people"; *yon-nin*, "four people," etc.

In the case of one or two persons, there is still another way of counting based on the native Japanese system of counting from 1 through 10. "One person" is often referred to as *hitori* (he-toe-ree), from *hitotsu;* and two persons is often *futari* (fuu-tah-ree), from *futatsu.*

When to use *ichi-nin* or *hitori*, or *ni-nin* or *futari*, can be a little tricky, but *hitori* and *futari* are the most common in general conversation, and you are more likely to be correct if you use them any time you refer to one or two persons.

The numerative for counting animals and fish is *hiki* (he-kee), which may also be pronounced *piki* or *biki. Ip-piki* refers to one animal or fish; *ni-hiki* to two animals or fish, etc.

When counting books, magazines, and other bound publications, the numerative is *satsu* (sot-sue). One copy is *is-satsu* (ees-sot-sue); two is *ni-satsu*.

Hon (hone), which literally means "trunk," is used when counting round, slender objects such as poles, pens, chopsticks, fingers, ropes, legs, etc. *Ip-pon* is one; *ni-hon* is two; *sam-bone* is three, etc.

Mai (my) is the numerative used to count flat things, such as sheets of paper, stamps, boards, plates, slices of bread. *Ichi-mai* is one; *ni-mai* is two; *san-mai* is three; *yon-mai* is four.

Hai (hie) is used to count cups or glasses of liquid. One cup or glass full of something is *ip-pai*; two is *ni-hai*; three, *sam-bai*; four, *yom-bai*; five, *go-hai,* etc.

Days of the Week

"Day" in Japanese is *hi* (he) in ordinary usage and *yobi* (yoe-bee) when referring to the days of the week.

The days of the week are:

Monday **Getsuyobi** (gate-sue-yoe-bee)
Tuesday **Kayobi** (kah-yoe-bee)
Wednesday **Suiyobi** (sue-e-yoe-bee)
Thursday **Mokuyobi** (moe-kuu-yoe-bee)
Friday **Kinyobi** (keen-yoe-bee)
Saturday **Doyobi** (doe-yoe-bee)
Sunday **Nichiyobi** (nee-chee-yoe-bee)

Counting Days

When counting days in Japanese, it is common to use a derivation of the Japanese numeral system for two to 10 days, and the Chinese system for one day and from 11 on. When the Japanese system is used, "day" is read as *ka* and the word *kan* is attached to indicate the time factor:

2 days **futsuka-kan** (futes-kah-kahn)
3 days **mikka-kan** (meek-kah-kahn)
4 days **yokka-kan** (yoke-kah-kahn)
5 days **itsuka-kan** (eets-kah-kahn)
6 days **muika-kan** (muu-e-kah-kahn)
7 days **nanoka-kan** (nah-no-kah-kahn)
8 days **yohka-kan** (yohh-kah-kahn)
9 days **kokonoka-kan** (koe-koe-no-kah-kahn)
10 days **tohka-kan** (tohh-kah-kahn)

1 day **ichi-nichi** (e-chee-nee-chee)
11 days **ju-ichi-nichi**
12 days **ju-ni-nichi,** etc.

Example Sentences

I am going to stay two days.
Futsuka-kan tomarimasu.
(Futes-kah-kahn toe-mah-ree-mahss.)

What day (of the week) is today?
Kyo wa nan yobi desu ka?
(K'yoe wah nahn yoe-bee dess kah?)

Today is Sunday.
Kyo wa Nichiyobi desu.
(K'yoe wah Nee-chee-yoe-bee dess.)

I hate Mondays.
Watakushi wa Getsuyobi ga kirai desu.
(Wah-tock-she wah Gate-sue-yoe-bee gah kee-rye dess.)

But I love Fridays.
Keredomo, Kinyobi ga suki desu.
(Kay-ray-doe-moe, Keen-yoe-bee gah ski dess.)

Let's go to Las Vegas Saturday morning.
Doyobi no asa Rasu Begasu ni ikimasho.
(Doe-yoe-bee no ah-sah Rahss Bay-gahss nee e-kee-mah-show.)

What is today's date?
Kyo wa nan nichi desu ka?
(Kyo wah nahn nee-chee dess kah?)

What date will Friday be?
Kinyobi wa nan nichi desu ka?
(Keen-yoe-bee wah nahn nee-chee dess kah?)

Day / Night

> today **kyo** (k'yoe)
> this morning **kesa** (kay-sah)
> morning **asa** (ah-sah)
> midday **hiru** (he-rue)
> daytime **hiru** (he-rue)
> afternoon **gogo** (go-go)
> this evening **komban** (kome-bahn)
> tonight **komban** (kome-bahn)
> night **yoru** (yoe-rue)
> last night **yube** (yuu-bay)

Tomorrow / Yesterday

> tomorrow **ashita** (ahsh-tah)
> day after tomorrow **asatte** (ah-sot-tay)

19

yesterday **kino** (kee-no)
day before yesterday **ototoi** (oh-toe-toy)

The Week

The Japanese word for "week" is *shu*, which is pronounced just like "shoe." Adding *kan* to *shu* expresses the concept of weekly or one week's time—*shukan* (weekly).

1 week **isshukan** (ee-shuu-kahn)
2 weeks **ni-shukan**
3 weeks **san-shukan**
4 weeks **yon-shukan**

To add "half" to a week or weeks, use the already familiar *han*: two and a half weeks: *ni-shukan-han* (nee-shuu-kahn-hahn); a week and a half: *isshukan-han*.

Other variations of the week:

this week **kon shu** (kone shuu)
next week **rai shu** (rye shuu)
last week **sen shu** (sane shuu)
every week **mai shu** (my shuu)
once a week **isshukan ichido** (es-shuu-kahn ee-chee-doe)
twice a week **isshukan nido** (ees-shuu-kahn nee-doe)
all this week **kon shu ippai** (kone-shuu eep-pie)
week after next **sa rai shu** (sah-rye-shuu)

Example Sentences

How many weeks will you be here?
Koko ni nan shukan gurai orimasu ka?

(Koe-koe nee nahn shuu-kahn guu-rye oh-ree-mahss kah?)

I'll be here for three weeks.
San shukan orimasu ("I" and "here" are understood.)
(Sahn shuu-kahn oh-ree-mahss.)

The Months

The Japanese word for "month" is *gatsu* (got-sue). When used to count months, in combination with numbers, and also in other compounds, *gatsu* becomes *getsu* (gate-sue).

As can readily be seen, the names of the months consist of the numerals 1 through 12, plus the word *gatsu*.

January **Ichigatsu** (ee-chee-got-sue)
February **Nigatsu** (nee-got-sue)
March **Sangatsu** (sahn-got-sue)
April **Shigatsu** (she-got-sue)
May **Gogatsu** (go-got-sue)
June **Rokugatsu** (roe-kuu-got-sue)
July **Shichigatsu** (she-chee-got-sue)
August **Hachigatsu** (hah-chee-got-sue)
September **Kugatsu** (kuu-got-sue)
October **Jugatsu** (juu-got-sue)
November **Juichigatsu** (juu-e-chee-got-sue)
December **Junigatsu** (juu-nee-got-sue)

Counting months in Japanese requires three ingredients: the numbers, the numbering factor *ka* (kah), and *getsu* (gate-sue), instead of *gatsu* (got-sue).

In other words:

1 month **ikagetsu** (ee-kah-gate-sue)
2 months **nikagetsu** (nee-kah-gate-sue)
3 months **sankagetsu** (sahn-kah-gate-sue)
4 months **yonkagetsu** (yoan-kah-gate-sue)
5 months **gokagetsu** (go-kah-gate-sue)
6 months **rokkagetsu** (roak-kah-gate-sue)
Etc.

To add "half" to a month or months, attach *han* (hahn)—one and a half months is thus *ikagetsu-han* (ee-kah-gate-sue-hahn).

this month **kon getsu** (kone gate-sue)
last month **sen getsu** (sane gate-sue)
next month **rai getsu** (rye gate-sue)

Dates

When referring to days of the month or dates, the system used is similar to counting days. (There is a special word for the first day of the month.)

1st **tsui-tachi** (t'sue-e-tah-chee)
2nd **futsuka** (futes-kah)
3rd **mikka** (meek-kah)
4th **yokka** (yoke-kah)
5th **itsuka** (eet-sue-kah)
6th **muika** (muu-e-kah)
7th **nanoka** (nah-no-kah)
8th **yohka** (yohh-kah)
9th **kokonoka** (koe-koe-no-kah)
10th **tohka** (tohh-kah)
11th **ju-ichi-nichi**
12th **ju-ni-nichi**
15th **ju-go-nichi**
23rd **ni-ju-san-nichi,** etc.

Example Sentences

Today is the first of January.
Kyo wa ichigatsu no tsuitachi desu.
(K'yoe wah ee-chee-got-sue no t'sue-e-tachi dess.)

Thursday will be February 15th.
Mokuyobi wa Nigatsu no jugonichi desu.
(Moe-kuu-yoe-bee wah Nee-got-sue no juu-go-nee-chee dess.)

Yesterday was the 10th.
Kino wa tohka deshita.
(Kee-no wah toh-kah desh-tah.)

Tomorrow will be the 18th.
Ashita wa juhachinichi desu.
(Ahhsh-tah wa juu-hah-chee-nee-chee dess.)

When are you going to Tokyo?
Tokyo e itsu ikimasu ka?
(Tokyo eh eet-sue e-kee-mahss kah?)

The Year

The word for "year" is *toshi* (toe-she) or *nen* (nane), depending on the usage.

This year **kotoshi** (koe toe-she)
next year **rai nen** (rye nane)
last year **kyo nen** (k'yoe nane)

Next year I am going to Japan.
Rai nen Nihon e ikimasu.
(Rye nane Nee-hone eh ee-kee-mahss.)

I went to Japan last year.
Kyo nen Nihon e ikimashita.
(K'yoe nane Nee-hone eh e-kee-mahssh-tah.)

The Seasons

  spring **haru** (hah-rue)
  summer **natsu** (not-sue)
  fall **aki** (ah-kee)
  winter **fuyu** (fuu-you)

Is Tokyo cold in the winter?
Fuyu ni Tokyo wa samui desu ka?
(Fuu-you nee Tokyo wah sah-muu-e dess kah?)

Does it rain a lot in the spring?
Haru ni ame ga takusan furimasu ka?
(Hah-rue nee ah-may gah tock-sahn fuu-ree-mahss kah?)

About Names

  The Japanese word for "name" is *namae* (nah-my),
or *O'namae* (oh-nah-my) in its more polite form. (The
similarity between the spelling of the English word
"name" and *namae* is coincidental.) The polite form
of the word should be used when you are asking
someone their name (unless it is a child).

  When referring to your own name or the name of
a member of your family, the regular form, *namae,*
should be used.

What is your name?
O'namae wa nan desu ka? (The "you" is under-
stood)
(Oh-nah-my wah nahn dess kah?)

My name is De Mente.
Watakushi no namae wa De Mente desu.
(Wa-tock-she no nah-my wah De Mente dess.)

The Japanese customarily say and write their family name first, followed by their given name.

When addressing or referring to anyone other than their own children and very close friends in very informal situations, the Japanese attach the honorific *San* (*sahn*) to every name they use. *San* has the meaning of Mr., Mrs., or Miss, whichever the case may be. (The concept of "Ms." has not penetrated the Japanese culture or language.)

In other words, *Suzuki-San* may be Mr. Suzuki, Mrs. Suzuki, or Miss Suzuki. If the meaning is not clear from the context of the sentence, you must specify which individual you are referring to by saying Mr. Suzuki's Wife (*Suzuki-San no Oku-San*); Mr. (or Mrs.) Suzuki's daughter (*Suzuki-San no musume*); or Mr. (or Mrs.) Suzuki's son (*Suzuki-San no musuko*); and so on.

Keep clearly in mind that it is *not* proper for a person to use *San* when referring to himself or herself. It would be grossly impolite for me to say, "My name is De Mente-San," or "This is De Mente-San calling."

The rule is: *always* use *San* when referring to someone else: *never* use *San* when referring to yourself.

The proper way to introduce or refer to yourself is: *Watakushi wa De Mente desu* (Wah-tock-she wah De Mente dess). If someone asks your name, all you need to say is *De Mente desu*. Keep in mind that the Japanese generally do not address each other by their first names except within families and among very close, young friends in informal situations.

An older woman who has employed another woman for many years might use her first name, but men who have worked together for 50 years still address each other by their last names with the honorific *San* attached.

Foreigners can and often do get away with calling Japanese by their first names, but it should be done with special care, and should be limited to people your own age and social level or below, with whom you have developed a personal relationship—and then only in informal situations.

In a business setting, for example, a Japanese would never call another person by his or her first name no matter how close or old the relationship. (This age-old custom *is* beginning to slowly change among younger Japanese businessmen, particularly when they are dealing with Westerners.)

When a person has a title, the Japanese will almost always use the title in preference to a name. The president of a company is referred to as *Shacho* (shah-choe). A department head is referred to as *Bucho* (buu-choe); a teacher, professor, or doctor as *Sensei* (sane-say-e).

Women (but usually not men) will sometimes attach *San* to *Shacho*, *Bucho*, and similar titles if they know the individual well enough to be informal and personal, and the situation is an emotional one.

Example Sentences

What is your name?
Anata no namae wa nan desu ka?
(Ah-nah-tah no nah-my wah nahn dess kah?)

What is his/her name?
Anohito no namae wa nan desu ka?
(Ah-no-ssh-toe no nah-my wah nahn dess kah?)

Please sign your name here.
Koko de namae wo kaite kudasai.
(Koe-koe day nah-my oh kite-tay kuu-dah-sie.)

Are you Mr. Watanabe?
Anata wa Watanabe-San desu ka?
(Ah-nah-tah wah Wah-tah-nah-bay-Sahn dess kah?)

How do you spell your name?
O'namae wa do yu fu ni kakimasu ka?
(Oh-nah-my wah doe yuu fuu nee kah-kee-mahss kah?)

What is your last name?
Myoji wa nan desu ka?
(Me-yoe-jee wah nahn dess kah?)

Which one is your family name?
Dore ga myoji desu ka?
(Doe-ray gah me-yoe-jee dess kah?)

Personal Pronouns

I **Watakushi** (wah-tock-she)

There are a number of other ways of expressing the personal pronoun "I." Women often abbreviate *watakushi* to *watashi* (wah-tah-she). Men often use the masculine *boku* (boe-kuu) or *ore* (oh-ray)—both, however, require care in their usage. *Boku* is polite enough but is very informal and generally not used in formal or official situations.

Ore, though not vulgar, is used only in *very* informal situations among close friends and associates—most often in a drinking or recreational situation—

by young students exercising their machoism, and by lower-class workers and gangster types.

we
watakushi-tachi
(wah-tock-she-tah-chee)

you (plural)
anata-tachi
(ah-nah-tah-tah-chee)

he or her (common)
anohito
(ah-no-ssh-toe)

they (common)
ano-hito-tachi
(ah-no-ssh-toe-tah-chee)

you (singular)
anata
(an-nah-tah)

he or her (polite)
anokata
(ah-no-kah-tah)

she
kanojo
(kah-no-joe)

they (polite)
anokata-gata
(ah-no-kah-tah-gah-tah)

*NOTE: In Japanese it is very common (typical, in fact) to leave out the personal pronouns "I" and "you," and often "he," "him," and "she," when the meaning is clear.

For example: In "Are you going shopping?" *Anata wa kaimono ni ikimasu ka?* the *anata wa* or "you" is usually left out.

The Four Main Japanese Islands

Hokkaido **Hoke-kie-doe**
Honshu **Hone-shuu**
Kyushu **Que-shuu**
Shikoku **She-koe-kuu**

Major Cities & Towns in Japan

Aomori Ah-oh-moe-ree
Atami Ah-tah-me
Beppu Bape-puu
Chitose Chee-toe-say
Enoshima Eh-no-she-mah
Fukuoka Fuu-kuu-oh-kah
Gifu Ghee-fuu
Hakodate Hah-koe-dah-tay
Hakone Hah-koe-nay
Himeji He-may-jee
Hiroshima He-roe-she-mah
Ito Ee-toe
Itsukushima Eet-sue-kuu-she-mah
Kagoshima Kah-go-she-mah
Kamakura Kah-mah-kuu-rah
Kanazawa Kah-nah-zah-wah
Kita-Kyushu Kee-tah-Que-shuu
Kobe Koe-bay
Kumamoto Kuu-mah-moe-toe
Kyoto Ke-yoe-toe

Miyajima Me-yah-jee-mah
Moji Moe-jee
Morioka Moe-ree-oh-kah
Nagasaki Nah-gah-sah-kee
Nagoya Nah-go-yah
Nara Nah-rah
Nikko Neek-koe
Osaka Oh-sah-kah
Sapporo Sop-poe-roe
Sendai Sin-die
Shimonoseki She-moe-no-say-kee
Takamatsu Tah-kah-mot-sue
Tokushima Toe-kuu-she-mah
Tokyo Toe-ke'yoe
Wakayama Wah-kah-yah-mah
Yokohama Yoe-koe-hah-mah
Zushi Zuu-she

Famous Tokyo Area Names

Akasaka (Ah-kah-sah-kah)—A popular night club, cabaret, geisha-inn, restaurant, hotel and shopping area adjoining central Tokyo.

Akasaka Mitsuke (Ah-kah-sah-kah Meet-sue-kay)—A famous intersection in Akasaka, near the Otani, Akasaka Prince, Akasaka Tokyu and New Japan Hotels.

Akihabara (Ah-kee-hah-bah-rah)—A popular tourist attraction, this is a big electrical appliance and electronic equipment wholesale district a few minutes north of downtown Tokyo.

Aoyama (Ah-oh-yah-mah)—A large, elevated area just southwest of downtown Tokyo; with famous residential, business, and shopping areas.

Asakusa (Ah-sock-sah)—A noted entertainment/shopping district on the northeastern side of Tokyo, and a terminal for one of the popular train lines to the famous mountain town of Nikko.

Ginza (Geen-zah)—Probably the best-known of Tokyo's shopping entertainment districts; downtown.

Hakozaki-cho (Hah-koe-zah-kee-choe)—This is the location of the Tokyo City Air Terminal, which serves the New Tokyo International Airport with limousine bus service. It is 10 to 15 minutes from downtown.

Harajuku (Hah-rah-juu-kuu)—On the western loop of Tokyo's famous Yamate (Yah-mah-tay) commuter train line, Harajuku is the gateway to the spectacular Meiji Shrine, an apparel design and boutique center, a restaurant area, and a noted weekend hangout for the young—especially the avant-garde.

Hibiya (He-bee-yah)—Between the Ginza district and the huge Imperial Palace grounds, Hibiya is one of Tokyo's premiere theater, restaurant, office-building, and shopping areas.

Ikebukuro (Ee-kay-buu-kuu-roe)—Some 30 minutes from downtown Tokyo on the northwest side, Ikebukuro is a major commuter terminal, shopping, restaurant, and entertainment center.

Kanda (Kahn-dah)—One of the oldest districts in Tokyo, Kanda is noted for its universities, bookstores, publishing companies, and office buildings.

Kyobashi (K'yoe-bah-she)—In central Tokyo adjoining the Ginza, this is an office building and shopping district.

Marunouchi (Mah-rue-no-uu-chee)—In central Tokyo across from the Imperial Palace Grounds, Marunouchi is one of the city's major business/financial areas, and includes Tokyo Station, the Central Post Office, and numerous other major office buildings.

Narita (Nah-ree-tah)—This is the location of the

New Tokyo International Airport, some 40 miles northeast of central Tokyo on Chiba Peninsula.

Nihonbashi (Nee-hone-bah-she)—Once the center of Japan, Nihonbashi ("Japan Bridge") is now a noted business, financial, and department store area.

Otemachi (Oh-tay-mah-chee)—Otemachi, adjoining Marunouchi on the north, is also a major banking and business center—with several hotels in the vicinity.

Meiji Koen (May-e-jee Koe-inn)—This is Meiji Park, once the grand estate of a Daimyo lord, now a beautiful recreational/museum area in central Tokyo.

Roppongi (Rope-pong-ghee)—A noted restaurant and night club district on a low hill 10 to 15 minutes southwest of downtown Tokyo. A movie-star hangout.

Shibuya (She-buu-yah)—Another of Tokyo's many "cities within a city," Shibuya is a huge transportation terminal, shopping, dining, and entertainment center; 25 to 30 minutes southwest of downtown.

Shimbashi (Sheem-bah-she)—A commuter station, geisha district, and restaurant-bar area adjoining the Ginza. Just south of the Imperial Palace grounds.

Shinagawa (She-nah-gah-wah)—A major train stop between Tokyo Central and Yokohama; with several major hotels (Pacific, Takanawa Prince, the New Takanawa Prince) in the immediate vicinity.

Shinjuku (Sheen-juu-kuu)—An extraordinary complex of high-rise hotels and office buildings, theaters, bars, cabarets, restaurants, and the biggest and busiest commuter station in Japan—30 minutes west of the downtown area.

Yurakucho (Yuu-rah-kuu-choe)—A small area sandwiched between Hibiya, Marunouchi, the Imperial Palace grounds, and the Ginza, Yurakucho is within the heart of Tokyo, with shops, department stores, restaurants, theaters, and offices.

Sukiyabashi (Sue-kee-yah-bah-she)—This is the major intersection-gateway to and from the Ginza, Hibiya, and Yurakucho. The area abounds in shops, restaurants, bars, etc.

Tsukiji (T'sue-kee-jee)—Adjoining the Ginza on the east, this area is noted for the Kabuki Theater, a number of hotels and restaurants, and the huge Tokyo Fish & Produce Market.

Names of Famous Department Stores

Isetan Ee-say-tahn
Matsuzakaya Mot-sue-zah-kah-yah
Mitsukoshi Meet-sue-koe-she
Takashimaya Tah-kah-she-mah-yah
Toyoko Toe-yoe-koe
Marui Mah-rue-ee
Tokyu Toe-que
Seibu Say-buu

Names of Famous Tokyo Hotels

Akasaka Prince Hotel
(Ah-kah-sah-kah Puu-reen-sue Hoe-tay-rue)

Akasaka Tokyu Hotel
(Ah-kah-sah-kah Toe-que Hoe-tay-rue)

Capitol Tokyu
(Cah-pee-toe-ruu Toe-que)

Ginza Dai-ichi Hotel
(Geen-zah Die-ee-chee Hoe-tay-rue)

Ginza Marunouchi Hotel
(Geen-zah Mah-rue-no-uu-chee Hoe-tay-rue)

Haneda Tokyu Hotel
(Hah-nay-dah Toe-que Hoe-tay-rue)

Hilton Hotel
(He-rue-tone Hoe-tay-rue)

Hotel Century Hyatt
(Hoe-tay-rue Sin-chuu-ree Hie-ah-toe

Hotel Grand Palace
(Hoe-tay-rue Guu-rahn-doe Pah-ray-sue)

Hotel Pacific
(Hoe-tay-rue Pah-she-fee-kuu

Hotel Takanawa
(Hoe-tay-rue Tah-kah-nah-wah)

Imperial Hotel/Teikoku Hoteru
(Tay-e-koe-kuu Hoe-tay-rue)

Keio Plaza Hotel
(Kay-e-oh Puu-rah-zah Hoe-tay-rue)

Miyako Hotel
(Me-yah-koe Hoe-tay-rue)

New Otani Hotel
(New Oh-tah-nee Hoe-tay-rue)

New Takanawa Prince Hotel
(New Tah-kah-nah-wah Puu-reen-sue)

Okura Hotel
(Oh-kuu-rah Hoe-tay-rue)

Shimbashi Dai-ichi Hotel
(Sheem-bah-she Die-ee-chee Hoe-tay-rue)

Takanawa Prince Hotel
(Tah-kah-nah-wah Puu-reen-sue)

Names of Popular Japanese Foods

Gohan Go-hahn (Rice)
Mizu-taki Me-zoo-tah-kee (Chicken, leeks, tofu in a broth)
Nori No-ree (Dried, seasoned seaweed)
Sashimi Sah-she-me (Slices of raw fish)
Soba Soe-bah (Buckwheat noodles)
Sukiyaki Sue-kee-yah-kee (Beef, tofu, leeks, and other vegetables, in soy sauce)
Sushi Sue-she (Raw seafood on buns of rice)
Tempura Tim-puu-rah (Deep-fried breaded seafood, vegetables)
Teppan-yaki Tape-pahn-yah-kee (Grilled meat, vegetables)
Tofu Toe-fuu (Soybean curd boiled or fried)
Tonkatsu Tone-kot-sue (Breaded pork steak)
Udon Uu-doan (Long, thick, wheat-flour noodles)
Yaki-soba Yah-kee-soe-bah (Fried noodles with goulash topping)
Yakitori Yah-kee-toe-ree (Barbecued chicken, vegetables)

Key Words and Sample Sentences

Who?
Donata?
(Doe-nah-tah?)

Who is it? / Who are you?
Donata desu ka?
(Doe-nah-tah dess kah?)

What?
Nani?
(Nah-nee?)

What is it?
Nan desu ka?
(Nahn dess kah?)

What do you want to do?
Nani wo shitai no desu ka?
(Nah-nee oh she-tie no dess kah?)

What do you want to buy?
Nani wo kaitai no desu ka?
(Nah-nee oh kie-tie no dess kah?)

What do you want to eat?
Nani wo tabetai no desu ka?
(Nah-nee oh tah-bay-tie no dess kah?)

When?
Itsu?
(Eet-sue?)

When are you coming?
Itsu kimasu ka?
(Eet-sue kee-mahss kah?)

When are you going?
Itsu ikimasu ka?
(Eet-sue ee-kee-mahss kah?)

When will it be ready?
Itsu dekimaksu ka?
(Eet-sue day-kee-mahss kah?)

Where?
Doko?
(Doe-koe?)

Where are you going?
Doko e ikimasu ka?
(Doe-koe eh ee-kee-mahss kah?)

Where do you want to go?
Doko e ikitai no desu ka?
Doe-koe eh ee-kee-tie no dess kah?)

Where is it?
Doko ni arimasu ka?
(Doe-koe nee ah-ree-mahss kah?)

Common Expressions

Yes **Hai** (Hie)
No **Iie** (Ee-eh)

(*Iie* is not commonly used in Japanese. "No" is generally expressed with the negative of the appropriate verb. For example: *Tabemasu ka?* [Are you going to eat? or Do you want to eat?] *Tabemasen* [I am not going to eat.])

Hello (for use on the telephone and
to attract attention).
Moshi-moshi
(Moe-she-moe-she)

Thank you.
Arigato gozaimasu
(Ah-ree-gah-toe go-zie-mahss)

Thank you very much.
Domo arigato gozaimasu
(Doe-moe ah-ree-gah-toe go-zie-mahss)

(*Domo* is often used alone to mean "thank you." Its usage is very informal and emphatic.)

Don't mention it.
Doitashimashite
(Doe-ee-tah-she-mahssh-tay)

Good morning.
Ohaiyo gozaimasu
(Oh-hie-yoe go-zie-mahss)

Good afternoon.
Konnichi wa
(Kone-nee-chee wah)

Good evening.
Konban wa
(Kone-bahn wah)

Good night.
Oyasumi nasai
(Oh-yah-sue-me nah-sie)

Welcome.
Irrashaimase
(Ee-rah-shy-mah-say)

Please come in.
Dozo, ohairi kudasai
(Doe-zoe, oh-hie-ree kuu-dah-sie)

Excuse me! (calling attention or apologizing)
Sumimasen!
(Sue-me-mah-sin)

Excuse me/I'm sorry (apology).
Gomenasai
(Go-may-nah-sie)

Just a moment, please.
Chotto matte kudasai
(Chote-toe mot-tay kuu-dah-sie)

It's a nice day, isn't it!
Ii otenki desu, ne!
(Ee oh-tane-kee dess, nay!)

It's hot, isn't it!
Atsui desu, ne!
(Aht-sue-ee dess, nay!)

It's cold, isn't it!
Samui desu, ne!
(Sah-muu-ee dess, nay!)

What time is it?
Nan-ji desu ka?
(Nahn-jee dess kah?)

How are you?
O'genki desu ka?
(Oh-gane-kee dess kah?)

I'm fine. How about you?
Genki desu. Anata wa?
(Gane-kee dess. Ah-nah-tah wah?)

Do you speak English?
Eigo ga hanasemasu ka?
(Aa-ee-go gah han-nah-say-mahss kah?)

Do you speak Japanese?
Nihon-go ga hanasemasu ka?
(Nee-hone-go gah han-nah-say mahss kah?)

I understand a little.
Sukoshi wakarimasu
(Sue-koe-she wah-kah-ree-mahss)

What is your name?
Anata no namae wa nan desu ka?
(Ah-nah-tah no nah-my wah nahn dess kah?)

May I take a/your picture?
Shashin wo totte ii desu ka?
(Shah-sheen oh tote-tay ee dess kah?)

Please come with me.
Watakushi to issho ni kite kudasai
(Wah-tock-she toe ee-show-nee ke-tay kuu-dah-sie)

May I go with you?
Issho ni itte ii desu ka?
(Ee-show nee eat-tay ee dess kah?)

Shall I go with you?
Issho ni ikimasho ka?
(Ee-show-nee ee-kee-mah-show kah?)

Please wait here.
Koko de matte kudasai
(Koe-koe day mot-tay kuu-dah-sie)

May I see your room key, please?
Heya no kagi wo misete kudasai?
(Hay-yah no kah-ghee oh me-say-tay kuu-dah-sie?)

I am the bus driver.
Watakushi ga basu no untenshu desu
(Wah-tock-she gah bah-sue no uun-tane-shuu dess)

I will check your baggage.
Nimotsu wo azukarimasu
(Nee-mote-sue oh ah-zoo-kah-ree-mahss)

Please board the bus.
Basu ni notte kudasai
(Bah-sue nee note-tay kuu-dah-sie)

We will board in 4 or 5 minutes.
Ato shi-go-hun de basu ni norimasu
(Ah-toe she-go-hoon day bah-sue nee no-ree-mahss)

Where do you want to get off?
Doko de oritai desu ka?
(Doe-koe day oh-ree-tie dess kah?)

This is your hotel.
Kore wa anata no hoteru desu
(Koe-ray wah ah-nah-tah-no hoe-tay-rue dess)

Are you ready (to go, etc)?
Yoi dekimashita ka?
(Yoe-e day-kee-mahssh-tah kah?)

Please get ready quickly.
Hayaku yoi-shite kudasai
(Hah-yah-kuu yoe-e ssh-tay kuu-dah-sie)

Show me your passport, please.
Pasupoto wo misete kudasai
(Pah-sue-poe-toe oh me-say-tay kuu-dah-sie)

Welcome to Phoenix.
Phoenix e irrashaimase
(Phoenix eh ee-rah-shy mah-say)

How many days will you be staying?
Nan-nichi gurai orimasu ka?
(Nahn-nee-chee guu-rye oh-ree-mahss kah?)

Are you here on business?
Shigoto de kimashita ka?
(She-go-toe day kee-mahssh-tah kah?)

Is this all (of our/your baggage, etc.)?
Kore de zembu desu ka?
(Koe-ray day zim-buu dess kah?)

Please open this one.
Kore wo akete kudasai
(Koe-ray oh ah-kay-tay kuu-dah-sie)

Please open all of them.
Zembu akete kudasai
(Zim-buu ah-kay-tay kuu-dah-sie)

How many (pieces) do you have?
Ikutsu arimasu ka?
(Ee-kute-sue ah-ree-mahss kah?)

That's fine. Thank you.
Kekko desu. Domo arigato.
(Keck-koe dess. Doe-moe ah-ree-gah-toe.)

Shall I help you?
Tetsudai masho ka?
(Tate-sue-die mah-show kah?)

Where do you want to go?
Doko e ikitai no desu ka?
(Doe-koe eh ee-kee-tie no dess kah?)

Do you want to go by taxi?
Takushi de ikitai desu ka?
(Tah-kuu-shee day ee-kee-tie dess kah?)

Do you want to go by bus?
Basu de ikitai desu ka?
(Bah-sue day ee-kee-tie dess kah?)

Do you have reservations?
Yoyaku wo totte arimasu ka?
(Yoe-yah-kuu oh tote-tay ah-ree-mahss kah?)

Shall I make a reservation for you?
Yoyaku wo totte agemasho ka?
(Yoe-yah-kuu oh tote-tay ah-gay-mah-show kah?)

There is a taxi stand in front of the hotel.
Hoteru no mae ni takushi noriba ga arimasu
(Hoe-tay-rue no my nee tah-kuu-shee no-ree-bah gah ah-ree-mahss)

Special Expressions

Itadakimasu (Ee-tah-dah-kee-mahss)
Said just before eating or drinking when someone else is the host, as an expression of thanks.

Gochiso-sama deshita (Go-chee-so-sah-mah deesh-tah)
Said to the host after eating or drinking, as an expression of thanks.

Oishikatta (Oh-e-she-kot-tah)
This means "It (or that) was delicious" and is said anytime after eating or drinking something good.

O'somatsu-sama (Oh-so-mot-sue-sah-mah)
This is often said by the host as a response to being thanked by someone for treating them to a meal. It means something like, "It was really nothing—but thank you for mentioning it."

Gomen kudasai (Go-mane kuu-dah-sie)
Said to call attention to your presence when entering the foyer of a home, or shop, especially when no one is visible. Basically, it means "excuse me."

Ojama shimasu (Oh-jah-mah she-mahss)
Said when invited to enter a home, and sometimes when entering an office. It means, "I am intruding."

Ojama shimashita (Oh-jah-mah she-mahssh-tah)
"I have intruded" or "inconvenienced you," said upon leaving a home or office.

Omachido-sama deshita (Oh-mah-chee-doe-sah-mah desh-tah)
Figuratively, "I am sorry to have kept you waiting."

Shitsurei shimasu (Sheet-sue-ray-e she-mahss)
"Excuse me." Said when passing in front of someone (in a theater, for example), cutting through a line, etc.

Shitsurei shimashita (Sheet-sue-ray-e she-mahsshta)
Past tense of the above, said when you bump

someone or interfere with someone or some situation, and meaning, "I'm sorry–excuse me."

Gokuro-san (Go-kuu-roe-sahn)
Said to a person or to people after they have put in a long, hard day's work or completed any difficult task. It means something like, "Thanks for going above and beyond the call of duty."

O'kage sama de (Oh-kah-gay sah-mah day)
This figuratively means, "Thanks to you," and is said when someone asks you how you are or if things are going well. It's a way of being very polite and complimentary by giving the other person credit for your own well-being (or someone else's they might have asked about).

Parts of the Body

   Head **Atama** (Ah-tah-mah)
   Forehead **Odeko** (Oh-day-koe)
   Ear(s) **Mimi** (Me-me)
   Eyebrows **Mayuge** (Mah-yuu-gay)
   Eye(s) **Me** (May)
   Nose **Hana** (Hana)
   Mouth **Kuchi** (Kuu-chee)
   Lips **Kuchibiru** (Kuu-chee-bee-rue)
   Tooth (teeth) **Ha** (Hah)
   Chin **Ago** (Ah-go)
   Neck **Kubi** (Kuu-bee)
   Throat **Nodo** (No-doe)
   Shoulders **Kata** (Kah-tah)
   Back **Senaka** (Say-nah-kah)
   Chest **Mune** (Muu-nay)
   Bust **Baasto** (Bahss-toe)

Stomach **I** (Ee); *also* **Onaka** (Oh-nah-kah)
Arm(s) **Ude** (Uu-day)
Wrist(s) **Te-kubi** (Tay-kuu-bee)
Hand(s) **Te** (Tay)
Finger(s) **Yubi** (Yuu-bee)
Thumb **Oyayubi** (Oh-yah-yuu-bee)
Little finger **Koyubi** (Koe-yuu-bee)
Ring finger **Kusuri yubi** (Kuu-sue-ree yuu-bee)
Fingernail(s) **Yubi no tsume** (Yuu-bee no t'sue-may)
Leg(s) **Ashi** (Ah-she)
Foot (feet) **Ashi** (Ah-she)
Ankle **Kurubushi** (Kuu-rue-buu-she)
Heart **Shinzo** (Sheen-zoe)
Lung(s) **Hai** (Hie)
Liver **Kanzo** (Kahn-zoe)
Kidney(s) **Jinzo** (Jeen-zoe)
Rear **O'shiri** (Oh-she-ree)

Health Words

What is the matter? **Doh shimashita ka?** (Doe she-mah-sshta kah?)
Allergy **Arerugi** (Ah-ray-rue-ghee)
Asthma **Zensoku** (Zen-soe-kuu)
Bandage **Hotai** (Hoe-tie)
Constipation **Bempi** (Bame-pee)
Cough **Seki ga deru** (Say-kee gah day-rue)
Diabetes **Tonyobyo** (Tone-yoe-b'yoe)
Diarrhea **Geri** (Gay-ree)
Earache **Mimi ga itai** (Me-me gah e-tie)
Eye drops **Me gusuri** (May guu-sue-ree)
First-aid kit **Kyukyu bako** (Que-que bah-koe)
Heart attack **Shinzo mahi** (Sheen-zoe mah-hee)
Nausea **Hakike** (Hah-kee-kay)

Stomachache **Onaka ga itai** (Oh-nah-kah gah e-tie)

Ulcers **Kaiyoh** (Kie-yoe)

Food Names

Apple(s) **Ringo** (Reen-go)

Apple pie **Appuru pai** (Ahp-puu-rue pie)

Asparagus **Asuparagasu** (Ah-sue-pah-rah-gah-sue)

Bacon **Bekon** (Bay-kone)

Bean(s) **Mame** (Mah-may)

Beef **Biifu** (Bee-fuu)

Beef steak **Biifu suteki** (Bee-fuu sue-tay-kee)

Bread **Pan** (Pahn); **Buredo** (Buu-ray-doe)

Breaded chicken **Chikin katsu** (Chee-keen kot-sue)

Breaded pork cutlet **Tonkatsu** (Tone-kot-sue)

Butter **Bata** (Bah-tah)

Cabbage **Kyabetsu** (Ke-yah-bate-sue)

Cake **Keki** (Kay-kee)

Carrot(s) **Ninjin** (Neen-jeen)

Cauliflower **Karifurawaa** (Kah-ree-fuu-rah-wah)

Chestnut(s) **Kuri** (Kuu-ree)

Chicken **Chikin** (Chee-keen); **Tori** (Toe-ree)

Celery **Serori** (Say-roe-ree)

Corn **Tomorokoshi** (Toe-moe-roe-koe-she); **Koon** (Kone)

Crab **Kani** (Kah-nee)

Cucumber **Kyuri** (Que-ree)

Eggs **Tamago** (Tah-mah-go)

Fish **Sakana** (Sah-kah-nah)

Fruit **Kudamono** (Kuu-dah-moe-no)

Garlic **Ninniku** (Neen-nee-kuu)

Grape(s) **Budo** (Buu-doe)

Grapefruit **Gurepu-furutsu** (Guu-rape-fuu-root-sue)

Green Peas **Gurin pisu** (Guu-reen pee-zuu)

Green pepper **Piiman** (Pee-mahn)

Ham **Hamu** (Hah-muu)

Hamburger **Hanbaagu** (Hahn-bah-guu)

Ice cream **Aisu kurimu** (Ice kuu-ree-muu)

Ketsup **Kechapuu** (Kay-chah-puu)

Lemon **Remon** (Ray-mone)

Lettuce **Retasu** (Ray-tah-sue)

Lobster **Ise-ebi** (E-say a-bee)

Meat **Niku** (Nee-kuu)

Mushroom(s) (Japanese type) **Shiitake** (She-e-tah-kay)

Mushrooms **Masshurumu** (Mah-shuu-room-muu)

Mustard **Masutado** (Mahss-tah-doe)

Onion(s) **Tamanegi** (Tah-mah-nay-ghee)

Orange **Orenji** (Oh-range-jee)

Peach(es) **Momo** (Moe-moe)

Pear(s) **Nashi** (Nah-she)

Pepper **Kosho** (Koe-show)

Persimmon **Kaki** (Kah-kee)

Pie **Pai** (Pie)

Potato(es) **Jagaimo** (Jah-gie-moe); **Poteto** (Poe-tay-toe)

Rice (cooked) **Gohan** (Go-hahn)

Salt **Shio** (She-oh)

Sausage **Soseji** (Soe-say-jee)

Sauce **Sosu** (Soe-sue)

Sugar **Sato** (Sah-toe)

Salad **Sarada** (Sah-rah-dah)

Soup **Supu** (Sue-pue)

Tangerine(s) **Mikan** (Mee-kahn)

Toast **Tosuto** (Tose-toe)

Tomato(es) **Tomato** (Toe-mah-toe)

Vegetables **Yasai** (Yah-sie)

Implements

Chopsticks **Hashi** (Hah-she)
Fork **Foku** (Foe-kuu)
Knife **Naifu** (Nie-fuu)
Spoon **Supuun** (Su-pune); **Saji** (Sah-jee)

Beverages

Beer **Biru** (Bee-rue)
Coca Cola **Koka Kora** (Koe-kah Koe-rah)
Coffee **Kohi** (Koe-hee)
Milk **Miruku** (Mee-rue-kuu)
Milk, cold **Tsumetai miruku** (T'sue-may-tie me-rue-kuu)
Milk shake **Miruku sheki** (Mee-rue-kuu shay-kee)
Orange juice **Orenji jusu** (Oh-range-jee juu-sue)
Pepsi Cola **Pepushi Kora** (Pep-she Koe-rah)
Tea, black **Kocha** (Koe-chah)
Tea, green **Ocha** (Oh-chah)
Tea, black with lemon **Remon ti** (Ray-mone tee)
Water, cold **Ohiya** (Oh-hee-yah)

In a Restaurant

How many of you (are there)?
Nan mei sama desu ka?
(Nahn may-e sah-mah dess kah?)

There are three of us.
San nin desu
(Sahn neen dess)

This way, please.
Dozo, kochira e
(Doe-zoe, koe-chee-rah-eh)

Would you like coffee?
Kohi ikaga desu ka?
(Koe-hee ee-kah-gah dess kah?)

Japanese tea (green tea), please.
Nihon cha wo kudasai
(Nee-hone chah oh kuu-dah-sie)

What do you have for dessert?
Dezaato ni wa nani ga arimasu ka?
(Day-zah-toe nee wah nah-nee gah ah-ree-mahss kah?)

What would you like to have?
Nan-ni nasaimasu ka?
(Nahn-nee nah-sie-mahss kah?)

May I have a menu, please.
Menyu wo kudasai
(Mane-yuu oh kuu-dah-sie)

(To call a waiter or waitress)
Onegaishimasu!
(Oh-nay-guy-she-mahss!)

Please cook it well-done.
Yoku yaite kudasai
(Yoe-kuu yite-tay kuu-dah-sie)

The bill, please.
Okanjo kudasai
(Oh-kahn-joe kuu-dah-sie)

Part Two: Glossary of Useful Vocabulary

A

A

[There is no equivalent of the article "a" in Japanese. It is "understood."]

Abalone *Awabi* **(Ah-wah-bee)**

Do you have abalone? *Awabi ga arimasu ka?* (Ah-wah-bee gah ah-ree-mahss kah?) Yes, we have. *Hai, arimasu.* (Hie, ah-ree-mahss.) Do you like abalone? *Awabi wo suki desu ka?* (Ah-wah-bee oh ski dess kah?) Yes, I like it. *Hai, suki desu.* (Hie, ski dess.) I'm not that fond of it. *Sonnani suki ja nai desu.* (Sone-nah-nee ski jah nie dess.)

Acupuncture *Harikyu* **(Hah-ree-que)**

I would like to have an acupuncture treatment. Is there a clinic in this area? *Harikyu no chiryo wo yatte moraitai desu. Kono hen ni kuriniku ga arimasu ka?* (Hah-ree-que no chee-rio oh yat-tay moe-rie-tie dess. Koe-no hane nee kuu-ree-nee-kuu gah ah-ree-mahss kah?) Will acupuncture really help? *Harikyu wa honto ni kikimasu ka?* (Hah-ree-que wah hone-toe nee kee-kee-mahss kah?)

À la carte *Ippin ryori* **(Eep-peen rio-ree)**

How about à la carte? *Ippin ryori wa ikaga desu ka?* (Eep-peen rio-ree wah e-kah-gah dess kah?) I prefer à la carte. *Ippin ryori no hoh ga ii desu.* (Eep-peen rio-ree no hoe gah ee dess.)

About *Gurai* **(Guu-rye)**

About how much do you have (is there?) *Dono gurai arimasu ka?* (Doe-no guu-rye ah-ree-mahss kah?) About how many people are there? *Nan nin gurai imasu ka?* (Nahn neen guu-rye ee-mahss kah?) [When referring to time, "about" is *goro* in Japanese.] About one o'clock. *Ichi-ji-goro.* (E-chee-jee go-roe.) Let's leave (go out) about six o'clock. *Rokuji goro ni dekakemasho.* (Roe-kuu-jee go-roe nee day-kah-kay-mah-show.) About what time will you return? *Nanji goro ni kaeri-masu ka?* (Nahn-jee go-roe nee kie-ree-mahss kah?)

Accessories *Soshokuhin* **(Soe-show-kuu-heen)**

Where is the accessory department? *Soshokuhin no uriba wa doko desu ka?* (Soe-show-kuu-heen no uu-ree-bah wah doe-koe dess kah?) [The Japan-ized version of this word is also used: *akusesari* (ah-kuu-say-sah-ree).]

Accident *Jiko* **(Jee-koe)**

There has been an accident. *Jiko ga arimashita.* (Jee-koe gah ah-ree-mahssh-tah.) Please call an ambulance. *Kyukyusha wo yonde kudasai.* (Que-que-shah oh yone-day kuu-dah-sie.) I've had an accident. Please help me. *Jiko ni aimashita. Tetsu-datte kudasai.* (Jee-koe nee aye-mahssh-tah. Tate-sue-dot-tay kuu-dah-sie.)

Address *Jusho* **(Juu-show)**

What is your address? *Anato no jusho wa doko desu ka?* (Ah-nah-tah no juu-show wah doe-koe dess

kah?) Please write your address here. *Jusho wa
koko ni kaite kudasai.* (Juu-show wah koe-koe nee
kite-tay kuu-dah-sie.) My address is . . . *Watakushi no jusho wa . . . desu. (Wah-tah-kuu-she no
juu-show wah . . . dess.)*

Admission fee *Nyujo ryo* **(Knew-joe rio)**
How much is the admission fee? *Nyujo ryo wa
ikura desu ka?* (Knew-joe rio wah ee-kuu-rah dess
kah?) It is three dollars. *San doru desu.* (Sahn
doe-rue dess.) It is five hundred yen. *Go hyaku
en desu.* (Go he-yah-kuu inn dess.)

Adult *Otona* **(Oh-toe-nah)**
Two adult tickets, please. *Otona-no kippu ni-mai
kudasai.* (Oh-toe-nah-no keep-pu nee-my kuu-
dah-sie.) How much is adult fare? *O-tona no ryokin wa ikura desu ka?* (Oh-toe-nah-no rio-keen
wah ee-kuu-rah dess kah?) Two adults; one
child. *Otona futari; kodomo hitori.* (Oh-toe-nah
fuu-tah-ree; koe-doe-moe ssh-toe-ree.)

Aerogram letter *Kokushokan* **(Koe-kuu-show-
khan)**
Ten aerogram forms, please. *Kokushokan wo ju-
mai kudasai.* (Koe-kuu-show-khan oh juu-my
kuu-dah-sie.)

Age *Toshi* **(Toe-she)**
How old are you? *Otoshi wa ikutsu desu ka?* (Oh-
toe-she wah ee-koot-sue dess kah?) I'm 26. *Ni-
ju-roku desu.* (Nee-juu-roe-kuu dess.) You don't
look your age. *Otoshi ni wa miemasen.* (Oh-toe-she
nee wah me-aa-mah-sin.) [*Toshi* literally means
"years." The word for age is *sai* (sie). What age
are you is *Nan sai desu ka?* (Nahn sie dess kah?)
Thus, "I'm 26." can also be *Ni-ju-roku sai desu.*
(Nee-juu-roe-kuu sie dess.)]

Agent (company) *Dairiten* **(Die-ree-tane)**
Do you have an agent in the U.S.? *Amerika ni dairiten ga arimasu ka?* (Ah-may-ree-kah nee die-ree-tane gah ah-ree-mahss kah?)

Agent (individual) *Dairi-nin* **(Die-ree-neen)**
What is your agent's name? *Dairi-nin no namae wa nan desu ka?* (Die-ree-neen-no nah-my wah nahn dess kah?)

Air-conditioner *Reibo* **(Ray-e-boe);** also *Kucho* (Kuu-choe) and *Eakon* (A-ah-kone)
[The latter word is a Japanese-English abbreviation of air-conditioner.] Please turn on the AC. *Reibo wo kakete kudasai.* (Ray-e-boe oh kah-kay-tay kuu-dah-sie.) Please turn the AC off. *Eakon wo kiite kudasai.* (A-ah-kone oh keet-tay kuu-dah-sie.)

Airline (company) *Koku-kaisha* **(Koe-kuu-kie-shah)**
Which airline are you taking? *Dono koku-kaisha ni norimasu ka?* (Doe-no koe-kuu-kie-shah nee no-ree mahss kah?) That airline does not go to Chicago. *Sono koku-kaisha wa shikago wo torimasen.* (Soe-no koe-kuu-kie-shah wah she-kah-go oh toe-ree-mah-sin.)

Airmail *Koku-bin* **(Koe-kuu-bean)**
Please send this by airmail. *Kore wo kokubin de dashite kudasai.* (Koe-ray oh koe-kuu-bean day dahsh-tay kuu-dah-sie.) I want to send it by airmail. *Kokubin de dashitai no desu.* (Koe-kuu-bean day dah-she-tie no dess.)

Airplane *Hikoki* **(He-koe-kee)**
Is my plane a Jumbo 747? *Watakushi no hikoki wa Jumbo no nana-yon-nana desu ka?* (Wah-tock-she-no he-koe-kee wah Jumbo-no nah-nah-yone- nah-

nah dess kah?) The plane is late. *Hikoki wa okurete imasu.* (He-koe-kee wah oh-kuu-rate-tay e-mahss.) Is the plane going to be crowded? *Hikoki wa komimasu ka?* (He-koe-kee wah koe-me-mahss kah?)

Airport *Kuko* (Kuu-koe)

How far is the airport? *Kuko wa dono gurai no kyori ga arimasu ka?* (Kuu-koe wah doe-no guu-rye no k'yoe-ree gah ah-ree-mahss kah?) What time are you leaving for the airport? *Kuko e nanji ni demasu ka?* (Kuu-koe eh nahn-jee nee day-mahss kah?) Is this the right terminal for Japan Air Lines? *Kore wa Nihon Koku no taminaru desu ka?* (Koe-ray wah Nee-hone Koe-kuu no tah-me-nah-rue dess kah?)

Airport lobby *Kuko robi* (Kuu-koe roe-bee)

I will meet you in the airport lobby. *Kuko no robi de aimasu.* (Kuu-koe-no roe-bee day aye-mahss.)

All *Minna* (Mean-nah); also *Zembu* (Zim-buu)

[*Zembu* is usually used when referring to things; *Minna* when referring to people.] Everybody! Let's go! *Minna-San! Ikimasho!* (Mean-nah-Sahn! E-kee-mah-show!) Is this all? *Kore wa zembu desu ka?* (Koe-ray wah zim-buu dess kah?) I'll take all of them/it. *Zembu moraimasu.* (Zim-buu moe-rye-mahss.)

All right (OK) *Daijobu* also *Yoroshii* (Die-joe-buu / Yoe-roe-she-e)

Are you okay? *Daijobu desu ka?* (Die-joe-buu dess kah?) I'm all right. *Daijobu desu.* (Die-joe-buu dess.) Is that all right? *Sore wa yoroshii desu ka?* (Soe-ray wah yoe-roe-she-e dess kah?)

Alone *Hitori* **(He-toe-ree)**
Are you alone? *O'hitori desu ka?* (Oh-he-toe-ree
dess kah?) Are you going alone? *Hitori de ikimasu ka?* (He-toe-ree day e-kee-mahss kah?) *I'm
alone. Hitori desu.* (He-toe-ree dess.) [Remember,
do not use the honorific "O" when referring to
yourself.]

Altitude *Kaibatsu* **(Kie-bot-sue)**
What is the altitude in Denver? *Denba-no-kaibatsu
wa ikutsu desu ka?* (Dane-bah-no kie-bot-sue wah
ee-koot-sue dess kah?) The altitude in Phoenix
is about 1,000 feet. *Phoenix no kaibatsu wa daitai i-
sen fiito desu.* (Fee-nake-sue-no kie-bot-sue wah
die-tie e-sin fee-toe dess.)

America *Amerika* **(Ah-may-ree-kah);** also *Beikoku*
(Bay-e-koe-kuu)
[The latter literally means "Rice Country," because in the early days of Japan–U.S. relations,
the U.S. shipped a lot of rice to Japan.] Have
you been to America before? *Mae ni Amerika e itta
koto ga arimasu ka?* (My nee Ah-may-ree-kah eh
eat-tah koe-toe gah ah-ree-mahss kah?) I am an
American. *Watakushi wa America-jin desu.* (Wah-
tock-she wah Ah-may-ree-kah-jeen dess.)

Announce *Happyo-shimasu* **(Hop-p'yoe-she-
mahss);** also *Anaunsu* (Ah-nah-uun-sue)
Please announce that the bus is leaving. *Basu ga
ima sugu deru to happyo shite kudasai.* (Bah-sue gah
e-mah sue-guu day-rue toe hop-p'yoe sssh-tay
kuu-dah-sie.) Did you hear that announcement?
Ima-no happyo wo kikimashita ka? (E-mah-no hop-
p'yo oh kee-kee-mahssh-tah kah?) When will
you make the announcement? *Itsu happyo wo shimasu ka?* (Eat-sue hop-p'yoe oh she-mahss kah?)

Answer *Henji* **(Hane-jee)**

I'm sorry, I cannot answer you in Japanese. *Su-mimasen, Nihongo de henji ga dekimasen.* (Sue-me-mah-sin, Nee-hone-go day hane-jee gah day-kee-mah-sin.) I will answer you later. *Ato-de henji wo shimasu.* (Ah-toe-day hane-jee oh she-mahss.) Please give me your answer soon. *Sugu henji wo shite kudasai.* (Sue-guu hane-jee oh ssh-tay kuu-dah-sie.)

Antiques (relic) *Jidai-mono* **(Jee-die-mo-no);** (art object) *Bijutsu-hin* (Bee-jute-sue-heen); (curio) *Kotto-hin* (koat-toe-heen)

Is there an antiques (curio) dealer in this area? *Kono hen ni kotto-ya ga arimasu ka?* (Koe-no hane nee koat-toe-yah gah ah-ree-mahss kah?)

Apartment *Apato* **(Ah-pah-toe)**

Do you live in an apartment? *Anata wa apato ni sunde imasu ka?* (Ah-nah-tah wah ah-pah-toe nee soon-day e-mahss kah?) I also live in an apartment. *Watakushi mo apato ni sunde imasu.* (Wah-tock-she moe ah-pah-toe nee soon-day e-mahss.)

Apparel, Western style *Yofuku* **(Yoe-fuu-kuu)**

What kind of apparel/clothing should I take? *Donna yofuku wo motte iku ho ga ii desu ka?* (Doan-nah yoe-fuu-kuu oh moat-tay e-kuu hoe gah ee dess kah?) Can I go (dressed) like this? *Kore day ikemasu ka?* (Koe-ray day e-kay-mahss kah?)

Appetizer *Zensai* **(Zen-sigh)**

How about some appetizers? *Zensai wa ikaga desu ka?* (Zen-sigh wah e-kah-gah dess ka?) [For Western-type appetizers, hors d'oeuvres (*odo-buru*) is more likely to be used.] What kind of hors d'oeuvres do you have? *Donna odo-buru ga arimasu ka?* (Doan-nah oh-doe-buu-rue gah ah-ree-mahss kah?)

Apply *Moshikomu* **(Moe-she-koe-muu)**
I want to apply for a visa. *Bisa wo moshikomitai desu.* (Bee-sah oh moe-she-koe-me-tie dess.)
May I have an application form? *Moshikomi sho wo itadekemasu ka?* (Moe-she-koe-me show oh e-tah-dah-kay-mahss kah?)

Appointment *Yakusoku* **(Yah-kuu-soe-kuu);** also
Apointo (Ah-poe-in-toe)
Do you have an appointment? *Yakusoku ga arimasu ka?* (Yah-kuu-soe-kuu gah ah-ree-mahss kah?) I have an appointment at 8 o'clock. *Hachi-ji ni yakusoku ga arimasu.* (Hah-chee-jee nee yah-kuu-soe-kuu gah ah-ree-mahss.) Please make an appointment. *Yakusoku wo torisukete kudasai.* (Yah-kuu-soe-ku oh toe-ree-skay-tay kuu-dah-sie.) I want to make an appointment. *Yakusoku wo torisuketai desu.* (Yah-kuu-soe-kuu oh toe-ree-skay-tie dess.)

April *Shigatsu* **(She-got-sue)**
I'm going to Japan in April. *Shigatsu ni Nihon e ikimasu.* (She-got-sue nee Nee-hone eh e-kee-mahss.) The weather is fine in April. *Shigatsu ni wa tenki ga ii desu.* (She-got-sue ni wah tane-kee gah ee dess.)

Arcade (shopping) *Akeido* **(Ah-kay-e-doe)**
Is there a shopping arcade in this hotel? *Kono ho-teru ni akeido ga arimasu ka?* (Koe-no hoe-tay-rue nee ah-kay-e-doe gah ah-ree-mahss kah?) Yes, there is. It's in the basement. *Hai, arimasu. Chika ni arimasu.* (Hie, ah-ree-mahss. Chee-kah nee ah-ree-mahss.)

Arrange (get ready) *Junbi* (June-bee)
Let's get ready. *Junbi shimasho.* (June-bee she-mah-show.) Please get ready by seven o'clock. *Shichi-ji made ni junbi wo shite kudasai.* (She-chee jee mah-day nee june-bee oh ssh-tay kuu-dah-sie.) I'm ready. *Junbi dekite imasu.* (June-bee deck-tay ee-mahss.)

Arrival gate *Tochaku geito* (Toe-chah-kuu gay-e-toe)
What is the number of the arrival gate? *Tochaku geito no bango wa nan ban desu ka?* (Toe-chah-kuu gay-e-toe no bahn-go wah nahn bahn dess kah?)

Arrive (plane/Train) Tochaku (Toe-chah-kuu)
My plane arrives at 3:00 P.M. *Watakushi no hikoki wa gogo no sanji ni tochaku shimasu.* (Wah-tock-she no he-koe-kee wah go-go no sahn-jee nee toe-chah-kuu she-mahss.) We will be arriving momentarily. *Mamonaku tochaku shimasu.* (Mah-moe-nah-kuu toe-chah-kuu she-mahss.) Has the Bullet Train arrived from Osaka? *Osaka kara no Shinkansen wa tochaku shimashita ka?* (Oh-sah-kah kah-rah no Sheen-khan-sin wah toe-chah-kuu-she-mahssh-tah kah?)

Arriving passengers *Go-tochaku no kata* (Go-toe-cha-kuu no kah-tah)
Arriving passengers this way, please! *Go-tochaku no kata, kochira e!* (Go toe-chah-kuu no kah-tah, koe-chee-rah eh!)

Ask *Kikimasu* (Kee-kee-mahss)
If you have any questions, please ask. *Shitsumon ga attara, dozo kiite kudasai.* (Sheet-sue-moan gah aht-tah-rah, doe-zoe keet-tay kuu-dah-sie.)

Please ask at the Information Desk. *Uketsuke de kiite kudasai.* (Uu-kay-t'sue-kay day keet-tay kuu-dah-sie.) Please ask him/her. *Anohito ni kiite kudasai.* (Ah-no ssh-toe nee keet-tay kuu-dah-sie.)

As soon as possible *Narubeku hayaku* (Nah-rue-bay-kuu hah-yah-kuu)
Please get ready as soon as possible. *Narubeku hayaku junbi wo shite kudasai.* (Nah-rue-bay-kuu hah-yah-kuu june-bee oh ssh-tay kuu-dah-sie.)

At company expense *Kaisha mochi de* (Kai-shah moe-chee day)
I am not traveling at company expense! *Kaisha mochi de ryoko shite imasen!* (Kie-shah moe-chee day rio-koe ssh-tay e-mah-sin!)

Attraction *Yobimono* (Yoe-bee-moe-no)
Are there any special attractions in this area? *Kono hen ni tokubetsu no yobimono ga arimasu ka?* (Koe-no hane nee toe-kuu-bate-sue no yoe-bee-moe-no gah ah-ree-mahss kah?)

Attractive (person) *Miryoku-no-aru hito* (Me-rio-kuu-no-ah-rue ssh-toe)
That woman is very attractive. *Sono onna-no-hito wa taihen miryoku ga arimasu.* (Soe-no own-nah-no-ssh-toe wa tie-hane me-rio-kuu gah ah-ree-mahss.)

August *Hachigatsu* (Hah-chee-got-sue)
I'm going to Tokyo on August 15th. *Hachigatsu-no ju-go-nichi ni Tokyo e ikimasu.* (Hah-chee-got-sue-no juu-go-nee-chee nee Tokyo eh e-kee-mahss.) Is it hot in August? *Hachigatsu ni wa atsui desu ka?* (Hah-chee-got-sue nee wah aht-sue-e dess kah?) Yes, it is hot. *Hai, atsui desu.* (Hie, aht-sue-e dess.)

Aunt *Oba-San* (Oh-bah-Sahn)

This is my aunt. *Konohito wa watakushi no oba desu.* (Koe-no-ssh-toe wah wah-tock-she-no oh-bah dess.)

Automatic *Jido* (Jee-doe)

In Japan all taxi doors are automatic. *Nihon de wa takushi no doa wa zembu jido desu.* (Nee-hone day wah tak-kuu-shee no doe-ah wah zim-buu jee-doe dess.) They open automatically. *Jido-teki ni akimasu.* (Jee-doe-tay-kee nee ah-key-mahss.) American taxis do not have automatic doors. *Amerika no taxi wa jido doa ga arimasen.* (Ah-may-ree-kah no takushi wah jee-doe doe-ah gah ah-ree-mah-sin.)

B

Back (of/behind) *Ushiro* (Uu-she-roe)

It is just behind the hotel. *Chodo hoteru no ushiro ni arimasu.* (Choe-doe hoe-tay-rue no uu-she-roe nee ah-ree-mahss.) Behind you. *Anata-no ushiro ni.* (Ah-nah-tah-no uu-she-roe nee.) Behind that box. *Sono hako no ushiro ni.* (Sone-no hah-koe no uu-she-roe nee.)

Bacon *Beikon* (Bay-e-kone)

Would you like some bacon? *Beikon wa ikaga desu ka?* (Bay-e-kone wah ee-kah-gah dess kah?) Yes. Please make it well-done. *Hai. Yoku yaite kudasai.* (Yoe-kuu yie-e-tay kuu-dah-sie.) Bacon and eggs, please. *Beikon eggu kudasai.* (Bay-e-kone a-guu kuu-dah-sie.)

Bad *Warui* **(Wah-rue-e)**
Unfortunately, the weather is bad today. *Ainiku, kyo-no tenki wa warui desu.* (Aye-nee-kuu, k'yoe-no tane-kee wah wah-rue-e dess.) This road is bad. *Kono michi wa warui desu.* (Koe-no mee-chee wah wah-rue-e dess.) That's no good. *Sore wa warui desu.* (Soe-ray wah wah-rue-e dess.)

Bad (taste) *Mazui* **(Mah-zuu-ee)**
How is the meat? *Niku wa doh desu ka?* (Nee-kuu wah doh dess kah?) It tastes bad. *Mazui desu.* (Mah-zuu-ee dess.)

Bag *Bagu* **(Bah-guu)**
Whose bag is this? *Kore wa donato-no bagu desu ka?* (Koe-ray wah doe-nah-tah-no bah-guu dess kah?) Have you seen my bag? *Watakushi-no bagu wo mimashita ka?* (Wah-tock-she no bah-guu oh me-mahssh-tah kah?) I've lost my bag. *Bagu wo nakushimashita.* (Bah-guu oh nah-kuu-she-mahssh-tah.)

Baggage *Nimotsu* **(Nee-moat-sue)**
Please take your baggage with you. *Nimotsu wo issho ni motte itte kudasai.* (Nee-moat-sue oh es-sho nee moat-tay eat-tay kuu-dah-sie.) Please check (hold) my baggage. *Nimotsu wo azukatte kudasai.* (Nee-moat-sue oh ah-zuu-kot-tay kuu-dah-sie.) Where is my baggage? *Watakushi-no nimotsu wa doko desu ka?* (Wah-tock-she-no nee-moat-sue wah doe-koe dess kah?) The bellboy took it. *Beruboi ga motte ikimashita.* (Bay-rue boy gah moat-tay ee-kee-mahssh-tah.)

Baggage cart *Bageji kaato* **(Bah-gay-jee kahh-toe)**
Are there baggage carts here? *Bageji kaato arimasu ka?* (Bah-gay-jee kahh-toe ah-ree-mahss kah.) May I use this baggage cart? *Kono kaato wo tsu-*

katte moh ii desu ka? (Koe-no kah-toe oh t'sue-kot-tay moe ee dess kah?)

Baggage room *Nimotsu azukarijo* (Nee-moat-sue ah-zuu-kah-ree-joe)
Where is the baggage check-room? *Nimotsu azu-kari-jo wa doko desu ka?* (Nee-moat-sue ah-zuu-kah-ree-joe wah doe-koe dess kah?)

Bank *Ginko* (Gheen-koe)
Is there a bank near here? *Kono chikaku ni ginko ga arimasu ka?* (Koe-no chee-kah-kuu nee gheen-koe gah ah-ree-mahss kah?) What time does it open? *Nanji ni akimasu ka?* (Nahn-jee nee ah-key-mahss kah?)

Bar *Baa* (Baah); also *Nomiya* (No-me-yah)
[*Nomiya* is the generic term for drinking place. When used in this context, *baa* is standard.] Let's go to a bar. *Baa ni ikimasho.* (Baah nee ee-kee-mah-show.) What time does the bar close? *Baa wa nanji ni shimarimasu ka?* (Bah wah nahn-jee nee she-mah-ree-mahss kah?)

Barbecue *Sumiyaki* (Sue-me-yah-kee); also *Babekyu* (Bah-bay-que)
[*Sumiyaki* is primarily used in reference to Japanese style barbecued dishes. In a Western context, *babekyu* is used.] Let's have a barbecue. *Babekyu shimasho.* (Bah-bay-que, she-mah-show.)

Barber *Tokoya* (Toe-koe-yah)
Where is the closest barber shop? *Ichiban chikai tokoya wa doko desu ka?* (Ee-chee-bahn chee-kie toe-koe-yah wah doe-koe dess kah?) Is there a barber in this hotel? *Kono hoteru ni tokoya-san ga arimasu ka?* (Koe-no hoe-tay-rue nee toe-koe-yah-sahn gah ah-ree-mahss kah?)

Bargain sale *Oyasu uri* **(Oh-yah-sue uu-ree);** also
Baagen seiru (Bah-gane say-e-rue)
When is your next bargain sale? *Tsugi-no bagen
seiru wa itsu desu ka?* (T'sue-ghee-no bah-gane
say-e-rue wah eat-sue dess kah?)

Bartender *Baatenda* **(Bah-tane-dah)**
Ask the bartender. *Baatenda ni kiite kudasai.* (Bah-
tane-dah nee keet-tay kuu-dah-sie.) He knows
everything. *Kare wa nandemo shite imasu.* (Kah-ray
wah nahn-day-moe ssh-tay ee-mahss.)

Basement *Chika* **(Chee-kah)**
[Japanese office buildings generally have several
basements, where shops and restaurants are often located.] Where are the restaurants? *Shokudo
wa doko ni arimasu ka?* (Show-kuu-doe wah doe-
koe nee ah-ree-mahss kah?) On the first basement. *Chika-no ikkai ni arimasu.* (Chee-kah-no
eek-kie nee ah-ree-mahss.)

Bath *Ofuro* **(Oh-fuu-roe);** also *Baasu* (Bah-sue)
Are you going to take a bath? *Ofuro ni hairimasu
ka?* (Oh-fuu-roe nee hie-ree-mahss kah?) Let's
take a bath. *Ofuro ni hairimasho.* (Oh-fuu-roe nee
hie-ree-mah-show). [A family-sized bath is *Ka-
zoku buro* (Kah-zoe-kuu buu-roe.)] Will the bath
be ready soon? *Ofuro wa sugu hairemasu ka?* (Oh-
fuu-roe wah sue-guu hie-ray-mahss kah?)

Battery *Denchi* **(Dane-chee)**
I need a new battery for my camera. *Kamera ni
atarashii denchi ga irimasu.* (Kah-may-rah nee ah-
tah-rah-she-e dane-chee gah e-ree-mahss.)
Where can I buy one? *Doko de kaemasu ka?* (Doe-
koe day kah-eh-mahss kah?)

Beach *Kaigan* **(Kie-ghan);** also *Biichi* (Bee-chee)
[When referring to a swimming/sunbathing beach, *biichi* is most commonly used.] All the beaches on Waikiki are public. *Waikiki no biichi wa zembu kokai sarete imasu.* (Waikiki-no bee-chee wah zim-buu koe-kie sah-ray-tay-ee-mahss.)

Beautiful *Utsukushi* **(Uut-sue-kuu-she)**
It is beautiful. *Utsukushi desu.* You are beautiful. *Anata wa utsukushi desu.* (Ah-nah-tah wah uut-sue-kuu-she dess.) A beautiful woman. *Bijin* (Bee-jeen.) Beauty contest. *Bijin kontesuto.* (Bee-jeen kone-tessuu-toh.)

Beauty salon *Biyoin* **(Bee-yoe-een)**
Is there a beauty salon in the hotel? *Hoteru ni biyoin ga arimasu ka?* (Hoe-tay-rue nee bee-yoh-een gah ah-ree-mahss kah?) I want to go to a beauty salon. *Biyoin ni ikitai no desu.* (Bee-yoh-een nee ee-kee-tie no dess.)

Be careful *Kiwotsukete* **(Kee-oh-skate-tay)**
Be careful when crossing the street. *Michi wo wataru toki kiwotsukete kudasai.* (Me-chee oh wah-tah-rue toe-kee kee-oh-skate-tay kuu-dah-sie.) Be careful! *Kiwotsukete!* (Kee-oh-skate-tay!)

Bed *Shindai* **(Sheen-die);** also *Betto* (Bet-toe).
Double bed *Daburu betto* (Dah-buu-rue bet-toe); Twin bed *Tsuin betto* (T'sue-een bet-toe); Single *Shinguru* (Sheen-guu-rue)
Do you sleep on a bed or on a floor-mattress? *Shindai ni nemasu ka soretomo futon ni nemasu ka?* (Sheen-die nee nay-mahss kah soe-ray-toe-moe fuu-tone nee nay-mahss kah?)

Bedtime *Neru-jikan* **(Nay-rue-jee-kahn)**
It's my bedtime. *Watakushi-no neru jikan dess.* (Wah-tock-she-no nay-rue jee-kahn dess.) Is it

67

already bedtime? *Mo, neru-jikan desu ka?* (Moe, nay-rue-jee-kahn dess kah?)

Beef stew *Biifu shichu* **(Bee-fuu ssh-chew)**
Do you have beef stew? *Biifu shichu arimasu ka?* (Bee-fuu ssh-chew ah-ree-mahss kah?)

Beer *Biru* **(Bee-rue)**
Would you like a beer? *Biru ikaga desu ka?* (Bee-rue ee-kah-gah dess kah?) What kind of beer do you have? *Donna shurui ga arimasu ka?* (Doan-nah shuu-rue-e gah ah-ree-mahss kah?) Do you have draft beer? *Nama biru arimasu ka?* (Nah-mah bee-rue ah-ree-mahss kah?)

Bellboy *Beru Boi* **(Bay-rue Boy)**
Please send a bellboy to my room. *Watakushi no heya ni beru boi wo yokoshite kudasai.* (Wah-tock-she-no hay-yah ni bay-rue boy oh yoe-koe-ssh-tay kuu-dah-sie.) I'm checking out. *Chekku outo shimasu.* (Check-ku ou-toe she-mahss.)

Bell desk *Beru desuku* **(Bay-rue desk-ku)**
Leave your bags at the bell desk. *Nimotsu wo beru desuku ni oite kudasai.* (Nee-moat-sue oh bay-rue desk-ku nee oh-ee-tay kuu-dah-sie.)

Beside (near) *Soba* **(Soe-bah)**
It's beside the station. *Eki no soba ni arimasu.* (Aa-kee-no soe-bah nee ah-ree-mahss.) Sit beside me. *Watakushi no soba ni suwatte kudasai.* (Wah-tock-she-no soe-bah nee swat-tay kuu-dah-sie.)

Besides *No hoka ni* **(No hoe-kah nee)**
Do you have anything besides this? *Kore no hoka ni arimasu ka?* (Koe-ray no hoe-kah nee ah-ree-mahss kah?)

Best *Ichiban* **(Ee-chee-bahn)**
I want the best (one). *Ichiban ii no ga hoshii desu.*
(Ee-chee-bahn ee no gah hoe-she-e dess.)
Which one is the best? *Dore ga ichiban ii desu ka?*
(Doe-ray gah ee-chee-bahn ee dess kah?)

Bicycle *Jitensha* **(Jee-tane-shah)**
Do you have (a/any) bicycles? *Jitensha ga arimasu
ka?* (Jee-tane-shah gah ah-ree-mahss kah?) I
would like to rent a bicycle. *Jitensha wo karitai
desu.* (Jee-tane-shah oh kah-ree-tie dess.)

Big *Okii* **(Oh-keee)**
It's big, isn't it! *Okii desu, ne!* (Oh-keee dess,
nay!) That's too big. *Sore wa okii sugimasu.* (Soe-
ray wah oh-keee sue-ghee-mahss.)

Big car *Ogata sha* **(Oh-gah-tah shah)**
I would like to rent a large car. *Ogata sha wo karitai desu.* (Oh-gah-tah shah oh kah-ree-tie dess.)
Medium-sized car: *chugata sha* (chuu-gah-tah
shah); small-sized car: *kogata sha* (koe-gah-tah
shah).

Bill (for purchase) *Okanjo* **(Oh-kahn-joe)**
The bill, please. *Okanjo onegaishimasu.* (Oh-kahn-
joe oh-nay-guy-she-mahss.) Where do I pay it?
Doko de haraimasu ka? (Doe-koe day hah-rye-
mahss kah?)

Blanket *Mofu* **(Moe-fuu)**
Please bring me one more blanket. *Mofu mo ichi-
mai motte kite kudasai.* (Moe-fuu moe e-chee my
mote-tay kee-tay kuu-dah-sie.)

Block (as in street block)
[Note: The Japanese do not use any such term as
"street block" in reference to distance or the lo-

cation of a building, because of inconsistencies in "block" lengths and direction. Short distances within towns and cities are normally given in meters or minutes.]

Blood pressure *Ketsu-atsu* **(Kate-sue-aht-sue)**
My blood pressure is high. *Watakushi no ketsu-atsu wa takai desu.* (Wah-tock-she no kate-sue-aht-sue wah tah-kie dess.) Is your blood pressure low? *Anata no ketsu-atsu wa hikui desu ka?* (Ah-nah-tah no kate-sue-aht-sue wa he-kuu-e dess kah?)

Boarding pass *Tojo ken* **(Toe-joe ken)**
Do you have your boarding pass? *Tojo ken motte imasu ka? (Toe-joe ken moat-tay ee-mahss kah?)* Please show me your boarding pass. *Tojo ken wo misete kudasai.* (Toe-joe ken oh me-sate-tay kuu-dah-sie.)

Boat (outboard motor or oars) *Boto* **(Boe-toe)**
Is there a boat rental place near here? *Kono chi-kaku ni boto wo kasu tokoro ga arimasu ka?* (Koe-no chee-kah-kuu nee boe-toe oh kah-sue toe-koe-roe gah ah-ree-mahss kah?) We have boats for rent. *Kashi boto ga arimasu.* (Kah-she boe-toe gah ah-ree-mahss.) Ferry boat: *Watashi bune* (Wah-tah-she buu-nay). Sail boat: *Hokake bune* (hoe-kah-kay buu-nay).

Book *Hon* **(Hone)**
Do you have any English-language books about Japan? *Nihon ni tsuite no Eigo no hon ga arimasu ka?* (Nee-hone nee t'sue-e-tay no Aa-e-go no hone gah ah-ree-mahss kah?) Is this your book?

Kore wa anato no hon desu ka? (Koe-ray wah ah-nah-tah no hone dess kah?)

Bookstore *Hon ya* **(Hone-yah)**
Is there a bookstore in the hotel? *Hoteru ni hon ya ga arimasu ka?* (Hoe-tay-rue nee hone yah gah ah-ree-mahss kah?)

Border (between countries/states) *Kokkyo* **(Koke-yoe)**
Is the border very far from here? *Kokkyo wa koko kara toi desu ka?* (Koke-yoe wah koe-koe kah-rah toy dess kah?)

Bottle *Bin* **(Bean)**
Do you have any bottled water? *Bin-iri no mizu ga arimasu ka?* (Bean-ee-ree no mee-zuu gah ah-ree-mahss kah?)

Bottle opener *Sen nuki* **(Sane new-kee)**
I need a bottle opener. *Sen nuki ga irimasu.* (Sane new-kee gah e-ree-mahss.) Do you have one? *Arimasu ka?* (Ah-ree-mahss kah?)

Bottoms up! (drinking toast) *Kampai* **(Kahm-pie!)**
Let's drink a toast! *Kampai shimasho!* (Kahm-pie she-mah-show!) Cheers! Here's to you! etc. *Kampai!* (Kahm-pie)

Bought *Kaimashita* **(Kie-mahssh-tah)**
Have you already bought all of the gifts you want? *Omiyage wo mo zembu kaimashita ka?* (Oh-me-yah-gay oh moe zim-buu kie-mahssh-tah kah?)

Bourbon *Babon* **(Bah-bone)**
Bourbon, please. *Babon, kudasai.* (Bah-bone kuu-dah-sie.) Bourbon and water, please. *Babon-no*

mizu-wari kudasai. (Bah-bone-no mee-zuu-wah-ree kuu-dah-sie.)

Bowl (container) *Domburi* (Dome-buu-ree)
Bring me a bowl, please. *Domburi wo motte kite kudasai.* (Dome-buu-ree oh mote-tay ke-tay kuu-dah-sie.)

Bowling *Boringu* (Boe-ring-guu)
Have you ever bowled before? *Boringu wo yatta koto ga arimasu ka?* (Boe-ring-guu oh yaht-tah koe-toe gah ah-ree-mahss kah?) Is there a bowling alley nearby? *Kono hen ni boringu senta ga arimasu ka?* (Koe-no hane nee boe-ring-guu sin-tah gah ah-ree-mahss kah?)

Box *Hako* (Hah-koe)
I need a box about this big. Do you have one? *Kono okisa no hako ga irimasu. Arimasu ka?* (Koe-no oh-kee-sah no hah-koe gah e-ree-mahss. Ah-ree-mahss kah?)

Brassiere *Burajaa* (Buu-rah-jah)

Bread *Pan* (Pahn)
Bread or rice, which do you prefer? *Pan ka gohan, dochi ga ii desu ka?* (Pahn kah go-hahn, doe-chee gah ee dess kah?) [Note: Rice is also commonly called *raisu* (rye-sue) and is understood by all in the proper context.]

Breakdown (vehicle) *Kosho* (Koe-show)
My car has broken down. Will you please call a repair shop? *Watakushi no jidosha ga kosho shimashita. Shuri-ya wo yonde itadakemasen ka?* (Wah-tock-she no jee-doe-shah gah koe-show-she-

mahssh-tah. Shu-ree-yah oh yone-day ee-tah-
dah-kay-mah-sin kah?)

Breakfast *Asa-gohan* **(Ah-sah-go-hahn)**
Have you already had breakfast? *Asa-gohan wo
mò tabemashita ka?* (Ah-sah-go-hahn oh moe tah-
bay-mahssh-tah kah?)   What time is breakfast?
Asa-gohan wa nanji desu ka? (Ah-sah-go-hahn wah
nahn-jee dess kah?)   What would you like for
breakfast? *Asa-gohan ni nani ga ii desu ka?* (Ah-
sah-go-hahn nee nah-nee gah ee dess kah?)
Breakfast is from 7:00 A.M. to 9:00 A.M. *Asa-gohan
wa shichi-ji kara kuji made desu.* (Ah-sah-go-hahn
wah she-chee-jee kah-rah kuu-jee mah-day
dess.)

Briefcase *Kaban* **(Kah-bahn)**
Don't forget your briefcase! *Kaban wo wasurenai
de!* (Kah-bahn oh wah-sue-ray-nie day!)   It's in
my briefcase. *Kaban ni haitte imasu.* (Kah-bahn
nee hite-tay ee-mahss.)

Bring *Motte kimasu* **(Mote-tay kee-mahss)**
Please bring (it) with you. *Issho ni motte kite kudasai.* (E-show-nee mote-tay kee-tay kuu-dah-
sie.)   I'll bring it. *Motte kimasu.* (Mote-tay kee-
mahss.)

Brochure *Panfuretto* **(Pahn-fuu-rate-toe)**
Do you have any brochures about Kyoto? *Kyoto
no panfuretto ga arimasu ka?* (Kyoto no pahn-fuu-
rate-toe gah ah-ree-mahss kah?)

Brother *Otoko-no kyodai* **(Oh-toe-koe-no k'yoe-
die)**
This is my younger brother. *Kore wa watakushi no
ototo desu.* (Koe-ray wah wah-tock-shee no oh-

toe-toe dess.) My older brother is in Dallas. *Wa-takushi no ani wa Darasu ni orimasu.* (Wah-tock-she-no ah-nee wah Dah-rah-sue nee oh-ree-mahss.)

Brush *Burashi* **(Buu-rah-shee);** also *Hea burashi* (Hay-ah buu-rah-she)
I want to buy a hairbrush. *Hea burashi wo kaitai desu.* (Hay-ah buu-rah-she oh kie-tie dess.)

Buddhism *Bukkyo* **(Buke-yoe)/Buddhist** *Bukkyo-to* **(Buke-yoe-toe)**
Are there many Buddhists in Japan? *Nihon ni Bukkyo-to ga takusan imasu ka?* (Nee-hone nee Buke-yoe-toe gah tock-sahn e-mahss kah?)

Budget *Yosan* **(Yoe-sahn)**
How much is your budget? *Yosan wa dono gurai arimasu ka?* (Yoe-sahn wah doe-no guu-rye ah-ree-mahss kah?) It's all gone! *Nakunarimashita!* (Nah-kuu-nah-ree-mahssh-tah!)

Buffet *Bufe* **(Buu-fay)**
In this hotel breakfast is always buffet style. *Kono hoteru no asa-gohan wa itsumo bufe sutairu desu.* (Koe-no hoe-tay-rue no ah-sah-go-han wah eat-sue-moe buu-fay sty-rue dess.)

Building *Tatemono* **(Tah-tay-moe-no);** also *Biru* (Bee-rue) and *Birudingu* (Bee-rue-ding-guu)
I am looking for the Sony Building. *Sony Biru wo sagashite imasu.* (Sony Bee-rue oh sah-gah-ssh-tay e-mahss.) What is that tall building? *Ano takai tatemono wa nan desu ka?* (Ah-no tah-kie tah-tay-moe-no wah nahn dess kah?)

Burn (scald) *Yakedo* **(Yah-kay-doe)**
I burned my hand. *Te wo yakedo shimashita.* (Tay oh yah-kay-doe she-mahss-tah.) Do you have any medicine? *Kusuri ga arimasu ka?* (Kuu-sue-ree gah ah-ree-mahss kah?)

Bus *Basu* **(Bah-sue)**
We are going by bus. *Basu de ikimasu.* (Bah-sue day e-kee-mahss.) Please board the bus. *Basu ni notte kudasai.* (Bah-sue nee note-tay kuu-dah-sie.) Which bus? *Dono basu?* (Doe-no bah-sue?)

Bus driver *Basu no untenshu* **(Bah-sue no uun-tane-shuu)**
This is the driver. *Konhito wa untenshu desu.* (Koe-no-ssh-toe wah uun-tane-shuu dess.) His name is Baker. *Kare no namae wa Beka desu.* (Kah-ray no nah-my wah Bay-kah dess.)

Bus fare *Basu dai* **(Bah-sue die)**
How much is the bus fare? *Basu dai wa ikura desu ka?* (Bah-sue die wah e-kuu-rah dess kah?) When do I pay the bus fare? *Basu dai wo itsu haraimasu ka?* (Bah-sue die oh eat-sue hah-rye-mahss kah?)

Bus stop *Teiryu jo* **(Tay-re-yuu joe);** also *Sutoppu* (Stope-puu); *Basu noriba* (Bah-sue no-ree-bah)
Where is the bus stop? *Basu sutoppu wa doko desu ka?* (Bah-sue stope-puu wah doe-koe dess kah?)

Business *Shobai* **(Show-by);** also *Bijinesu* (Bee-jee-nay-sue); *Shigoto* (She-go-toh)
What is your business? *Anata no shigoto wa nan desu ka?* (Ah-nah-tah no she-go-toh wah nahn dess kah?) Are you here on business? *Shigoto de kimashita ka?* (She-go-toh day kee-mahssh-tah kah?)

Business hours *Eigyo jikan* **(Egg-yoe jee-kahn)**
What are your business hours? *Eigyo jikan wa nanji kara nanji made desu ka?* (Egg-yoe jee-kahn wah nahn-jee kah-rah nahn-jee mah-day dess kah?)

Busy (telephone) *Hanashi-chu* **(Hah-nah-ssh-chew)**
It is busy. Just a moment, please. *Hanashi-chu desu.* (Hah-nah-ssh-chew dess.) *Chotto matte kudasai.* (Chote-toe mot-tay kuu-dah-sie.)

Butter *Bata* **(Bah-tah)**
May I have some more butter, please. *Bata wo mo sukoshi kudasai.* (Bah-tah oh moe sko-she kuu-dah-sie.)

Buy *Kaimasu* **(Kie-mahss)**
I want to buy a pair of thongs. *Zori wo kaitai desu.* (Zoe-ree oh kie-tie dess.) Why don't you buy a pair of cowboy boots? *Doshite kauboi buutsu wo kaimasen ka?* (Doe-ssh-tay cowboy boot-sue oh kie-mah-sin kah?)

By (means of) *De* **(Day)**
Do you want to go by taxi? *Takushi de ikitai desu ka?* (Tah-kuu-she day e-kee-tie dess kah?) It's better to walk. It's only two or three minutes on foot. *Aruku ho ga ii desu. Aruite ni-san-pun dake desu.* (Ah-rue-kuu hoe gah ee dess. Ah-rue-ee-tay nee-sahn-poon dah-kay dess.)

By myself / yourself *Hitori de* **(Hee-toe-ree day)**
I am going by myself. *Hitori de ikimasu.* (Hee-toe-ree day e-kee-mahss.) Are you traveling by yourself? *Hitori de ryoko shite imasu ka?* (Ssh-toe-ree day rio-koe ssh-tay e-mahss kah?)

C

Caddy *Kyadei* (K'yah-day)

How much are caddies per hour? *Kyadei wa ichiji-kan de ikura desu ka?* (K'yah-day wah ee-chee-jee-kahn day ee-kuu-rah dess kah?)   Are all caddies in Japan women? *Nihon de kyadei wa minna onna-no-hito desu ka?* (Nee-hone day k'yah-day wah meen-nah own-nah-no-ssh-toe dess kah?)   Yes, they are. *Hai, so desu.* (Hie, soe dess.)

Cafeteria *Kafeteriya* (Kah-fay-tay-ree-yah)

Are there many cafeterias in Japan? *Nihon ni kafeteriya ga takusan arimasu ka?* (Nee-hone nee kah-fay-tay-ree-yah gah tock-sahn ah-ree-mahss kah?)   No. They are rare. *Iie. Sukunai desu.* (Ee-eh. Sue-kuu-nie dess.)

Cake (Western) *Keki* (Kay-kee)

Would you like some cake? *Keki wa ikaga desu ka?* (Kay-kee wah e-kah-gah dess kah?)

Call (telephone) *Denwa shimasu* (Dane-wah she-mahss)

Please call me at 6 o'clock. *Rokuji ni denwa wo shite kudasai.* (Roe-kuu-jee nee dane-wah oh ssh-tay kuu-dah-sie.)   What time would you like to be called? *Nanji ni denwa wo shimasho ka?* (Nahn-jee nee dane-wah oh she-mah-show kah?)

Camera *Kamera* (Kah-may-rah)

I forgot my camera. *Kamera wo wasuremashita.* (Kah-may-rah oh wah-sue-ray-mahssh-tah.)   Whose camera is this? *Kore wa donata no kamera desu ka?* (Koe-ray wah doe-nah-tah no kah-may-rah dess kah?)

Camp *Kyampu* **(K'yahm-puu);** Camper (vehicle)
Kyampu kaa (K'yahm-puu kah)
Is it all right to camp here? *Koko de kyampu shite mo ii desu ka?* (Koe-koe day k'yahm-puu ssh-tay moe ee dess kah?)

Can buy *Kaemasu* **(Kah-eh-mahss)**
Where can I buy a kimono? *Kimono wo doko de kaemasu ka?* (Kee-moe-no oh doe-koe day kah-eh-mahss kah?)

Cancel *Torikeshi* **(Toe-ree-kay-she)**
Please cancel my reservations. *Watakushi no yoyaku wo torikeshite kudasai.* (Wah-tock-she-no yoe-yah-kuu oh toe-ree-kay-she-tay kuu-dah-sie.) Do you have a cancellation charge? *Torikeshi-ryo ga arimasu ka?* (Toe-ree-kay-she-rio gah ah-ree-mahss kah?)

Can do *Dekimasu* **(Day-kee-mahss)**
Can (you) do it? *Dekimasu ka?* (Day-kee-mahss kah?) When can you do it? *Itsu dekimasu ka?* (Eat-sue day-kee-mahss kah?) I can do it by the day after tomorrow. *Asatte made ni dekimasu.* (Ah-sot-tay mah-day nee day-kee-mahss.)

Candle *Rosoku* **(Roe-soe-kuu)**
If there is an electrical outage, use these candles. *Teiden ga attara, kono rosoku wo tsukatte kudasai.* (Tay-e-dane gah aht-tah-rah, koe-no roe-soe-kuu oh scot-tay kuu-dah-sie.)

Candy (Western) *Kyande* **(K'yahn-day);** (Japanese)
Ame (Ah-may)
Would you like some candy? *Kyande wo tabemasu ka?* (K'yahn-day oh tah-bay-mahss ka?)

Canoe *Kanu* **(Kah-new)**
I want to rent a canoe. *Kanu wo karitai desu.* (Kah-new oh kah-ree-tie dess.)

Car *Jidosha* **(Jee-doe-shah);** also *Kuruma* (Kuu-rue-mah)
Do you have a car? *Jidosha wo motte imasu ka?* (Jee-doe-shah oh mote-tay e-mahss kah?) Let's go by car. *Jidosha de ikimasho.* (Jee-doe-shah day e-kee-mah-show.)

C/O (Care Of) *Kata* **(Kah-tah)**
Please send this in care of Mr. Suzuki. *Kore wo Suzuki-San kata de dashite kudasai.* (Koe-ray oh Sue-zuu-kee-Sahn kah-tah day dahssh-tay kuu-dah-sie.)

Carry (take to) *Motsu/Motte iku* **(Mote-sue/ mote-tay e-kuu)**
Please carry this to my room. *Kore wo watakushi no heya e motte itte kudasai.* (Koe-ray oh wah-tock-she-no hay-yah eh mote-tay eat-tay kuu-dah-sie.)

Cash *Genkin* **(Gain-keen)**
I will pay cash. *Genkin de haraimasu.* (Gain-keen day hah-rye-mahss.) Do you have any cash? *Genkin ga arimasu ka?* (Gain-keen gah ah-ree-mahss kah?) Please cash this. *Kore wo genkin ni shite kudasai.* (Koe-ray oh gain-keen nee ssh-tay kuu-dah-sie.)

Cashier **Reji (Reh-jee)**
Please pay the cashier. *Reji ni haratte kudasai.* (Reh-jee nee hah-rot-tay kuu-dah-sie.) The cashier is next to the front entrance. *Reji wa genkan no doa no soba desu.* (Reh-jee wah gain-kahn no doe-ah no soe-bah dess.)

Cassette *Kasetto* **(Kah-set-toe)**
I am looking for a cassette radio. *Kasetto no rajio wo sagashite imasu* (Kah-set-toe no rah-jee-oh oh sah-gah-ssh-tay e-mahss.)

Castle *Shiro* **(She-roe)**
I would like to see some of Japan's famous castles. *Nihon no yumei na shiro wo mitai desu.* (Nee-hone no yuu-may-e nah she-roe oh me-tie dess.) [Note: when used in conjunction with a specific castle, *shiro* becomes *jo*. For example, Osaka Castle = *Osaka Jo.*]

Catch (get on) *Norimasu* **(No-ree-mahss)**
I want to catch the next train. *Kono tsugi no ressha ni noritai desu.* (Koe-no t'sue-ghee no ray-shah nee no-ree-tie dess.) Catch (a cold) *Kaze wo hiku* (Kah-zay oh he-kuu). I caught a cold. *Kaze wo hikimashita.* (Kah-zay oh he-kee-mahssh-tah.)

Cavity (in tooth) *Mushiba* **(Muu-she-bah)**
I have a cavity. *Mushiba ga arimasu.* (Muu-she-bah gah ah-ree-mahss.) It hurts. *Itai desu.* (E-tie dess.) Where can I find a dentist. *Haisha-san wa doko ni arimasu ka?* (Hie-shah-sahn wah doe-koe nee ah-ree-mahss kah?)

Celebration (party) *Oiwai* **(Oh-e-wie)**
Let's celebrate. *Oiwai wo shimasho.* (Oh-e-wie oh she-mah-show). What kind of celebration are you having? *Donna oiwai desu ka?* (Doan-nah oh-e-wie dess kah?)

Cent *Sento* **(Sin-toe)**
Do you have ten cents in change? *Ju sento no komakai okane ga arimasu ka?* (Juu-sin-toe no koe-moe-kie oh-kah-nay gah ah-ree-mahss kah?)

Center *Chushin* **(Chuu-sheen);** *Mannaka* **(Mahn-nah-kah)**
I would like to go to the center of town. *Machi no chushin ni ikitai desu.* (Mah-chee no chuu-sheen nee e-kee-tai dess.) Sit in the center (middle).

Mannaka ni suwatte kudasai. (Mahn-nah-kah nee swat-tay kuu-dah-sie.)

Champagne *Champen* **(Shawm-pane)**
Do you like champagne? *Shampen suki desu ka?* (Shawm-pane ski dess kah?)   Yes, I like it. *Hai, suki desu.* (Hie, ski dess.)

Change (money) *O'tsuri* **(Oh-t'sue-ree);** small coins *komakai okane* (koe-mah-kie oh-kah-nay); Change currency *Okane wo kaeru* (Oh-kah-nay oh kie-rue)
Don't forget your change! *O'tsuri wo wasurenaide!* (Oh't-sue-ree oh wah-sue-ray-nie-day!)   Do you have any small coins? *Komakai okane arimasu ka?* (Koe-mah-kie oh-kah-nay ah-ree-mahss kah?)   I want to change dollars (into yen). *Doru wo kaetai desu.* (Doe-rue oh kie-tie dess.)

Change buses *Basu wo norikaemasu* **(Bah-sue oh no-ree-kie-mahss)**
We will change buses in Hakone. *Hakone de basu wo norikaemasu.* (Hah-koe-nay day basu oh no-ree-kie-mahss.)

Change planes *Hikoki wo norikaemasu* **(He-koe-kee oh no-ree-kie-mahss)**
Do I have to change planes? *Hikoki wo norikaemasu ka?*   Where do I change? *Doko de norikaemasu ka?* (Doe-koe day no-ree-kie-mahss kah?)

Channel (TV) *Chaneru* **(Chah-nay-rue)**
Which channel is best for news. *Nuzu no chaneru to shite dore ga ichiban ii desu ka?* (New-zoo no chan-nay-rue to ssh-tay doe-ray gah e-chee-bahn ee dess kah?)

Charge (cost) *Hiyo* **(He-yoe)**
How much is the charge? *Hiyo wa ikura desu ka?*
(He-yoe wa e-kuu-rah dess kah?) Charge to
Tsukemasu. Charge it to my bill. *Watakushi no
kanjo ni tsukete kudasai.* (Wah-tock-she no kahn-
joe nee skate-tay kuu-dah-sie.)

Charter *Chata* **(Chah-tah);** *Kashikiri* **(Kah-she-kee-
ree)**
We are going by chartered bus. *Chata basu de ikimasu.* (Chah-tah bah-sue day e-kee-mahss.)
Where can I charter a small plane? *Chiisai hikoki
wa doko de chata dekimasu ka?* (Cheee-sie he-koe-
kee wah doe-koe day chah-tah day-kee-mahss
kah?)

Cheap *Yasui* **(Yah-sue-ee)**
This is really cheap. *Kore wa honto ni yasui desu.*
(Koe-ray wah hone-toe nee yah-sue-ee dess.) Is
that one cheaper? *Sore wa motto yasui desu ka?*
(Soe-ray wah mote-toe yah-sue-ee dess kah?)

Check (clothing/baggage) *Azukarimasu* **(Ah-zuu-
kah-ree-mahss)**
Please check this. *Kore wo azukatte kudasai.* (Koe-
ray oh ah-zuu-kot-tay kuu-dah-sie.) Do you
have your check-stub? *Azukari-sho arimasu ka?*
(Ah-zuu-kah-ree-sho ah-ree-mahss kah?)

Check (look into) *Shirabemasu* **(She-rah-bay-
mahss)**
Please check on my reservations. *Watakushi no
yoyaku wo shirabete kudasai.* (Wah-tock-she no yoe-
yah-kuu oh she-rah-bate-tay kuu-dah-sie.)

Check (money) *Kogitte* **(Koe-geet-tay)**
Will a check be all right? *Kogitte demo yoroshii
desu ka?* (Koe-geet-tay day-moe yoe-roe-shee dess
kah?) Please cash this check. *Kono kogitte wo*

genkin ni shite kudasai. (Koe-no koe-geet-tay oh gane-keen nee ssh-tay kuu-dah-sie.)

Check in *Chekku in* **(Chek-kuu een)**
Good morning. Are you checking in? *Ohaiyo gozaimasu. Chekku in shimasu ka?* (Oh-hie-yoe gozie-mahss. Chek-kuu-een she-mahss kah?)
Have you already checked in? *Mo Chekku in shimashita ka?* (Moe chek-kuu-een she-mahssh-tah kah?)

Check out *Chekku outo* **(Che-kuu ou-toe)**
What is the check-out time? *Chekku outo jinkan wa nanji desu ka?* (Chek-kuu ou-toe jee-kahn wah nahn-jee dess kah?) Are you checking out? *Chekku outo desu ka?* (Che-kuu ou-toe dess kah?)

Cheese *Chizu* **(Chee-zuu)**
What kind of cheese do you have? *Chizu no shurui wa nani ga arimasu ka?* (Chee-zuu no shuu-rue-e wah nah-nee gah ah-ree-mahss kah?)

Cherry blossoms *Sakura-no hana* **(Sah-kuu-rah-no hah-nah)**
When do the cherry blossoms bloom in Tokyo? *Tokyo de sakura no hana ga itsu sakimasu ka?* (Tokyo day sah-kuu-rah-no hah-nah gah eat-sue sah-kee-mahss kah?) I want to go cherry-blossom viewing. *Hanami ni ikitai desu.* (Hah-nah-me nee e-kee-tie dess.)

Chicken *Niwatori* **(Nee-wah-toe-ree)**
Do you have barbecued chicken? *Yaki-tori ga arimasu ka?* (Yah-kee-toe-ree gah ah-ree-mahss kah?) How about fried chicken? *Chikin furai wa do desu ka?* (Chee-keen fuu-rye wah doe dess kah?)

Japanese in Plain English

Child/Children   *Kodomo* (Koe-doe-moe)
What is the charge for a child? *Kodomo no ryokin wa ikura desu ka?* (Koe-doe-moe no rio-keen wah e-kuu-rah dess kah?)   Children are free. *Kodomo wa muryo desu.* (Koe-doe-moe wah muu-rio dess.)

Chili pepper   *Togarashi* (Toe-gah-rah-she)
I can't eat chili pepper. *Togarashi wo taberaremasen.* (Toe-gah-rah-shee oh tah-bay-rah-ray-mah-sin.)

China   *Chugoku* (Chuu-go-kuu)
Have you ever been to China? *Chugoku ni itta koto ga arimasu ka?* (Chuu-go-kuu nee eat-tah koe-toe gah ah-ree-mahss kah?)

Chinese (person)   *Chugoku-jin* (Chuu-go-kuu-jeen)
He/she is Chinese. *Anohito wa Chugoku-jin desu.* (Ah-no-ssh-toe wah Chuu-go-kuu-jeen dess.)   I am not Chinese; I'm Japanese. *Watakushi wa Chugoku-jin dewa arimasen; Nihon-jin desu.* (Wa-tock-she wah Chuu-go-kuu-jeen day-wah ah-ree-mah-sin; Nee-hone-jeen dess.)

Chinese food   *Chugoku ryori* (Chuu-go-kuu rio-ree);   *Chuka ryori* (Chuu-kahh rio-ree)
Let's eat Chinese food tonight. *Komban Chugoku ryori wo tabemasho.* (Kome-bahn Chuu-go-kuu rio-ree oh tah-bay-mah-show.)

Chocolate   *Chokoreto* (Choe-koe-rate-toe)
Do you have any chocolate cake? *Chokoreito keki arimasu ka?* (Choe-koe-rate-toe kay-kee ah-ree-mahss kah?)   How about hot chocolate (drink)? *Kokoa wa?* (Koe-koe-ah wah?)

Chopsticks   *O'hashi* (Oh-hah-she)
Please give me chopsticks. *O'hashi kudasai.* (Oh-hah-she kuu-dah-sie.)   Can you eat with chop-

84

sticks? *O'hashi de taberaremasu ka?* (Oh-hah-she day tah-bay-rah-ray-mahss kah?)

City *Shi* **(She);** *also* Metropolis *Toh* (Toh)
Yokohama is a city but Tokyo is a metropolis. *Yokohama wa shi desu ga, Tokyo wa toh desu.* (Yoe-koe-hah-mah wah she dess gah, Tokyo wah toh dess.)

Clean *Kirei* **(Kee-ray-e)**
Please clean my room. *Heya wo kirei ni shite kudasai.* (Hay-yah oh kee-ray nee ssh-tay kuu-dah-sie.) This is not clean. *Kore wa kirei dewa arimasen.* (Koe-ray wah kee-ray-e day-wah ah-ree-mah-sin.)

Clerk (in a shop) *Ten-in* **(Tane-een);** in a bank *Ginko-in* (Gheen-koe-een); in an office *Jimu-in* (Jee-muu-een)
Let's ask a clerk. *Ten-in ni kikimasho.* (Tane-een nee kee-kee-mah-show.)

Clinic *Kuriniku* **(Kuu-ree-nee-kuu)**
Where is the nearest clinic? *Ichiban chikai kuriniku wa doko desu ka?* (Ee-chee-bahn chee-kie kuu-ree-nee-kuu wah doe-koe dess kah?) Please take me there. *Asoko ni tsurete itte kudasai.* (Ah-soe-koe nee t'sue-ray-tay eet-tay kuu-dah-sie).

Clock (watch) *Tokei* **(Toe-kay-e)**
Is there a clock in the room? *Heya ni tokei ga arimasu ka?* (Hay-yah nee toe-kay-e gah ah-ree-mahss kah?)

Close (near) *Chikai* **(Chee-kie)**
Is it near? *Chikai desu ka?* (Chee-kie dess kah?)

Close (shut) *Shimemasu* **(She-may-mahss)**
Please close the door. *Doa wo shimete kudasai.* (Doe-ah oh she-may-tay kuu-dah-sie.) What

time do you close? *Nanji ni shimemasu ka?* (Nahn-jee nee she-may-mahss kah?)

Closed *Shimatte imasu* (She-mot-tay e-mahss)
Department stores are closed today. *Depaato wa kyo shimatte imasu.* (Day-paa-toe wah k'yoe she-mot-tay e-mahss.)

Clouds *Kumo* (Kuu-moe); cloudy *kumotte imasu* (kuu-mote-tay e-mahss)
It's really a shame, but it's cloudy this morning. *Honto ni zannen desu kedo, kesa wa kumotte imasu.* (Hone-toe nee zahn-nahn dess kay-doe, kay-sah wah kuu-mote-tay e-mahss.)

Coach (of a train) *Go-sha* (Go-shah); also *Kyaku-sha* (Kyack-shah)
We are in coach number one. *Watakushitachi wa ichi-go-sha ni orimasu.* (Wah-tock-she-tah-chee wah e-chee-go-shah nee oh-ree-mahss.) What is your coach number. *Anato wa nan go-sha desu ka?* (Ah-nah-tah wa nahn go-shah dess kah?)

Coca Cola *Koku* (Koe-kuu); also *Koka Kora* (Koe-kah Koe-rah)
A Coke, please. *Koku, kudasai.* (Koe-kuu, kuu-dah-sie.)

Cocktail *Kakuteru* (Kah-kuu-tay-rue)
Would you like a cocktail? *Kakuteru wa ikaga desu ka?* (Kah-kuu-tay-rue wah e-kah-gah dess kah?)

Coffee *Kohi* (Koe-he)
Would you like coffee? *Kohi desu ka?* (Koe-he dess kah?) Cream and sugar? *Kurimu to O'sato wa?* (Kuu-ree-muu toe Oh-sah-toe wah?)

Coffee shop *Kissaten* **(Kees-sah-tane)**; also *Kohi shoppu* (Koe-he shope-puu)
In Japan there are over a dozen different kinds of coffee shops. *Nihon ni wa ichi dasu ijo no kissaten no shurui ga arimasu.* (Nee-hone nee wah e-chee dah-sue e-joe no kees-sah-tane no shuu-rue-e gah ah-ree-mahss.)

Coins (money) *Koka* **(Koe-kah)**
I need some coins. Would you change this please? *Koka ga irimasu. Kore wo kuzushite itadake-masen ka?* (Koe-kah gah e-ree-mahss. Koe-ray oh kuu-zuu-ssh-tay e-tah-dah-kay-mah-sin kah?)

Cold (to the touch) *Tsumetai* **(T'sue-may-tie)**
This coffee is cold. *Kono kohi wa tsumetai desu.* (Koe-no koe-he wah t'sue-may-tie dess.)

Cold (weather) *Samui* **(Sah-muu-ee)**
It's really cold today, isn't it! *Kyo wa honto ni samui desu, ne!* (K'yoe wah hone-toe nee sah-muu-ee dess, nay!) Are you cold? *Samui desu ka?* (Sah-muu-ee dess kah?) I'm cold. *Samui desu.* (Sah-muu-ee dess.)

Collect call (telephone) *Senpo barai* **(Sane-poe bah-rye)**
I would like to make a collect call to Minneapolis. *Mineaporisu ni senpo barai no denwa wo kaketai desu.* (Me-nay-ah-poe-ree-sue nee sane-poe bah-rye no dane-wah oh kah-kay-tie dess.)

Colors *Iro* **(E-roe)**; Beige *Beiju* (Bay-e-juu); blue *buru* (buu-ruu); black *kuroi* (kuu-roy); brown *chairo* (chah-e-roe); green *gurin* (guu-reen); pink *pinku* (peen-kuu); purple *murasaki* (muu-rah-sah-kee); red *akai* (ah-kie); white *shiroi* (she-roy); yellow *kiiro* (kee-e-roe) What color is it? *Nani iro desu ka?* (Nah-nee e-roe dess kah?) Do you have any other colors? *Hoka-no iro ga arimasu ka?* (Hoe-kah-no e-roe gah ah-ree-mahss kah?)

Comb *Kushi* (Kuu-she)
I lost my comb. Where can I buy a new one? *Kushi wo nakushimashita. Atarashii no wa doko de kaemasu ka?* (Kuu-she oh nah-kuu-she-mahssh-tah. Ah-tah-rah-she no oh doe-koe day kie-mahss kah?)

Come *Kimasu* (Kee-mahss)
Are you coming (with us/me)? *Kimasu ka?* (Kee-mahss kah?) No, I'm not. *Ikimasen.* (E-kee-mah-sin.) Please come this way. *Dozo, kochira e kite kudasai.* (Doe-zoe, koe-chee-rah eh kee-tay kuu-dah-sie.)

Come again *Mata dozo* (Mah-tah doe-zoe)
Please come again. *Mata dozo.* (Mah-tah doe-zoe.)

Come in, please *Dozo, haitte kudasai* (Doe- zoe hite-tay kuu-dah-sie)
May I come in? *Haitte mo ii desu ka?* (Hite-tay moe ee dess kah?)

Commission *Tesuryo* (Tay-sue-ree-yoe)
How much is your commission? *Tesuryo wa ikura desu ka?* (Tay-sue-ree-yoe wah e-kuu-rah dess kah?) It is 10 percent. *Ju pasento desu.* (Juu pah-sin-toe dess.)

Company (business) *Kaisha* (Kie-shah)
What is the name of your company? *Kaisha no namae wa nan desu ka?* (Kie-shah no nah-my wah nahn dess kah?) What is your company address? *Kaisha no jusho wa nan desu ka?* (Kie-shah no juu-show wah nahn dess kah?)

Concert *Ongaku-kai* (**Own-gah-kuu-kie**); also *Konsato* (Kone-sah-toh)
There is a concert tonight. *Komban ongakukai ga arimasu.* (Kome-bahn own-gah-kuu-kie gah ah-ree-mahss.)

Confirm *Kakunin shimasu* (**Kah-kuu-neen she-mahss**)
Please confirm my reservations. *Watakushi no yoyaku wo kakunin shite kudasai.* (Wah-tock-she no yoe-yah-kuu oh kah-kun-neen ssh-tay kuu-dah-sie.)

Confirmation slip *Kakunin sho* (**Kah-kuu-neen show**)
This is your confirmation slip. Don't lose it. *Kore wa anata no kakunin sho desu. Naku sanai de kudasai.* (Koe-ray wah ah-nah-tah no kah-kuu-neen show dess. Nah-kuu sah-nie day kuu-dah-sie.)

Connecting flight *Nori-tsugi-bin* (**No-ree-t'sue-ghee-bean**)
What time does my connecting flight leave? *Watakushi no nori-tsugi-bin wa nanji ni demasu ka?* (Wah-tock-she no no-ree-t'sue-ghee-bean wah nahn-jee nee day-mahss kah?)

Connecting Passenger Information *Noritsugi Kyaku Annai* (**No-reet-sue-ghee Kyack-kuu Ahn-nie**)
Please ask at the Connecting Passenger Information Desk/Counter. *Noritsugi Kyaku Annaisho de kiite kudasai.* (No-reet-sue-ghee Kyack-kuu Ahn-nie-sho de keet-tay kuu-dah-sie.)

Constipation *Bempi* (**Bame-pee**)
I'm constipated! *Bempi shite imasu!* (Bame-pee ssh-tay e-mahss!)

Consulate *Ryoji-kan* **(Rio-jee-kahn)**
Do you want to go to the Japanese Consulate?
Nihon no Ryoji-kan ni ikitai desu ka? (Nee-hone no
Rio-jee-kahn nee e-kee-tie dess kah?)

Contact *Renraku* **(Rane-rah-kuu)**
Please contact me when you arrive in Denver.
Denba e tsuku to denwa de renraku shite kudasai.
(Dane-bah eh t'sue-kuu toe dane-wah day rane-
rah-kuu ssh-tay kuu-dah-sie.)   I'll contact you
later. *Ato de renraku shimasu.* (Ah-toe day rane-
rah-kuu she-mahss.)

Contract *Keiyaku* **(Kay-e-yah-kuu)**
When will you sign the contract? *Keiyaku wo itsu
sain shimasu ka?* (Kay-e-yah-kuu oh eat-sue sah-
een she-mahss kah?)

Cool (weather) *Suzushii* **(Sue-zuu-she-e)**
It's cool today, isn't it! *Kyo wa suzushii desu, ne!*
(K'yoe wah sue-zuu-she-e dess, nay!)

Corn flakes *Kon fureikusu* **(Kone fuu-ray-e-
kuu-sue)**
Have you ever eaten corn flakes? *Kon fureikusu
wo tabeta koto ga arimasu ka?* (Kone fuu-ray-ei-ku-
sue oh tah-bay-tah koe-toe gah ah-ree-mahss
kah?)

Corned beef *Kon bifu* **(Kone bee-fuu)**
Please give me a corned beef sandwich and a
glass of milk. *Kon bifu sando to miruku wo kudasai.*
(Kone bee-fuu sahn-doe toe me-rue-kuu oh kuu-
dah-sie.)

Corner *Kado* **(Kah-doe)**
The shop is right on the street corner. *Mise wa
chodo michi no kado ni arimasu.* (Me-say wah choe-

doe me-chee no kah-doe nee ah-ree-mahss.)
Which corner? *Dono kado?* (Doe-no kah-doe?)

Counter *Kaunta* (Kah-un-tah)
Please pay at the counter. *Kaunta de haratte kuda-sai.* (Kah-un-tah day hah-rot-tay kuu-dah-sie.)

Couple (husband and wife) *Fufu* (Fuu-fuu)
Is that man and woman husband and wife? *Sono otoko to onna wa fufu desu ka?* (Soe-no oh-toe-koe toe own-nah wah fuu-fuu dess kah?)

Country (nation) *Kuni* (Kuu-nee); Country (rural area) *Inaka* (E-nah-kah)
Japan is a very small country. *Nihon wa taihen chiisai kuni desu.* (Nee-hone wah tie-hane chee-sie kuu-nee dess.) He is a country-bumpkin. *Ano-hito wa inaka-pei desu.* (Ah-no-ssh-toe wah e-nah-kah-pay-e dess.)

Cover charge *Seki ryo* (Say kee rio); also *Kaba chaji* (Kah-bah chah-jee)
Do you have a cover charge? *Seki ryo wa arimasu ka?* (Say kee rio wah ah-ree-mahss kah?)

Crab *Kani* (Kah-nee)
Let's order some crab soup. *Kani no supu wo chu-mon shimasho.* (Kah-nee no suu-puu oh chuu-moan she-mah-show.) This crab is delicious. *Kono kani wa oishii desu.* (Koe-no kah-nee wah oh-ee-she dess.)

Crater *Kako* (Kah-koe)
This crater was made by a giant meteor. *Kono kako wa okii no inseki de tsukuraremashita.* (Koe-no kah-koe wah oh-kee-e no inn-say-kee day t'sue-kuu-rah-ray-mah-ssh-tah.)

Cream pie *Kurimu pai* (Kuu-ree-muu pie)
Cream pie and a cup of coffee, please. *Kurimu pai to kohi wo kudasai.* (Kuu-ree-muu pie toe koe-he oh kuu-dah-sie.)

Credit card *Kurejito kado* (Kuu-ray-jee-toe kah-doe)
Do you accept credit cards? *Kurejito kado wa yoroshii desu ka?* (Kuu-ray-jee-toe kah-doe wah yoe-roe-shee dess kah?)

Crown Prince (of Japan) *Kotaishi Denka* (Koe-tie-she Dane-kah)
Where does the Crown Prince live? *Kotaishi Denka wa doko ni sunde imasu ka?* (Koe-tie-she Dane-kah wah doe-koe nee soon-day e-mahss kah?)

Cry *Nakimasu* (Nah-kee-mahss)
Why are you crying? *Doshite naite imasu ka?* (Doh-ssh-tay nie-tay e-mahss kah?) Don't cry! *Nakanai de!* (Nah-kah-nie day!)

Cuff links *Kafusu botan* (Kah-fuu-sue boe-tahn)
I lost my cuff links. *Kafusu botan wo nakushimashita.* (Kah-fuu-sue boe-tahn oh nah-kuu-she-mahssh-tah.)

Curtain *Katen* (Kah-tane)
Shall I open the curtains? *Katen wo akemasho ka?* (Kah-tane oh ah-kay-mah-show kah?) No. Close them, please. *Iie. Shimete kudasai.* (Ee-eh. She-mate-tay kuu-dah-sie.)

Custom (habit) *Shukan* (Shuu-kahn)
Is this a Japanese custom? *Kore wa Nihon no shukan desu ka?* (Koe-ray wah Nee-hone no shuu-kahn dess kah?) It is a good custom. *Ii shukan desu.* (Ee shuu-kahn dess.)

Customer *O'kyaku* **(Oh-kyack-kuu)**
In Japan customers often get special service. *Nihon de wa kyaku wa tabi-tabi tokubetsu no sabisu wo moraimasu.* (Nee-hone day wah kyack-kuu wah tah-bee-tah-bee toe-kuu-bate-sue no sah-bee-sue oh moe-rye-mahss.)

Customs Office *Zeikan* **(Zay-kahn);** Customs Declaration *Zeikan Shinkoku-sho* (Zay-kahn Sheen-koe-kuu-show); Customs officer *Zeikan ri* (Zay-kahn ree)
Many Japanese go thru Customs in Honolulu. *Takusan no Nihon-jin ga Honoruru de Zeikan wo torimasu.* (Tock-sahn no Nee-hone-jeen gah Hoe-no-rue-rue day Zay-kahn oh toe-ree-mahss.)

D

Dad *O'To-San* **(Oh-Toe-Sahn);** Daddy *O'To-Chan* (Oh-Toe-Chahn)
[Note: Children and wives may or may not use the honorific "O" in addressing and referring to their father or spouses, depending on the situation. Both are common. The "O" is a little formal. It is often not used in more intimate, emotional situations.]

Dance (Japanese folk) *Odori* **(Oh-doe-ree);** To dance *Odorimasu* (Oh-doe-ree-mahss); *Dansu* (dahn-sue)
Shall we dance? *Odorimasho ka?* (Oh-doe-ree-mah-show kah?) I can't dance. *Odoremasen* (Oh-doe-ray-mah-sin.) Let's go dancing. *Dansu ni ikimasho.* (Dahn-sue nee e-kee-mah-show.)

Daughter *Musume* **(Muu-sue-may)**
This is my daughter. *Konohito wa watakushi no musume desu.* (Koe-no-ssh-toe wah wah-tock-she-no muu-sue-may dess.)

Dead-end (street) *Tsuki atari* **(Ski ah-tah-ree)**
This street is a dead-end. *Kono michi wa tsuki atarimasu.* (Koe-no me-chee wah t'ski ah-tah-ree-mahss.) Go to the dead-end and turn right. *Tsuki atatte, migi e magatte kudasai.* (T'ski ah-tot-tay, me-ghee eh mah-got-tay kuu-dah-sie.)

Deep *Fukai* **(Fuu-kie)**
Is the water deep? *Mizu wa fukai desu ka?* (Mee-zuu wah fuu-kie dess kah?)

Delicious *Oishii* **(Oh-e-she-e)**
It (the food) is really delicious. *Taihen oishii desu.* (Tie-hane oh-e-she-e dess.) Really? *Honto ni?* (Hone-toe nee?)

Deliver *Todokemasu* **(Toe-doe-kay-mahss)**
Can you deliver this to my hotel? *Kore wo watakushi no hoteru ni todokeru koto ga dekimasu ka?* (Koe-ray oh wah-tock-she-no hoe-tay-rue nee toe-doe-kay-rue koe-toe gah day-kee-mahss kah?)
Please deliver it. *Todokete kudasai.* (Toe-doe-kay-tay kuu-dah-sie.)

Deluxe *Gokana* **(Go-kah-nah);** *Derakusu* (Day-rah-kuu-sue)
The Imperial is a deluxe hotel. *Teikoku Hoteru wa derakusu no hoteru desu.* (Tay-e-koe-kuu Hoe-tay-rue wah day-rah-kuu-suu no hoe-tay-rue dess.)

Dentist *Haisha* **(Hie-shah)**
I have to go to a dentist. *Haisha ni ikanakereba narimasen.* (Hie-shah nee e-kah-nah-kay-ray-bah nah-ree-mah-sin.) Please take me. *Tsurete itte kudasai.* (T'sue-ray-tay eet-tay kuu-dah-sie.)

Department store *Depaato* (Day-paah-toe)
What time do department stores open? *Depaato wa nanji ni akimasu ka?* (Day-paah-toe wah nahn-jee nee ah-key-mahss kah?)

Departure *Shuppatsu* (Shupe-pot-sue); Departure (area sign); *Hassha* (Hah-sshah)
What time is your departure? *Shuppatsu wa nanji desu ka?* (Shupe-pot-sue wah nahn-jee dess kah?) I depart tomorrow at 2:30 P.M. *Shuppatsu wa ashita no go-go no ni-ji-han desu.* (Shupe-pot-sue wa ah-ssh-tah no go-go no nee-jee-hahn dess.)

Develop film *Genzo shimasu* (Gane-zoe she-mahss)
Please develop this film. *Kono firumu wo genzo shite kudasai.* (Koe-no fee-rue-muu oh gane-zoe ssh-tay kuu-dah-sie.)

Desert *Sabaku* (Sah-bah-kuu)
There are sand deserts in southern California. *Karifoniya no nan-to ni suna no sabaku ga arimasu.* (Kah-ree-foe-nee-yah no nahn-toe nee sue-nah no sah-bah-kuu gah ah-ree-mahss.)

Dessert *Dezato* (Day-zah-toe)
What kind of dessert do you like? *Donna dezato ga suki desu ka?* (Doan-nah day-zah-toe gah ski dess kah?) Would you like some dessert? *Dezato wa ikaga desu ka?* (Day-zah-toe wah e-kah-gah dess kah?)

Diagonally opposite *Suji mukai* (Sue-jee muu-kie)
The shop is diagonally opposite the Arizona Bank. *Sono mise wa Arizona Ginko no suji mukai desu.* (Soe-no me-say wah Ah-ree-zoe-nah Gheen-koe no sue-jee muu-kie dess.)

Dial (the phone) *Mawashimasu* **(Mah-wah-she-mahss)**
Dial 9 first. *Saisho ni kyu wo mawashite kudasai.* (Sie-show nee que oh mah-wahssh-tay kuu-dah-sie.)

Diarrhea *Geri* **(Gay-ree)**
I have diarrhea. Where can I buy some medicine? *Geri shite imasu. Kusuri wa doko de kaemasu ka?* (Gay-ree ssh-tay e-mahss. Kuu-sue-ree wah doe-koe day kie-mahss kah?)

Dictionary *Jibiki* **(Jee-bee-kee)**
Do you have an English-Japanese dictionary? *Ei-Wa jibiki wo motte imasu ka?* (A-E Wah jee-bee-kee oh mote-tay e-mahss kah?) I also need a Japanese English dictionary. *Wa-Ei jibiki mo irimasu.* (Wah-A-e jee-bee-kee moe e-ree-mahss.)

Diet (food intake) *Shokuji-ryoho* **(Show-kuu-jee rio-hoe)**
I'm on a diet. *Shokuji ryoho shite imasu.* (Show-kuu-jee rio-hoe ssh-tay e-mahss.)

Dining car (on train) *Shokudo sha* **(Show-kuu-doe shah)**
What number is the dining car? *Shokudo sha wa nan go-sha desu ka?* (Show-kuu-doe shah wa nahn go-shah dess kah?)

Dinner *Yuhan* **(Yuu-hahn);** *Yushoku* (Yuu-show-kuu)
What time is dinner? *Yuhan wa nanji desu ka?* (You-hahn wah nahn-jee dess kah?) Do you have a "set dinner" (full course)? *Teishoku ga arimasu ka?* (Tay-e-show-kuu gah ah-ree-mahss kah?) What is today's set dinner? *Kyo no teishoku wa nan desu ka?* (K'yoe no tay-show-kuu wah nahn dess kah?)

Direct flight *Chokko bin* **(Choke-koe bean)**
Is that a direct (non-stop) flight? *Sore wa chokko bin desu ka?* (Soe-ray wah choke-koe bean dess kah?)

Direction (way) *Hogaku* **(Hoe-gah-kuu)**
Which direction is Tokyo Station? *Tokyo Eki no hogaku wa dochira desu ka?* (Tokyo A-kee no hoe-gah-kuu wah doe-chee-rah dess kah?)

Direct line (telephone) *Chokutsu* **(Choke-t'sue)**
Does Mr. Tanaka have a direct line? *Tanaka-San wa chokutsu arimasu ka?* (Tah-nah-kah-Sahn wah choke-t'sue ah-ree-mahss kah?)

Dirty *Kitanai* **(Kee-tah-nie)**
This plate is dirty. *Kono sara wa kitanai desu.* (Koe-no sah-rah wah kee-tah-nie dess.)

Discount *Waribiki* **(Wah-ree-bee-kee)**
Will you give me a discount? *Waribiki shite kuremasu ka.* (Wah-ree-bee-kee ssh-tay kuu-ray mahss kah?) I'll give you a 15 percent discount. *Ju-go pasento no waribiki wo agemasu.* (Juu-go pah-sin-toe no wah-ree-bee-kee oh ah-gay-mahss.)

Dish *Sara* **(Sah-rah)**
Please bring one more dish. *Mo hitotsu no sara wo motte kite kudasai.* (Moe ssh-tote-sue no sah-rah oh mote-tay kee-tay kuu-dah-sie.)

Distance *Kyori* **(K'yoe-ree)**
What is the distance between here and those mountains? *Koko kara ano yama made no kyori wa dono gurai desu ka?* (Koe-koe kah-rah ah-no yah-mah mah-day no k'yo-ree wah doe-no guu-rye dess kah?)

Distant (far) *Toi* **(Toy)**

Is the shop far from here? *Mise wa toi desu ka?* (Me-say wah toy dess kah?) No, it isn't far. *Iie, toku-nai desu.* (E-e-eh, toe-kuu-nie dess.)

Dizzy *Memai* **(May-my)**

I feel dizzy. *Memai ga shimasu.* (May-my gah she-mahss.)

Doctor *Isha* **(E-shah)**

Is there a doctor in the hotel? *Hoteru ni isha ga orimasu ka?* (Hoe-tay-rue nee e-shah gah oh-ree-mahss kah?) Please take me to a doctor. *Isha e tsurete itte kudasai.* (E-shah eh t'sue-rate-tay eet-tay kuu-dah-sie.)

Dollar *Doru* **(Doe-rue)**

How much is that in dollars? *Doru de sore wa ikura desu ka?* (Doe-rue day soe-ray wah e-kuu-rah dess kah?) It is $25. *Niju-go doru desu.* (Nee-juu-go doe-rue dess.)

Door *To* **(Toh)**; *Doa* (Doe-ah)

Please open the door. *To wo akete kudasai.* (Toh oh ah-kay-tay kuu-dah-sie.) Please close the door. *Doa wo shimete kudasai.* (Doe-ah oh she-may-tay kuu-dah-sie.)

Double (room) *Daburu* **(Dah-buu-rue)**

Do you want a double room? *Daburu no heya wo hoshii desu ka.* (Dah-buu-rue no hay-yah oh hoe-she-e dess kah?)

Downtown *Machi-no chushin* **(Mah-chee-no chuu-sheen)**

I would like to see the downtown area. *Machi-no chushin wo mitai desu.* (Mah-chee-no chuu-sheen oh me-tie dess.) Which way is downtown? *Machi no chushin wa dochi desu ka?* (Mah-chee no chuu-sheen wah doe-chee dess kah?)

Do you have (is there)? *Arimasu ka* **(Ah-ree-
mahss kah?)**
Do you have any wrapping paper? *Tsutsumi gami
ga arimasu ka?* (T-sue-t'sue-me gah-me gah ah-
ree-mahss kah?)

Draft beer *Nama biru* **(Nah-mah bee-rue)**
Two draft beers, please. *Nama biru ni-hai kudasai.*
(Nah-mah bee-rue nee-hie kuu-dah-sie.)

Dress (Western style) *Yofuku* **(Yoe-fuu-kuu);**
Dress *Doresu* (Doe-ray-sue)
How much is this dress? *Kono doresu wa ikura
desu ka?* (Koe-no doe-ray-sue wah e-kuu-rah dess
kah?) Do you always wear Western-style clothing? *Anata wa itsumo yofuku wo kimasu ka?* (Ah-
nah-tah wah eat-sue moe yoe-fuu-kuu oh kee-
mahss kah?) Get dressed! *Yofuku wo kinasai!*
(Yoe-fuu-kuù oh kee-nah-sie!)

Dressing (for salad) *Doreshingu* **(Doe-ray-
sheeng-guu)**
What kind of dressing do you have? *Donna doreshingu ga arimasu ka?* (Doan-nah doe-ray-shing-
guu gah ah-ree-mahss kah?)

Drink *Nomimasu* **(No-me-mahss);** A drink *Nomimono* (No-me-moe-no)
Would you like something to drink? *Nani-ka nomimasu ka?* (Nah-nee-kah no-me-mahss kah?)
What do you want to drink? *Nani wo nomitai desu
ka?* (Nah-nee oh no-me-tie dess kah?) What do
you have to drink? *Nomimono wa nani ga arimasu
ka?* (No-me-moe-no wah nah-nee gah ah-ree-
mahss kah?)

Drinking water *Nomi mizu* **(No-me me-zuu)**
Is this drinking water? *Kore wa nomi mizu desu ka?*
(Koe-ray wah no-me me-zuu dess kah?)

Drive (a car) *Unten shimasu* **(Uun-tane she-mahss)**
Can you drive a car? *Jidosha no unten suru koto ga dekimasu ka?* (Jee-doe-shah no uun-tane sue-rue koe-toe gah day-kee-mahss kah?) Would you like to go for a drive? *Doraibu ni ikimasu ka?* (Doe-rye-buu nee e-kee-mahss kah?)

Driver *Untenshu* **(Uun-tane-shuu)**; *Doraiba* (Doe-rye-bah)
Are you the driver? *Anata wa doraiba desu ka?* (Ah-nah-tah wah doe-rye-bah dess kah?)

Driver's license *Menkyo sho* **(Mane-k'yoe show)**
Do you have your driver's license? *Menkyo sho wo motte imasu ka?* (Mane-k'yoe show oh mote-tay e-mahss kah?) Please let me see it. *Misete kudasai.* (Me-sate-tay kuu-dah-sie.)

Drugstore *Kusuri-ya* **(Kuu-sue-ree-yah)**
Is there a drugstore nearby? *Kono hen ni kusuri-ya ga arimasu ka?* (Koe-no hane nee kuu-sue-ree-yah gah ah-ree-mahss kah?)

Drunk (to be) *Yotte imasu* **(Yote-tay e-mahss)**
He is drunk. *Anohito wa yotte imasu.* (Ah-no-ssh-toe wah yote-tay e-mahss.)

Drunk person *Yopparai* **(Yope-pah-rye)**
Be careful of that drunk! *Ano yopparai ni kiwo-tsuke nasai!* (Ah-no yope-pah-rye nee kee-oh-t'sue-kay nah-sie!)

Dry (clothing) *Kawakashimasu* **(Kah-wah-kah-she-mahss)**
This clothing is not dry. *Kono yofuku wa mada kawaite imasen.* (Koe-no yoe-fuu-kuu wah mah-dah kah-wah-eh-tay e-mah-sin.)

Dry-cleaning *Dorai kuriningu* **(Do-rye kuu-ree-ning-guu)**
I would like to have these pants dry-cleaned. *Kono zubon wo dorai kuriningu wo shite moraitai desu.* (Koe-no zuu-bone oh doe-rye kuu-ree-ning-guu oh ssh-tay moe-rye-tie dess.)

Dust *Hokori* **(Hoe-koe-ree)**
This room is really dusty. *Kono heya wa honto ni hokorippoi desu.* (Koe-no hay-yah wah hone-toe nee hoke-koe-ree-poy dess.) Please dust (clean). *Soji wo shite kudasai.* (Soe-jee oh ssh-tay kuu-dah-sie.)

Duty-free shop *Men-zei ten* **(Mane-zay-e tane)**
I want to go shopping at a duty-free shop. *Men-zei ten de kaimono shitai desu.* (Mane-zay-e tane day kie-moe-no ssh-tie dess.)

E

Early *Hayai* **(Hah-yie);** Too early *Hayasugiru* (Hah-yah-sue-ghee-rue)
It is still early. *Mada hayai desu.* (Mah-dah hah-yie dess.) Do you get up early? *Hayaku okimasu ka?* (Hah-yah-kuu oh-kee-mahss kah?)

Earring *Mimi-kazari* **(Me-me kah-zah-ree)**
I would like to see some earrings. *Mimi-kazari wo mitai desu.* (Me-me kah-zah-ree oh me-tie dess.) We have some very nice earrings. *Totemo ii mimi-kazari ga arimasu.* (Toe-tay-moe ee me-me-kah-zah-ree gah ah-ree-mahss.)

East *Higashi* (He-gah-she)
Which exit is the East Exit? *Dono deguchi ga Higashi Guchi desu ka?* (Doe-no day-guu-chee gah He-gah-shee Guu-chee dess ka?) The East Exit is on the other side of the terminal. *Higashi Guchi wa tamineru no muko gawa desu.* (He-gah-she Guu-chee wah tah-me-nah-rue no muu-koe gah-wah dess.)

Eat *Tabemasu* (Tah-bay-mahss)
Would you like to eat now? *Ima tabemasu ka?* (E-mah tah-bay-mahss kah?) Have you already eaten? *Mo tabemashita ka?* (Moe tah-bay-mahssh-tah kah?) No, I haven't eaten yet. *Iie, mada tabeteimasen.* (Ee-eh, mah-dah tah-bay-tay-e-mah-sin.) What do you want to eat? *Nani wo tabetai desu ka?* (Nah-nee oh tah-bay-tie dess kah?)

Eggs *Tamago* (Tah-mah-go)
Do you eat eggs? *Tamago wo tabemasu ka?* (Tah-mah-go oh tah-bay-mahss kah?) How would you like your eggs cooked? *Do yu fu ni yaitara ii desu ka?* (Doe yuu fuu nee yie-tah-rah ee dess kah?) Boiled eggs *Yude tamago* (Yuu-day tah-mah-go); soft-boiled eggs *han-juku tamago* (hahn-juu-kuu tah-mah-go); fried eggs *furaido eggu* (fuu-rye-doe a-guu); scrambled eggs *sukuramburu eggu* (sue-kuu-rahm-buu-rue a-guu); sunnyside-up *medama yaki* (may-dah-mah yah-kee)

Electricity (light) *Denki* (Dane-kee)
Where are the electrical outlets? *Denki no soketto wa doko ni arimasu ka?* (Dane-kee no soe-ket-toe wah doe-koe nee ah-ree-mahss kah?) Electric bulb *denkyu* (dane-que); electric lamp *dento* (dane-toe); electric fan *sempuki* (same-puu-kee)

Elevator *Erebeta* **(A-ray-bay-tah)**
Where is the elevator? *Erebeta wa doko desu ka?* (A-ray-bay-tah wah doe-koe dess kah?)

Embassy *Taishikan* **(Tie-she-kahn)**
I must go to the Japanese Embassy. *Nihon no Taishikan ni ikanakereba narimasen.* (Nee-hone no Tieshe-kahn nee e-kah-nah-kay-ray-bah nah-reemah-sin.) Do you know where it is? *Doko ni aru ka shite imasu ka?* (Doe-koe nee ah-rue kah sshtay e-mahss kah?)

Emergency *Hijoji* **(He-joe-jee)** or *Kinkyu* **(Keenque)**
This is an emergency. *Kore wa hijoji desu.* (Koeray way he-joe-jee dess.) Please call the doctor. *O'isha-San wo yonde kudasai.* (Oh-e-shah-Sahn oh yone-day kuu-dah-sie.)

Emergency exit *Hijo guchi* **(He-joe guu-chee)**
Where is the emergency exit? *Hijo guchi wa dochira desu ka?* (He-joe guu-chee wah doe-chee-rah dess kah?)

Emperor (of Japan) *Tenno Heika* **(Tane-no Hay-e-kah)**
Is the Emperor in the Imperial Palace? *Tenno Heika wa ima Kyujo ni irrashaimasu ka?* (Tane-no Hay-e-kah wah e-mah Que-joe nee e-rah-shymahss kah?)

Endorse (a check) *Uragaki shimasu* **(Uu-rah-gah-kee she-mahss)**
Please endorse this check. *Kono kogitte wo uragaki shite kudasai.* (Koe-no koe-geet-tay oh uu-rah-gah-kee ssh-tay kuu-dah-sie.)

England *Eikoku* **(A-e-koe-kuu);** English person *Ei-koku jin* **(A-e-koe-kuu jeen)**
Have you ever been to England? *Eikoku ni itta*

koto ga arimasu ka? (A-e-koe-kuu nee eat-tah koe-toe gah ah-ree-mahss kah?)

English language   *Eigo* (A-e-go)
Do you speak English? *Eigo ga dekimasu ka?* (A-e-go gah day-kee-mahss kah?)   No, I cannot. *Dekimasen.* (Day-kee-mah-sin.)   Is there anyone here who can speak English? *Dare ka Eigo no dekiru kata wa irashaimasu ka?* (Dah-ray kah A-e-go no day-kee-rue kah-tah wah e-rah-shy-mahss kah?)

Enjoy   *Tanoshimimasu* (Tah-no-she-me-mahss)
Are you enjoying yourself? *Tanoshii desu ka?* (Tah-no-she-e dess kah?)   Yes, I am (enjoying myself)   *Hai, tanoshii desu.* (Hie, tah-no-she-e dess.)   I had a good time. *Tanoshikatta desu.* (Tah-no-she-kot-tah dess.)

Enlarge (film)   *Hikinobashimasu* (He-kee-no-bah-she-mahss)
Please enlarge this film. *Kono firumu wo hikinobashite kudasai.* (Koe-no fee-rue-muu oh hi-kee-no-bah-ssh-tay kuu-dah-sie.)

Enough   *Jubun* (Juu-boon)
Do you have enough? *Jubun arimasu ka?* (Juu-boon ah-ree-mahss kah?)   I have enough. *Jubun arimasu.* (Juu-boon ah-ree-mahss.)   This is more than enough. *Kore wa ju-ni-bun desu.* (Koe-ray wah juu-nee-boon dess.)

Entrance   *Iriguchi* (E-ree-guu-chee);   Entrance foyer to a Japanese house or inn   *Genkan* (Gane-kahn); Main entrance of a building *Shomen* (Show-mane);   Back entrance *Ura guchi* (Uu-rah guu-chee) Tokyo Station has many entrances. *Tokyo Eki wa takusan iriguchi ga arimasu.* (Tokyo A-kee wah tock-sahn e-ree-guu-chee gah ah-ree-mahss.) I will meet you in front of the main entrance. *Shomen no mae de aimasu.* (Show-mane no my day aye-mahss.)

Envelope (letter) *Futo* **(Fuu-toe)**
Do you have airmail envelopes? *Kokubin no futo arimasu ka?* (Koe-kuu-bean no fuu-toe ah-ree-mahss kah?)

Equator *Sekido* **(Say-kee-doe)**
We have just crossed the equator. *Chodo ima sekido wo watarimashita.* (Choe-doe e-mah say-kee-doe oh wah-tah-ree-mahssh-tah.)

Escalator *Esukareta* **(S-kah-ray-tah)**
In Tokyo many subway stations have escalators. *Tokyo ni takusan chikatetsu no eki wa esukareta ga arimasu.* (Tokyo nee tock-sahn chee-kah-tate-sue no a-kee wah es-kah-ray-tah gah ah-ree-mahss.)

Europe *Yoroppa* **(Yoe-rope-pah);** also *Oshu* (Oh-shuu)
European-made goods are very popular in Japan. *Yoroppa-sei no shinamono wa Nihon de ninki ga arimasu.* (Yoe-rope-pah-say no she-nah-moe-no wah Nee-hone day neen-kee gah ah-ree-mahss.)

Evening *Yugata* **(Yuu-gah-tah);** This evening *Komban* (Kome-bahn)
I'll be here until this evening. *Yugata made koko ni orimasu.* (Yuu-gah-tah mah-day koe-koe nee oh-ree-mahss.)

Every hour *Ichiji-kan goto ni* **(E-chee-jee-kahn go-toe-nee)**
The train leaves every hour. *Ressha wa ichiji-kan goto ni demasu.* (Ray-shah wa e-chee-jee-kahn go-toe nee day-mahss.)

Every 30 minutes *Sanjuppun oki ni* **(Sahn-jupe-poon oh-kee nee)**
There is a train leaving every 30 minutes. *Sanjuppun oki ni ressha wa demasu.* (Sahn-jupe-poon oh-kee nee ray-shah wah day-mahss.)

Everything *Zembu* **(Zim-buu)**
Is this everything? *Kore wa zembu desu ka?* (Koe-ray wah zim-buu dess kah?) Take everything. *Zembu motte itte kudasai.* (Zim-buu mote-tay eat-tay kuu-dah-sie.)

Exit (at airports, hotels) *Hijo Guchi* **(He-joe Guu-chee);** Exit of regular buildings, stations, etc.) *Deguchi* (Day-guu-chee)
[Note: *hijo guchi* actually means "emergency exit," but it is standard in airports and hotels in Japan.] Meet me in front of the exit. *Deguchi no mae de atte kudasai.* (Day-guu-chee no my day aht-tay kuu-dah-sie.)

Expense *Hiyo* **(He-yoe);** Travel expense. *Ryohi* (Rio-he); At one's own expense. *Jihi-de* (Jee-he-day)
I am traveling at my own expense. *Watakushi wa jihi-de ryoko shite imasu.* (Wah-tock-she wah jee-hee-day rio-koe ssh-tay e-mahss.)

Expensive *Takai* **(Tah-kie)**
This shop is expensive! *Kono mise wa takai desu!* (Koe-no me-say wah tah-kie dess!)

Expire *Kireru* **(Kee-ray-rue)**
Your visa has expired. *Anato no bisa ga kiremashita.* (Ah-nah-tah-no bee-sah gah kee-ray-mah-ssh-tah.) When does your visa expire? *Bisa ga itsu kiremasu ka?* (Bee-sah gah eat-sue kee-ray mahss kah?)

Extension (phone) *Naisen* **(Nie-sin)**
May I have extension 23, please. *Naisen no niju-san onegaishimasu.* (Nie-sin no nee-juu-sahn oh-nay-gie-she-mahss.) What is your extension number? *Anata no naisen wa nanban desu ka?* (Ah-nah-tah no nie-sin wah nahn-bahn dess kah?)

Eyeglasses *Megane* **(May-gah-nay)**
Where are my glasses? I can't see. *Megane wa doko desu ka? Miemasen!* (May-gah-nay wah doe-koe dess kah? Me-a-mah-sin!)

F

Factory *Kojo* **(Koe-joe)**
I would like to see an automobile factory. *Jidosha no kojo wo mitai desu.* (Jee-doe-shah no koe-joe oh me-tai dess.) Is your factory large? *Anato no kojo wa okii desu ka?* (Ah-nah-tah no koe-joe wah oh-kee-e dess kah?)

Fairway (golf) *Feauei* **(Fay-ah-way)**
Is this the right fairway? *Kore wa tadashii feauei desu ka?* (Koe-ray wah tah-dah-she-e fay-ah-way dess kah?)

Famous *Yumei* **(Yuu-may-e)**
Is that a famous person? *Anohito wa yumei na hito desu ka?* (Ah-no-ssht-toe wah yuu-may nah ssht-toe dess kah?) This bridge is famous in Japan. *Nihon de wa kono hashi wa yumei desu.* (Nee-hone day wah koe-no hah-she wah yuu-may-e dess.)

Famous (local) products *Meibutsu* **(May-e-boot-sue);** Famous place *Meisho* **(may-e-show)**
In Japan many regions have famous local pro-

ducts. *Nihon de wa chiho no meibutsu ga takusan arimasu.* (Nee-hone day wah chee-hoe no may-e-boot-sue gah tock-sahn ah-ree-mahss.) And famous places as well. *Sore to meisho mo arimasu.* (Soe-ray toe may-e-show moe ah-ree-mahss.)

Far *Toi* (Toy)
Is the embassy far from here? *Taishikan wa koko kara toi desu ka?* (Tie-she-kahn wah koe-koe kah-rah toy dess kah?) Yes, it is. *Hai, toi desu.* (Hie, toy dess.) I do not want to walk far. *Ammari toku arukitaku-nai.* (Ahm-mah-ree toe-kuu ah-rue-kee-tah-kuu-nie.)

Fashion (style) *Ryuko* (Ree-you-koe); *also* Fashion *Fasshon* (Fah-shone); Fashion model *Fasshon moderu* (Fah-shone moe-day-rue); Fashionable *Ryuko shite imasu* (Ree-you-koe ssh-tay e-mahss)
Is this the newest fashion? *Kore wa ichiban atarashii ryuko desu ka?* (Koe-ray way e-chee-bahn ah-tah-rah-she-e ree-you-koe dess kah?) That is old fashioned. *Sore wa ryuko okure desu.* (Soe-ray wah ree-you-koe oh-kuu-ray dess.)

Feast (banquet) *Gochiso* (Go-chee-soh)
That was really a feast! *Sore wa honto ni gochiso deshita!* (Soe-ray wah hone-toe nee go-chee-soh desh-tah!) [Note: after being treated to a meal, it is customary to say to the host: "*Gochiso Sama deshita*" (Go-chee-soh Sah-mah desh-tah.)]

February *Nigatsu* (Nee-got-sue)
In Japan's northern regions it is cold in February. *Nihon no kita no chiho de Nigatsu wa samui desu.* (Nee-hone no kee-tah no chee-hoe day Nee-got-sue wah sah-muu-e dess.) Today is the 10th of February. *Kyo wa Nigatsu no toh-ka desu.* (K'yoe wah Nee-got-sue no toh-kah dess.)

Feel bad *Kibun ga warui* **(Kee-boon gah wah-rue-e)**
Do you feel bad? *Kibun ga warui desu ka?* (Kee-oon gah wah-rue-e dess kah?) No, I feel good. *Iie, kibun ga ii desu.* (Ee-eh, kee-boon gah ee dess.)

Ferry boat *Renraku-sen* **(Rane-rah-kuu-sane)**
Is there a ferry boat from Tokyo to Oshima? *Tokyo kara Oshima made renraku-sen ga arimasu ka?* (Tokyo kah-rah Oh-she-mah mah-day rane-rah-kuu-sane gah ah-ree-mahss kah?)

Festival *Matsuri* **(Mot-sue-ree)**
Most of Japan's festivals have some connection with a shrine or temple. *Nihon no matsuri wa hotondo zembu otera ka jinja ni kankei arimasu.* (Nee-hone no mot-sue-ree wah hoe-tone-doe zim-buu oh-tay-rah kah jeen-jah nee kahn-kay-e gah ah-ree-mahss.) Are there any festivals going on today? *Kyo wa doko ka de matsuri wo yatte imasu ka?* (K'yoe wah doe-koe kah day mot-sue-ree oh yaht-tay e-mahss kah?)

Fever *Netsu* **(Nate-sue)**
Do you have a fever? *Netsu ga arimasu ka?* (Nate-sue gah ah-ree-mahss kah?) No, I'm just hot. *Iie, tada atsui desu.* (Ee-eh, tah-dah aht-sue-e dess.)

Fifteen *Jugo* **(Juu-go)**
Fifteenth floor, please. *Ju-go-kai O'negaishimasu.* (Juu-go-kie Oh-nay-guy-she-mahss.) It is 15 kilometers from here. *Koko kara jugo kiro desu.* (Koe-koe kah-rah juu-go kee-roe dess.)

First (ordinal number) *Ichibamme* **(E-chee-bahm-may);** First (of all) *Dai-ichi* (Die-e-chee); First (in time) *Saisho* (Sie-show); First time *Hajimete* (hah-jee-may-tay)

Will the first person please enter. *Ichi-bamme no kata ga haitte kudasai.* (E-chee-bahm-may no kah-tah gah hite-tay kuu-dah-sie.) Is this your first time? *Hajimete desu ka?* (Hah-jee-may-tay dess kah?) First let's go shopping. *Saisho kaimono ni ikimasho.* (Sie-show kie-moe-no nee e-kee-mah-show.)

Film *Firumu* **(Fee-rue-muu)**
Do you have any color film? *Kara no firumu ga arimasu ka?* (Kah-rah no fee-rue-muu gah ah-ree-mahss kah?); Black and white *Kuro to shiro* (Kuu-roe toe she-roe.)

Fine (good, acceptable) *Kekko* **(Keck-koe);** *Ii* (Ee)
That is fine. *Sore wa kekko desu.* (Soe-ray wah keck-koe dess.) It sure is fine weather today, isn't it! *Kyo wa honto ni ii otenki desu, ne!* (K'yoe wah hone-toe nee ee oh-tane-kee dess, nay!)

Fire *Hi* **(He);** Conflagration *Kaji* (Kah-jee); Fire alarm *Kasai hochi* (Kah-sie hoe-chee); Fireworks *Hanabi* (Hah-nah-bee)
Please put the fire (in a stove, etc.) out. *Hi wo keshite kudasai.* (He oh kay-ssh-tay kuu-dah-sie.) Fires are very dangerous in Japan. *Nihon de wa kaji wa taihen abunai desu.* (Nee-hone day wah kah-jee wah tie-hane ah-buu-nie dess.)

Fish *Sakana* **(Sah-kah-nah);** Raw fish *Nama zakana* (Nah-mah zah-kah-nah)
Do you like fish? *Sakana ga suki desu ka?* (Sah-kah-nah gah ski dess kah?) How would you like your fish cooked? *Do yu fu ni ryorishitara ii desu ka?* (Doe yuu fuu nee rio-ree-she-tah-rah ee dess kah?) Do you eat raw fish? *Nama zakana wo tabemasu ka?* (Nah-mah zah-kah-nah oh tah-bay-mahss kah?)

Fishing *Tsuri* **(T'sue-ree);** Fishing rod *Tsuri zao* (T'sue-ree zah-oh); Fishing line *Tsuri ito* (T'sue-ree e-toe)
Let's go fishing. *Tsuri ni ikimasho* (T'sue-ree nee e-kee-mah-show.)

Fit (clothing) *Aimasu* **(Aye-e-mahss);** Fitting room *Shichaku shitsu* (She-chah-kuu sheet-sue)
Do the shoes fit well? *Kutsu ga yoku aimasu ka?* (Kute-sue gah yoe-kuu aye-mahss kah?) Yes, they fit. *Hai, atte imasu.* (Hie, aht-tay e-mahss.)

Flashlight *Kaichu dento* **(Kie-chuu dane-toe)**
Bring a flashlight. *Kaichu dento wo motte kite kudasai.* (Kie-chuu dane-toe oh mote-tay kee-tay-kuu-dah-sie.)

Flight (airline) *Bin* **(Bean)**
What flight are you going on? *Nan bin ni norimasu ka?* (Nahn bean nee noe-ree-mahss kah?) Flight No. 1—*Ichi Bin* (E-chee Bean); flight No. 2—*ni bin* (nee bean); flight No. 16—*ju-roku bin* (juu-roe-kuu-bean); flight No. 560—*gohyaku roku-ju bin* (go-h'yack-ku roe-kuu juu bean.)

Flight number *Bin mei* **(Bean may-e)**
What is your flight number? *Bin mei wa nan desu ka?* (Bean may-e wah nahn dess kah?)

Float (in parade) *Dashi* **(Dah-she)**
How many floats will there be in the festival? *Matsuri ni ikutsu no dashi ga demasu ka?* (Mot-sue-ree nee e-kute-sue no dah-she gah day mahss kah?)

Floor (of a room) *Yuka* **(Yuu-kah);** One floor of a hotel or building *Kai* (Kie)
Set it on the floor. *Yuka ni oite kudasai.* (Yuu-kah nee oh-e-tay kuu-dah-sie.) What floor is your

room on? *O'heya wa nan-kai desu ka?* (Oh-hay-yah wa nahn-kie dess kah?) The 23rd floor. *Ni-ju-san kai desu.* (Nee-juu-sahn kie dess.)

Flower *Hana* **(Hah-nah)**; Flower shop *Hana ya* (Hah-nah yah)
I would like to send some flowers. *Hana wo okuritai desu.* (Hah-nah oh oh-kuu-ree-tie dess.)
Aren't those flowers beautiful! *Sono hana wa kirei desu, ne!* (Soe-no hah-nah wah kee-ray-e dess, nay!)

Flower arranging *Ikebana* **(Ee-kay-bah-nah)**
Have you studied flower arranging? *Ikebana wo benkyo shita koto ga arimasu ka?* (Ee-kay-bah-nah oh bane-k'yoe ssh-tah koe-toe gah ah-ree-mahss kah?)

Fog *Kiri* **(Kee-ree)**; Haze *Moya* (Moe-yah)
San Francisco often has lots of fog. *San Furanshisuko wa tama ni takusan kiri ga demasu.* (Sahn Fuu-rahn-she-sue-koe wah tah-mah nee tock-sahn kee-ree gah day-mahss.)

Folding screen *Byobu* **(B-yoe-buu)**
Where can I buy folding screens? *Byobu wo doko de kaemasu ka?* (B'yoe-buu oh doe-koe day kie-mahss kah?) What is the width of this folding screen? *Kono byobu no haba wa dono gurai desu ka?* (Koe-no b'yoe-buu no hah-bah wah doe-no guu-rye dess kah?)

Food (generic sense) *Shokuhin* **(Show-kuu-heen)**; Food (meal) *Shokuji* (Show-kuu-jee); Something to eat *Tabemono* (Tah-bay-moe-no); Japanese food *Nihon shoku* (Nee-hone show-kuu); Western food *Yo shoku* (Yoh show-kuu)
What kind of food do you want, Japanese or

Western? *Donna shokuji ga hoshii desu ka? Yo shoku? Nihon shoku?* (Doan-nah show-kuu-jee gah hoe-she-e dess kah? Yoh show-kuu? Nee-hone show-kuu?) Have you become accustomed to eating Western food? *Yo shoku ni narete imashita ka?* (Yoh show-kuu nee nah-ray-tay e-mahssh-tah kah?)

Food poisoning *Shoku chudoku* (**Show-kuu chuu-doe-kuu**)

I think I have food poisoning. Please take me to a doctor. *Shoku chudoku da to omoimasu. Isha ni tsurete itte kudasai.* (Show-kuu chuu-doe-kuu dah toe oh-moe-e-mahss. E-shah nee t'sue-ray-tay eet-tay kuu-dah-sie.)

Foreign *Gaikoku no* (**Guy-koe-kuu no**)

Is this (item) foreign? *Kono shinamono wa gaikoku no desu ka?* (Koe-no she-nah-moe-no wah guy-koe-kuu no dess kah?)

Foreigner *Gaikoku-jin* (**Guy-koe-kuu-jeen**) or *Gaijin* (**Guy-jeen**)

In Japan foreigners are really conspicuous. *Nihon de gaikoku-jin wa totemo hitome ni tsukimasu.* (Nee-hone day guy-koe-kuu-jeen wa tote-tay-moe ssh-toe-may nee t'sue-kee-mahss.) Who is that foreigner? *Sono gaijin wa donata desu ka?* (Soe-no guy-jeen wah doe-nah-tah dess kah?)

Fork *Foku* (**Foe-kuu**)

Would you like to have a fork? *Foku hoshii desu ka?* (Foe-kuu hoe-she-e dess kah?) Chopsticks will be fine. *Hashi de yoroshii desu.* (Hah-she day yoe-roe-she-e dess.) Please bring me a fork. *Foku wo motte kite kudasai.* (Foe-kuu oh mote-tay kee-tay kuu-dah-sie.)

Formal *Seishiki no* **(Say-e-she-kee no)**
It is not a formal party. Come as you are. *Seishiki no paati ja nai. Sono mama de kite kudasai.* (Say-e-she-kee no pah-tee jah nie. Soe-no mah-mah day kee-tay kuu-dah-sie.)

Fortune teller *Ura-nai shi* **(Uu-rah-nie she)**
In Tokyo fortune tellers come out in the evenings. *Tokyo de wa ura-nai shi wa yugata ni demasu.* (Tokyo day wah uu-rah-nie she wah yuu-gah-tah nee day-mahss.)

Fragile *Koware-yasui* **(Koe-wah-ray-yah-sue-e)**
This (package, etc.) is fragile. Please be careful. *Kore wa koware mono desu kara chui shite kudasai* (Koe-ray wah koe-wah-ray moe-no dess kah-rah chuu-e ssh-tay kuu-dah-sie.)

France *Furansu* **(Fuu-rahn-sue);** French (person) *Furansu-jin* (Fuu-rahn-sue-jeen)
This is made in France *Kore wa Furansu-sei desu.* (Koe-ray wah Fuu-rahn-sue-say-e dess.) Are you from France? *Anata wa Furansu-jin desu ka?* (Ah-nah-tah wah Fuu-rahn-sue-jeen dess ka?)

Free (no cost) *Muryo* **(Muu-rio);** also *Tada* (Tah-dah); Free (at leisure) *Hima* (He-mah)
Is this free? *Kore wa muryo desu ka?* (Koe-ray wah muu-rio dess kah?) This is a free sample. *Kore wa tada no mihon desu.* (Koe-ray wah tah-dah no me-hone dess.) Are you free now? *Ima hima desu ka?* (E-mah he-mah dess kah?)

Free seats (unreserved) *Jiyu seki* **(Jee-yuu say-kee)**
All of the seats on the first floor are "free." *Ikai no seiki wa zembu jiyu seki desu.* (E-kie no say-kee wah zim-buu jee-yuu say-kee dess.)

Friday *Kinyobi* **(Keen-yoe-bee)**
On Friday stores are open until 9:00 P.M. *Kinyobi ni mise wa yoru no ku-ji made aite imasu.* (Keen-yoe-bee nee me-say wah yoe-rue no kuu-jee mah-day aye-tay e-mahss.) Will you be checking out on Friday? *Kinyobi ni cheku-auto shimasu ka?* (Keen-yoe-bee nee chek-au-toe she-mahss kah?)

Front desk *Furonto* **(Fuu-rahn-toe);** Registration Desk (at Japanese inns) *Choba* (Choe-bah)
Front Desk, please [when on the phone]. *Furonto onegaishimasu.* (Fuu-rahn-toe oh-nay-guy-she-mahss.) This is the Front Desk. *Furonto desu.* (Fuu-rahn-toe dess.)

Fruit *Kudamono* **(Kuu-dah-moe-no);** Apple *Ringo* (Reen-go); Peach *Momo* (Moe-moe); Pear *Nashi* (Nah-she); Plum *Ume* (Uu-may); Tangerine *Mikan* (Me-kahn)
What kind of fruit do you like? *Donna kudamono ga suki desu ka?* (Doan-nah kuu-dah-moe-no gah ski dess kah?) I will just have some fruit. *Kudamono dake de kekko desu.* (Kuu-dah-moe-no dah-kay day keck-koe dess.) Are tangerines in season? *Mikan wa ima shun desu ka?* (Me-kahn wah e-mah shune dess kah?)

Full (of food, etc.) *Ippai* **(Eep-pie)**
Are you already full? *Mo ippai desu ka?* (Moe eep-pie dess kah?) I'm full. I can't eat anymore! *Ippai desu. Mo taberaremasen!* (Eep-pie dess. Moe tah-bay-rah-ray-mah-sin!)

Full (seats in theater, plane) *Manseki* **(Mahn-say-kee)**
Is it full? *Manseki desu ka?* (Mahn-say-kee dess kah?) Yes, it's full. *Manseki desu.* (Mahn-say-kee

dess.) There are still plenty of seats. *Mada taku-san seki ga arimasu.* (Mah-dah tock-sahn say-kee gah ah-ree-mahss.)

Full course (meal) *Furu Kosu* **(Fuu-rue Koe-suu)**
[Note: In Japan full-course meals are usually divided into Course A, Course B, etc. *A kosu, B kosu,* etc. (A koe-sue; B koe-sue).] B Course, please. *B Kosu wo kudasai.* (B koe-sue oh kuu-dah-sie.)

G

Garden *Niwa* **(Nee-wah);** *Gaaden* (Gahh-dane)
[Note: In Japan a garden *(niwa)* is synonymous with yard, and the typical garden is very small. Hotel gardens, however, are often large and beautifully landscaped.] I would like to have a garden but I have no room (space). *Niwa ga ho-shii kedo aita basho ga nai desu.* (Nee-wah gah hoe-shee kay-doe aye-tah bah-show gah nie dess.)

Garlic *Ninniku* **(Neen-nee-kuu)**
Is a lot of garlic used in Japan? *Nihon de wa taku-san ninniku wo tsukaimasu ka?* (Nee-hone day wah tock-sahn neen-nee-kuu oh t'sue-kie-e-mahss kah?) Is there any garlic in this? *Kore ni ninniku ga haitte imasu ka?* (Koe-ray nee neen-nee-kuu gah hite-tay e-mahss kah?) I don't like garlic. *Ninniku kirai desu.* (Neen-nee-kuu kee-rye dess.)

Gas *Gasu* **(Gah-sue);** also *Gasorin* (Gah-soe-reen)
Is gasoline expensive in Japan? *Nihon de gasorin wa takai desu ka?* (Nee-hone day gah-soe-reen wah tah-kie dess kah?) Yes, it is. *Hai, takai desu.* (Hie, tah-kie dess.) One liter costs about as

much as one American gallon. *Ichi rita wa Amerika no garon to onaji gurai desu.* (E-chee ree-tah wa Ah-may-ree-kah no gah-rone toe oh-nah-jee guu-rie dess.)

Gate *Mon* **(Moan);** Arrival gate *Tochaku guchi* (Toe-chah-kuu guu-chee); Departure gate *Tojo guchi* (Toe-joe guu-chee); *Geito* (Gay-e-toe) If the gate is closed, please ring the bell. *Mon ga shimatte itara, beru wo oshite kudasai.* (Moan gah she-mot-tay eat-tah-rah, bay-rue oh ohssh-tay kuu-dah-sie.) Gate No. 1 *Ichiban Geito* (E-chee-bahn Gay-e-toe); Gate No. 3 *Sanban Geito* (Sahn-bahn Gay-e-toe); Gate No. 69 *Rokujukyuban Geito* (Roe-kuu-juu-gue-bahn Gay-e-toe).

Gather (assemble) *Atsumarimasu* **(Aht-sue-mah-ree-mahss)**
Please gather in the lobby at 1:30 P.M. *Gogo no ichiji-han ni robi de atsumatte kudasai.* (Go-go no e-chee-jee-hahn nee roe-bee day aht-sue-mot-tay kuu-dah-sie.)

Genuine *Hommono* **(Home-moe-no)**
Is this genuine leather? *Kore wa hommono no kawa desu ka?* (Koe-ray wah home-moe-no no kah-wah dess kah?) No, it's imitation. *Iie, nise-mono desu.* (Ee-eh, nee-say-moe-no dess.)

German (person) *Doitsu-jin* **(Doe-eat-sue-jeen);** German (thing) *Doitsu-no* (Doe-eat-sue-no); German (language) *Doitsu Go* (Doe-eat-sue Go) Is that woman German? *Ano onna-no-hito wa Doitsu-jin desu ka?* (Ah-no own-nah-no-ssh-toe wah Doe-eat-sue-jeen dess kah?) She speaks German. *Kanojo wa Doitsu go wo hanasemasu.* (Kah-no-joe wah Doe-eat-sue go oh hah-nah-say-mahss).

Gift *Omiyage* (Oh-me-yah-gay)

Please accept this gift. *Dozo, kono omiyage wo osa-mete kudasai.* (Doe-zoe, koe-no oh-me-yah-gay oh oh-sah-may-tay kuu-dah-sie.) It is a gift for your mother. *Anata no Oka-San ni Omiyage desu.* (Ah-nah-tah no Oh-kah-Sahn ni Oh-me-yah-gay dess.) Thank you for the gift. *Omiyage wo domo arigato gozaimasu.* (Oh-me-yah-gay oh doe-moe ah-ree-gah-toe go-zie-mahss.) I still have to buy two gifts. *Mada futatsu no omiyage wo kawanakereba narimasen.* (Mah-dah fuu-tot-sue no oh-me-yah-gay oh kah-wah-nah-kay-ray-bah nah-ree-mah-sin.)

Gift-buying-going-away money *Senbetsu* (Sane-bate-sue)

[Note: It used to be very common for the Japanese to give money (in special envelopes) to friends leaving on trips—most of which was used to buy gifts. The word is still useful.]

Girl *Onna-no-ko* (Own-nah-no-koe); Young (unmarried) lady *O-jo-San* (Oh-joe-Sahn)

That girl is beautiful. *Ano onna-no-ko wa utsuku-shii desu.* (Ah-no own-nah-no-koe wah uut-sue-kuu-she-e dess.) Please introduce me to that girl. *Ano onna-no-ko ni shokai shite kudasai.* (Ah-no own-nah-no-koe nee show-kie ssh-tay kuu-dah-sie.)

Give *Agemasu* (ah-gay-mahss)

Please give this key to Mr. Suzuki. *Kono kagi wo Suzuki-San ni agete kudasai.* (Koe-no kah-ghee oh Suu-zuu-kee-Sahn nee ah-gay-tay kuu-dah-sie.) I'll give it to him tonight. *Komban Suzuki-San ni agemasu.* (Kome-bahn Suzuki-Sahn nee ah-gay-mahss.) I gave it to him yesterday. *Kino anohito ni agemashita.* (Kee-no ah-no-ssh-toe nee ah-gay-mahssh-tah.)

Glass (for drinking) *Koppu* (Kope-puu)
Please bring six glasses to my room. *Watakushi no heya e muttsu no koppu wo motte kite kudasai.* (Wah-tock-she no hay-yah eh mute-sue no kope-puu oh mote-tay kee-tay kuu-dah-sie.)

Glasses (eye) *Megane* (May-gah-nay)
Are these your glasses? *Kore wa anata no megane desu ka?* (Koe-ray wah ah-nah-tah no may-gah-nay dess kah?) No. I think they are Mr. Sato's. *Iie, Sato-San no to omoimasu.* (Ee-eh, Sah-toe-Sahn no toe oh-moy-mahss.)

Globe fish *Fugu* (Fuu-guu)
Have you ever eaten fugu? *Fugu wo tabeta koto ga arimasu ka?* (Fuu-guu oh tah-bay-tah koe-toe gah ah-ree-mahss kah?) Not yet, but I would like to try it. *Mada desu ga, tabete mitai desu.* (Mah-dah dess gah, tah-bay-tay me-tie dess.)

Gloves *Tebukuro* (Tay-buu-kuu-roe)
The wind is very cold today. You'd better take gloves. *Kyo no kaze ga sugoku tsumetai no de tebu-kuro wo motte iku ho ga ii desu.* (K'yoe no kah-zay gah sue-go-kuu t'sue-may-tie no day, tay-buu-kuu-roe oh mote-tay e-kuu hoh gah ee dess.)

Go *Ikimasu* (Ee-kee-mahss)
I'm going now. *Ima ikimasu.* (E-mah e-kee-mahss.) When are you going? *Itsu ikimasu ka?* (Eat-sue e-kee-mahss kah?) I went yesterday. *Kino ikimashita.* (Kee-no e-kee-mahssh-tah.) Let's go. *Ikimasho.* (E-kee-mah-show.)

Go out *Dekakemasu* (Day-kah-kay-mahss)
Are you going out tonight? *Komban dekakemasu ka?* (Kome-bahn day-kah-kay-mahss kah?)

119

He/she went out. *Dekakemashita.* (Day-kah-kay-mahssh-tah.)

Gold *Kin* **(Keen);** Gold mine *Kin zan* (Keen zahn)
Is this 24-carat gold? *Kore wa nijuyon karato no kin desu ka?* (Koe-ray wah nee-juu-yone kah-rah-toe no keen dess kah?) Do you have any gold coins? *Kinka arimasu ka?* (Keen-kah ah-ree-mahss Kah?)

Golf *Gorufu* **(Go-rue-fuu);** Golf course *Gorufu jo* (go-rue-fuu joe); Golf club *Gorufu kurabu* (Go-rue-fuu kuu-rah-buu); Green's fee *Gurin fii* (Guu-reen fee)
Golf is a very popular sport in Japan. *Nihon de gorufu wa taishuteki-na supotsu desu.* (Nee-hone day go-rue-fuu wa tie-shuu-tay-kee-nah sue-poat-sue dess.) Let's go play golf. *Gorufu wo yari ni ikimasho.* (Go-rue-fuu oh yah-ree nee e-kee-mah-show.)

Good afternoon *Konnichi wa* **(Kone-nee-chee wah)**
[Note: said from around noon until early evening, this expression is similar to "Good day."]

Goodbye *Sayonara* **(Sah-yoe-nah-rah)**
[The literal meaning of this beautiful word is "If it must be so!" It is used when parting for relatively short as well as long periods.]

Good evening *Komban wa* **(Kome-bahn wah)**
[Said from around dusk until the wee hours.]

Good morning *Ohaiyo gozaimasu* **(Oh-hie-yoe go-zie-mahss)**
[Said from very early until around 11:00 A.M. (Except by people who work at night. They say

"Good Morning" when they first meet in the evening.)]

Good night *Oyasumi nasai* **(Oh-yah-sue-me nah-sie)**
[The literal meaning of *Oyasumi nasai* is something like "Go to rest" or "Go to sleep."]

Grandfather *Ojii-San* **(Oh-jee-e-Sahn)**
Is your grandfather still alive? *Anato no Ojii-San wa mada ikite imasu ka?* (Ah-nah-tah no Oh-jee-e-Sahn wah mah-dah e-kee-tay e-mahss kah?) My grandfather is 81 years old. *Watakushi no Ojii-San ga hachiju-ichi sai desu.* (Wah-tock-she no Oh-jee-e-Sahn gah hah-chee-juu-e-chee sie dess.)

Grandmother *Obaa-San* **(Oh-bahh-Sahn);**
Grandparents *Sofubo* (Soe-fuu-boe)
Does your grandmother live with you? *Obaa-San ga anata to issho ni sunde imasu ka?* (Oh-bahh-Sahn gah ah-nah-tah toe e-sshow nee soon-day e-mahss kah?)

Grape(s) *Budo* **(Buu-doe);** Grape juice *Gurepu jusu* (guu-ray-puu juu-sue)
When is the grape season? *Budo no shun wa itsu desu ka?* (Buu-doe no shune wah eat-sue dess kah?)

Grapefruit (Japanese variety) *Natsu mikan* **(Not-sue me-kahn);** (Western variety) *Gurepu furutsu* (Guu-ray-puu fuu-rue-t'sue)
Is the grapefruit pink? *Gurepu furutsu wa pinku desu ka?* (Guu-ray-puu fuu-rue-t'sue wah peen-kuu dess kah?) We would both like grapefruit. *Futari tomo gurepu furutsu hoshii desu.* (Fuu-tah-ree toe-moe guu-ray-puu fuu-rue-t'sue hoe-shee dess.)

121

Group *Gurupu* **(Guu-rue-puu)**
Which is your group? *Anata no gurupu wa dochira desu ka?* (Ah-nah-tah no guu-rue-puu wah doe-chee-rah dess kah?) Please form a group here. *Koko de gurupu ni natte kudasai.* (Koke-koe day guu-rue-puu nee naht-tay kuu-dah-sie.)

Guarantee *Hosho shimasu* **(Hoe-show she-mahss);** Guarantor *Hosho nin* (Hoe-show neen) Will you guarantee me? *Anata wa watakushi wo hosho shite kuremasu ka?* (Ah-nah-tah wah wah-tock-she oh hoe-show ssh-tay kuu-ray-mahss kah?) Without a guarantor you cannot stay in Japan. *Hosho nin ga inai to Nihon ni iraremasen.* (Hoe-show neen gah e-nie toe Nee-hone nee e-rah-ray-mah-sin.) Will you guarantee this check? *Kono kogitte wo hosho shimasu ka?* (Koe-no ko-geet-tay oh hoe-show she-mahss kah?)

Guest *Okyaku-san* (Oh-k'yack-sahn); also *Gesuto* (Guesto); Guest room *Kyaku ma* (K'ya-kuu mah)
[Note: The Japanese typically refer to guests, individually and in groups, as *Okyaku-san* or "Honorable guest," which is both respectful and practical (since it is not necessary to know their names to address them in a very acceptable manner).] Would the guest like something to drink? *Okayku-san wa nani-ka nomimasu ka?* (Oh-k'yack-sahn wah nah-nee-kah no-me-mahss kah?)

Guide *Annai-sha* **(Ahn-nie-shah);** also *Gaido* (Gie-doe); To guide *Annai shimasu* (Ahn-nie she-mahss); English-speaking guide *Eigo no de-kiru gaido* (A-e-go no day-kee-rue gie-doe) Please guide me. *Annai shite kudasai.* (Ahn-nie ssh-tay kuu-dah-sie.) Are you our guide? *Anata wa watakushi-tachi no annai-sha desu ka?* (Ah-nah-

tah wah wah-tock-she-tah-chee no ahn-nie shah
dess kah?) I want to hire an English-speaking
guide. *Eigo no dekiru gaido wo tanomitai desu.* (A-e-
go no day-kee-rue gie-do oh tah-no-me-tie dess.)

Guidebook *Annai sho* **(Ahn-nie show);** also
Gaido buukuu (Gie-doe buu-kuu)
You can buy a guidebook in the hotel bookstore.
*Hoteru no buukuu shoppu de gaido buukuu wo kau
koto ga dekimasu.* (Hoe-tay-rue no buu-kuu shope-
puu day gie-doe buu-kuu oh kow koe-toe gah
day-kee-mahss.)

H

Habit *Shukan* **(Shuu-kahn);** also *Kuse* (Kuu-say)
Is that a Japanese habit? *Sore wa Nihon-jin no shu-
kan desu ka?* (Soe-ray wah Nee-hone-jeen no
shuu-kahn dess kah?) We have similar habits in
America. *Amerika ni onaji yo na shukan ga arimasu.*
(Ah-may-ree-kah nee oh-nah-jee yoh nah shuu-
kahn gah ah-ree-mahss.) Bad habit *Warui kuse*
(Wah-rue-e kuu-say).

Haggle *Negirimasu* **(Nay-ghee-ree-mahss)**
Come on! Let's haggle (about the price)! *Sa!
Negirimasho!* (Sah! Nay-ghee-ree-mah-show!)
I'm sorry. At this shop we cannot haggle. *Sumi-
masen ga. Kono mise de negiru koto gah dekimasen.*
(Sue-me-mah-sin gah. Koe-no me-say day nay-
ghee-rue koe-toe gah day-kee-mah-sin.)

Hair (on the head) *Kami* **(Kah-me);** *Kami-no ke*
(Kah-me-no kay)
I think long hair is beautiful. *Nagai kami ga kirei
da to omoimasu.* (Nah-guy kah-me gah kee-ray-e

123

dah toe oh-moy-mahss.) Don't get your hair cut
short. *Kami wo mijikaku katte wa ikenai.* (Kah-me
oh me-jee-kah-kuu kot-tay wah e-kay-nie.)

Half *Hambun* (Hahm-boon); Less than half
Hambun ika (Hahm-boon e-kah); Over half
Hambun ijo (Hahm-boon e-joe)
Just give me half of it, please. I have a small ap-
petite. *Hambun dake kudasai. Watakushi wa sho-
shoku desu.* (Hahm-boon dah-kay kuu-dah-sie.
Wah-tock-she wah show-show-kuu dess.)

Hall (large room) *Hiroma* (He-roe-mah); *Horu*
(Hoe-rue); Corridor *roka* (roe-kah)
I put my bags out in the hall. *Nimotsu wo roka ni
dashimashita.* (Nee-mote-tsu oh roe-kah nee
dah-she-mahssh-tah.) Last night we went to a
dance hall. *Yube watakushi-tachi wa dansu horu ni
ikimashita.* (Yuu-bay wah-tock-she-tachi wah
dahn-sue hoe-rue nee e-kee-mahssh-tah.)

Ham *Hahmu* (Hah-muu); Ham sandwich *Hamu
sando* (Hah-muu sahn-doe)
Do you eat ham? *Hamu wo tabemasu ka?* (Hah-
muu oh tah-bay-mahss kah?) I'll have ham and
eggs. *Hamu eggu ni itashimasu.* (Hah-muu eggu
nee e-tah-she-mahss.)

Hamburger *Hamubaga* (Hah-muu bah-gah)
Two hamburgers, please. *Hamubaga futatsu kudasai.* (Hah-muu-bah-gah fuu-tot-sue kuu-dah-
sie.) With onions. *Tamanegi nosete.* (Tah-mah-
nay-ghee no-say-tay.)

Hand (person's) *Te* (Tay)
Let me see your hand. *Te wo misete.* (Tay oh me-
say-tay). Use your right hand. *Migi no te wo tsukatte.* (Me-ghee no tay oh scot-tay.) Left hand—
Hidari no te (He-dah-ree no tay).

Handbag *Tesage* **(Tay-sah-gay);** *Handobakku*
(Hahn-doe bah-kuu)
Be careful with your handbag. *Handobakku ni
kiwotsukete.* (Hahn-doe-bah-ku nee kee-oh-
skay-tay.)

Hand baggage *Te-ni-motsu* **(Tay-nee-mote-sue)**
Please take all hand baggage with you. *Te-ni-
motsu wo zembu motte itte kudasai.* (Tay-nee-mote-
sue oh zim-buu mote-tay eat-tay kuu-dah-sie.)
Don't forget your hand baggage. *Te-ni-motsu wo
wasure nai de.* (Tay-nee-mote-sue oh wah-sure-ray
nie day.)

Handkerchief *Hankechi* **(Hahn-kay-chee)**
You dropped your handkerchief. *Hankechi wo oto-
shimashita.* (Hahn-kay-chee oh oh-toe-she-
mahssh-tah.)

Hangover *Futsuka-yoi* **(Futes-kah yoy)**
I always have hangovers so I don't drink very
much. *Watakushi wa itsumo futsuka-yoi shimasu
kara ammari nomimasen.* (Wah-tock-she wah eet-
sue-moe futes-kah yoy she-mahss kah-rah ahm-
mah-ree no-me-mah-sin.)

Happy (short-term) *Ureshii* **(Uh-ray-she-e);** Happy (long-term) *Shiawase* (She-ah-wah-say);
Happy/glad to do something *Yorokobimasu* (Yoe-
roe-koe-bee-mahss)
I'm really happy (to see you, hear about that,
etc.) *Ureshii desu.* (Uu-ray-she-e dess.) I'll be
happy to accompany you. *Yorokonde otomo shimasu.* (Yoe-roe-kone-day oh-toe-moe she-
mahss.)

Hard (to the touch) *Katai* **(kah-tie);** Hard (difficult) *Muzukashii* (Mu-zuu-kah-she-e)
This seat is hard. *Kono seki wa katai desu.* (Koe-no

say-kee wah kah-tie dess.) Is Japanese difficult?
Nihongo wa muzukashii desu ka? (Nee-hone-go
wah muu-zuu-kah-she-e dess kah?)

Have (meaning "to be" or "to exist") *Arimasu* (Ah-ree-mahss)

Is there any (some)? *Arimasu ka?* (Ah-ree-mahss
kah?) Do you have. . . ? Arimasu ka? (Ah-ree-mahss kah?)

Headache *Zutsu shimasu* (Zoot-sue she-mahss)

I have a headache. *Watakushi wa zutsu ga shite
imasu.* (Wah-tock-she wah zoot-sue gah ssh-tay
e-mahss.) Do you have any aspirin? *Asupurin ga
arimasu ka?* (Ahs-puu-reen gah ah-ree-mahss
kah?)

Health resort *Hoyo chi* (Hoe-yoe chee)

I'd like to see a health resort in the mountains.
Yama no naka no hoyo chi wo mitai desu. (Yah-mah
no nah-kah no hoe-yoe chee oh me-tie dess.)

Hear (listen) *Kikimasu* (Kee-kee-mahss)

Did you hear that? *Sore wo kikimashita ka?* (Soe-
ray oh kee-kee-mahssh-tah kah?) No, I didn't.
Iie, kikimasen deshita. (Ee-eh, kee-kee-mah-sin
desh-tah.) Can you hear? *Kikoemasu ka?* (Kee-
koe-eh-mahss kah?) Please listen. *Kiite kudasai.*
(Keet-tay kuu-dah-sie.)

Heart (medical) *Shinzo* (Sheen-zoe); Heart (ro-mantic/literary) *Kokoro* (Koe-koe-roe)

I think he's having a heart attack. *Shinzo ga mahi
wo shite iru to omoimasu.* (Sheen-zoe gah mah-he
oh ssh-tay e-rue toe oh-moy-mahss.) I thank
you with all my heart. *Kokoro kara orei wo moshia-
gemasu.* (Koe-koe-roe kah-rah oh-ray-e oh moe-
she-ah-gay-mahss.)

Heavy *Omoi* **(Oh-moy)**
My suitcase is heavy. Please help me. *Watakushi no sutsu kesu wa omoi desu. Tetsudatte kudasai.* (Wah-tock-she no soot-sue kay-sue wah oh-moy dess. Tate-sue-dot-day kuu-dah-sie.) This is too heavy for me. *Kore wa watakushi ni omosugimasu.* (Koe-ray wah wah-tock-she nee oh-moe-sue-ghee-mahss.)

Helicopter *Herikoputa* **(Hay-ree-kope-tah)**
I would like to fly over the beach in a helicopter. *Herikoputa de kaigan no ue wo tobitai desu.* (Hay-ree-kope-tah day kie-ghan no way oh toe-bee-tie dess.)

Hello (on the telephone) *Moshi-Moshi* **(Moe-she-Moe-she)**
[*Moshi-moshi* is also used to attract the attention of a waiter or someone who has dropped something, etc. See **Good Morning, Good Afternoon,** etc.]

Highway *Kaido* **(Kie-doe);** Expressway *Kosoku-doro* (Koe-soe-kuu-doe-roe)
Which expressway goes to Nagoya? *Nagoya yuki no kosokudoro wa dore desu ka?* (Nah-go-yah yuu-kee no koe-soe-kuu-doe-roe wah doe-ray dess kah?)

Historical Place *Kyu Seki* **(Que Say-kee)**
In Japan there are many Historical Places. *Nihon ni wa kyu seki ga takusan arimasu.* (Nee-hone nee wah que say-kee gah tock-sahn ah-ree-mahss.)

Holiday *Kyujitsu* **(Que-jeet-sue);** *Horidei* (Hoe-ree-day-e)
When is your next holiday? *Anata no tsugi no kyujitsu wa itsu desu ka?* (Ah-nah-tah no t'sue-ghee

no que-jeet-sue wah eat-sue dess kah?) Today is
a holiday. *Kyo wa horidei desu.* (K'yoe wah hoe-
ree-day-e dess.)

Home *Uchi* (Uu-chee)
I'm going home. *Uchi e kaerimasu.* (Uu-chee eh
kie-ree-mahss.) My wife is at home. *Kanai wa
uchi ni orimasu.* (Kah-nie wah uu-chee nee oh-re-
mahss.) My house is very small. *Watakushi no
uchi wa taihen chiisai desu.* (Wah-tock-she no uu-
chee wa tie-hane chee-sie dess.)

Honeymoon trip *Shinkon ryoko* (Sheen-kone rio-koe)
Is this your honeymoon trip? *Shinkon ryoko desu
ka?* (Sheen-kone rio-koe dess kah?)

Hors d'oeuvres (Japanese style) *Zensai* (Zen-sie); *Otsumami* (Oh-t'sue-mah-me)
[Note: *otsumami*—peanuts, dried beans, tiny
sembei crackers, etc.—are usually served with
drinks.] Please serve some hors d'oeuvres. *Zensai wo dashite kudasai.* (Zen-sie oh dah-ssh-tay
kuu-dah-sie.)

Hospital *Byooin* (B'yohh-een)
Where is the nearest hospital? *Ichiban chikai
byooin wa doko desu ka?* (E-chee-bahn chee-kai
b'yohh-een wah doe-koe dess kah?) I will take
you to a hospital. *Byooin e tsurete ikimasu.*
(B'yohh-een nee t'sue-ray-tay e-kee-mahss.)

Hostess (class restaurant) *Annai-gakari* (Ahn-nie-gah-kah-ree); Cabaret/Nightclub Hostess *Hosutesu* (hoess-tay-sue)
Please wait for the (restaurant) hostess. *Annai-
gakari wo matte kudasai.* (Ahn-nie-gah-kah-ree oh
mot-tay kuu-dah-sie.) Cabaret hostesses can be
charming companions, but expensive. *Kyabare no*

hosutesu wa chaamingu ga takai desu! (K'yah-bah-ray no hoess-tay-sue wah chah-meen-guu gah tah-kie dess!).

Hot (spicy) *Karai* (Kah-rye)
Is this (dish) spicy? *Kore wa karai desu ka?* (Koe-ray wah kah-rye desu kah?) I cannot eat spicy foods. *Karai tabemono wo taberaremasen.* (Kah-rye tah-bay-moe-no oh tah-bay-rah-ray-mah-sin.)

Hot (touch/weather) *Atsui* (Aht-sue-e)
Is it hot now in Tokyo? *Ima Tokyo wa atsui desu ka?* (E-mah Tokyo wah aht-sue-e dess kah?) Don't touch that! It's hot! *Sore ni sawaranai de! Atsui desu!* (Soe-ray nee sah-wah-rah-nie day! Aht-sue-e dess)

Hotel *Hoteru* (Hoe-tay-rue); *Yado* (Yah-doe)
[Note: Western-style hotels are always referred to in Japanese as *hoteru*.] What hotel are you staying at? *Dono hoteru ni tomatte imasu ka?* (Do-no hoe-tay-rue nee toe-mot-tay e-mahss kah?) Is that a good hotel? *Sore wa ii hoteru desu ka?* (Soe-ray wah ee hoe-tay-rue dess kah?)

Hotspring spa *Onsen* (Own-sin)
Japan has over one thousand hotspring spas. *Nihon wa isen ijo no onsen ga arimasu.* (Nee-hone wah e-sin e-joe no own-sin gah ah-ree-mahss.) Have you ever stayed at an *onsen*? *Onsen ni tomatta koto ga arimasu ka?* (Own-sin nee toe-mot-tah koe-toe gah ah-ree-mahss kah?)

Hour *Jikan* (Jee-kahn); One hour *Ichi jikan* (E-chee jee-kahn); Two hours *Ni jikan* (Nee jee-khan)
We will be here for about one hour. *Koko ni dai-tai ichi jikan gurai imasu.* (Koe-koe nee die-tie e-chee jee-kahn guu-rye e-mahss.)

House *Ie* **(E-eh)**
[Note: *Ie* refers more to the building or to the
family line; i.e., the House of Mitsui.] Next year
I will build a new house. *Rainen atarashii no ie wo
kenchiku shimasu.* (Rye-nane ah-tah-rah-she-e no
e-eh oh kane-chee-kuu she-mahss.)

House phone *Okunai denwa* **(Oh-kuu-nie dane-
wah)**
Where are the house phones? *Okunai denwa wa
doko ni arimasu ka?* (Oh-kuu-nie dane-wah wah
doe-koe nee ah-ree-mahss kah?)

How cooked *Yaki guai* **(Yah-kee gwie)**
How would you like it cooked? *Donna yaki guai
ga ii desu ka?* (Doan-nah yah-kee gwie gah ee
dess kah?) Well-done, please. *Yoku yaite kudasai.*
(Yoe-kuu yite-tay kuu-dah-sie.) Medium-well
Mediumm (May-dee-umm); rare *nama-yaki* (nah-
mah-yah-kee.)

How do you do (greeting) *Dozo yoroshiku* **(Doe-
zoe yoe-roe-she-kuu.)**

How many (persons) *Nan nin* **(Nahn neen)**
How many people (in your party)? *Nan nin desu
ka?* (Nahn neen dess kah?)

How many pieces (bags, etc.) *Nan-ko* **(Nahn-koe)**
How many bags do you have? *Nimotsu ga nan-ko
arimasu ka?* (Nee-mote-sue gah nahn-koe ah-ree-
mahss kah?)

How much (cost) *Ikura* **(E-kuu-rah)**
How much is it? *Ikura desu ka?* (E-kuu-rah dess
kah?)

Humidity *Shimerike* **(She-may-ree-kay)** or
Shitsudo (Sheet-sue-doe)
In Phoenix, Arizona the humidity is very low.

Arizona no Fenikkusu de wa shimerike ga taihen hikui desu. (Arizona no Fee-nee-kuu-sue day wah she-may-ree-kay gah tie-hane he-kuu-ee dess.) The humidity is high in Tokyo. *Tokyo de wa shimerike ga takai desu.* (Tokyo day wah she-may-ree-kay gah tah-kie dess.)

Humorous (funny) *Kokkei-na* (Koke-kay-e-nah)
He is very humorous. *Anohito wa taihen kokkei-na hito desu.* (Ah-no-ssh-toe wah tie-hane koke-kay-e-nah ssh-toe dess.)

Hungry *Onaka ga sukimasu* (On-nah-kah gah ski-mahss)
Are you hungry? *Onaka ga suite imasu ka?* (Oh-nah-kah-gah sue-e-tay e-mahss kah?) Yes, I am. *Hai, suite imasu.* (Hie, sue-e-taye-mahss.) No, I'm not. *Iie, suite imasen.* (Ee-eh, sue-e-tay e-mah-sin.)

Hurry *Hayaku* (Hah-yah-kuu); To be in a hurry *Isogimasu* (E-soe-ghee-mahss); Hurry! *Isoide!* (E-soy-e-day!)
We're late. Please hurry. *Osoku narimashita. Hayaku shite kudasai.* (Oh-soe-ku nah-ree-mahssh-tah. Hah-yah-kuu ssh-tay kuu-dah-sie.) Hurry! *Hayaku!* (Hah-yah-kuu) Are you in a hurry? *O'isogi desu ka?* (Oh-e-soe-ghee dess kah?)

Husband *Shujin* (Shuu-jeen); Your husband *Go-shujin* (Go-shuu-jeen)
Where is your husband? *Go-shujin wa doko ni irasshaimasu ka?* (Go-shuu-jeen wah doe-koe nee e-rah-shy-mahss kah?) This (person) is my husband. *Konohito wa watakushi no shujin desu.* (Koe-no-ssh-toe wah wah-tock-she no shuu-jeen dess.) How old is your husband? *Go-shujin wa o'ikutsu desu ka?* (Go-shuu-jeen wah oh-e-kut-sue

dess kah?)   That is none of your business. *Sore
wa anata to kankei arimasen.* (Soe-ray wah ah-nah-
tah toe khan-kay-e ah-ree-mah-sin.)

I

I   *Watakushi* **(Wah-tock-she);** also *Watashi* (Wah-
tah-she); *Boku (Boe-kuu);* and *Ore* (Oh-ray)
[*Watakushi* is used by both males and females in
formal and informal situations. *Watashi* is very
feminine and is used by young women. *Boku* is
used by boys and men in informal situations and
may be used informally by young women as an
affectation. *Ore* is used by boys and men, especially blue-collar workers and students, in informal conversation. The "I" is understood in many
cases and is not expressed directly—i.e.,"I want
to buy this." *Kore wo kaitai desu.* (Koe-ray oh kie-
tie dess.)   The full sentence would be: *Watakushi
wa kore wo kaitai desu.*   The possessive "my" is
formed by adding *no* to any of the forms of "I":
watakushi-no; watashi-no; boku-no; ore-no.]

I'm sorry   *Gomen nasai* **(Go-main nah-sie);**   also
Sumimasen (Sue-me-mah-sin)
[*Gomen nasai* is used when apologizing. *Sumimasen* is used to apologize as well as to attract attention (of a waitress, clerk, etc.).] Excuse me,
but what do you call that? *Sumimasen ga, sore wo
nanto iimasu ka?* (Sue-me-mah-sin gah, soe-ray oh
nahn-toe ee-mahss kah?) [There is a special expression used when you have kept someone
waiting: *Omachidosama deshita* (Oh-mah-chee-doe-
sah-mah desh-tah).]

Ice *Kori* **(Koe-ree)**
May I have some ice, please? *Kori wo itadakemasen ka?* (Koe-ree oh ee-tah-dah-kay-mah-sin kah?) Please put a little more ice in. *Mo sukoshi kori wo irete kudasai.* (Moe sue-koe-she koe-ree oh ee-ray-tay kuu-dah-sie.)

Ice cream *Aisu kurimu* **(Aye-sue kuu-ree-muu)**
Do you have chocolate ice cream? *Chokoreto aisu kurimu ga arimasu ka?* (Choe-koe-ray-toe aye-sue kuu-ree-muu gah ah-ree-mahss kah?) What kind of ice cream do you have? *Donna aisu kurimu ga arimasu ka?* (Doan-nah aye-sue kuu-ree-muu gah ah-ree-mahss kah?)

Identification *Mibunshomei* **(Me-boon-show-may-e)** Identification Card *Mibunshomei Sho* (Me-boon-show-may-e show); *Shomeisho Yo* (Show-may-e-show Yoe)
May I see your identification, please? *Mibunshomei wo misete itadakemasen ka?* (Me-boon-show-may-e oh me-say-tay ee-tah-dah-kay-mah-sin kah?)

Immediately *Ima sugu* **(Ee-mah sue-guu);** also *Sugu ni* (Sue-guu nee)
Let's leave immediately! *Sugu ni ikimasho!* (Sue-guu nee ee-kee-mah-show!) Right now! *Ima sugu!* (Ee-mah sue-guu!)

Immigration Office *Nyukoku Kanri Jimusho* **(Knew-koe-kuu Khan-ree Jim-show)**
I must go to the Immigration Office today. *Kyo Nyukoku Kanri Jimusho e ikanakereba narimasen.* (K'yoe Knew-koe-kuu Khan-ree Jim-show eh e-kah-nak-kay-ray-bah-nah-ree-mah-sin.) Please take me to the Immigration Office (to taxi driv-

er). *Nyukoku Kanri Jimusho e itte kudasai.* (Knew-
koe-kuu Khan-ree Jim-show eh eat-tay kuu-dah-
sie.)

Imperial *Teikoku* **(Tay-e-koe-kuu)**
I am staying at the Imperial Hotel. *Teikoku Hoteru
ni tomatte imasu.* (Tay-e-koe-kuu Hoe-tay-rue nee
toe-mot-tay ee-mahss.) I would like to see the
Imperial Palace. *Kyujo wo mitai desu.* (Que-joe oh
me-tie dess.)

Important *Taisetsu* **(Tie-sate-sue)**
This is an important matter. *Kore wa taisetsu na
koto desu.* (Koe-ray wah tie-sate-sue nah koe-toe
dess.) It is important. *Taisetsu desu.* (Tie-sate-sue
dess.)

In case of *No baai* **(No bah-ee)**
In case of rain, please cancel it. *Ame no baai ni wa
torikeshite kudasai.* (Ah-may no bah-ee nee wah
toe-ree-kay-ssh-tay kuu-dah-sie.)

Include *Fukumimasu* **(Fuu-kuu-me-mahss)**
Please include this. *Kore wo fukumete kudasai.*
(Koe-ray oh fuu-kuu-mah-ray-tay kuu-dah-sie.)
That is included in your bill. *Sore wa kanjo ni
haitte orimasu.* (Soe-ray wah kahn-joe nee hite-tay
oh-ree-mahss.)

Information *Joho* **(Joe-hoe);** *Tsuchi* **(T'sue-chee)**
Where can I get information about hotspring resorts? *Doko de onsen no joho wo eru koto ga dekimasu ka?* (Doe-koe day own-sin no joe-hoe oh
eh-rue koe-toe gah day-kee-mahss kah?)
Haven't you received any information about our
hotel reservations? *Hoteru no yoyaku ni tsuite nan*

no tsuchi mo uketotte imasen ka? (Hoe-tay-rue no yoe-yah-ku nee t'sue-e-tay nahn no t'sue-chee moe uu-kay-tote-tay ee-mah-sin kah?)

Information Desk/Counter *Annai Jo* **(Ahn-nie Joe);** also *Uketsuke* (Ou-kay-t'sue-kay) Where is the Information Desk? *Annai Jo wa doko desu ka?* (Ahn-nie Joe wah doe-koe dess kah?) Please ask at the Information Desk. *Annai Jo de kiite kudasai.* (Ahn-nie Joe day keet-tay kuu-dah-sie.) I'll meet you at the Information Desk. *Uketsuke de aimasho.* (Ou-kay-t'sue-kay day aye-mah-show.)

Injection *Chusha* **(chuu-shah)** I just received an injection. *Chusha wo ukemashita.* (Chuu-shah oh ou-kay-mah-ssh-tah.)

Inn *Ryokan* **(Rio-kahn)** Tonight I want to stay in an inn. *Komban ryokan ni tomaritai desu.* (Kome-bahn rio-kahn nee toe-mah-ree-tie dess.) Are inns cheaper than hotels? *Ryokan wa hoteru yori yasui desu ka?* (Rio-kahn wah hoe-tay-rue yoe-ree yah-sue-ee dess kah?)

Inside *Naka de* **(Nah-kah day)** Please wait inside the hotel. *Hoteru no naka day matte kudasai.* (Hoe-tay-ru no nah-kah day mot-tay kuu-dah-sie.) Let's go inside. *Naka e hairimasho.* (Nah-kah eh hie-ree-mah-sho.)

Inspect *Shirabemasu* **(She-rah-bay-mahss)** Will Customs inspect our baggage in Tokyo? *Tokyo de Zeikan wa watakushi-tachi no nimotsu wo shirabemasu ka?* (Tokyo day Zay-e-khan wah wah-tah-kuu-she-tah-chee no nee-mote-sue oh she-rah-bay-mahss kah?)

Insurance *Hoken* (Hoe-kane); Accident insurance *Shogai hoken* (Show-guy hoe-kane); Life
insurance *Seimei hoken* (Say-e-may-e hoe-kane);
Insurance company *Hoken kaisha* (Hoe-kane kie-
shah); Insurance agent *Hoken dairiten* (Hoe-
kane die-ree-tane)
What is the name of your insurance company?
Anato no hoken kaisha no namae wa nan desu ka?
(Ah-nah-tah no hoe-kane kie-shah no nah-my
wah nahn dess kah?) Do you have full cover-
age? *Kanzen hoken ga arimasu ka?* (Kahn-zen hoe-
kane gah ah-ree-mahss kah?)

Interesting *Omoshiroi* (Oh-moe-she-roy)
That (it) was interesting. *Sore wa omoshirokatta.*
(Soe-ray wah oh-moe-she-roe-kot-tah.) It is in-
teresting. *Omoshiroi desu.* (Oh-moe-she-roy dess.)

**Interesting place *Omoshiroi tokoro* (Oh-moe-she-
roy toe-koe-roe)**
Are there any unusually interesting places near
here? *Kono chikaku ni tokubetsu no omoshiroi tokoro
ga arimasu ka?* (Koe-no chee-kah-kuu nee toe-
kuu-bate-sue no oh-moe-she-roy toe-koe-roe gah
ah-ree-mahss kah?)

International *Kokusai* (Koke-sie)
You have an overseas phone call. *Kokusai denwa
ga kakatte imasu.* (Koke-sie dane-wah gah kah-
kot-tay-ee-mahss.) Are you the international
operator? *Anata wa kokusai kokanshu desu ka?* (Ah-
nah-tah wah koke-sie koe-khan-shuu dess
kah?) May I have the International Department,
please. *Kokusai Bu onegaishimasu.* (Koe-kuu-sie
Buu oh-nay-guy-she-mahss.)

International Arrival Area *Kokusai-sen Tochaku Jo* (Koke-sie-sin Toe-chah-kuu Joe)
We will meet you at the International Arrival Area. *Kokusai-sen Tochaku Jo de aimasu.* (Koke-sie Sin Toe-chah-kuu-joe day aye-mahss.)

International driver's license *Kokusai menkyo sho* (Koke-sie mane-k'yoe show)
I have an international driver's license. *Watakushi wa kokusai menkyo sho wo motte imasu.* (Wah-tah-kuu-she wah koke-sie mane-k'yoe show oh mote-tay ee-mahss.)

Interpreter *Tsuyaku* (T'sue-yah-kuu)
Please call an interpreter. *Tsuyaku wo yonde kudasai.* (T'sue-yah-kuu oh yone-day kuu-dah-sie.) Please wait. I will call an interpreter. *Matte kudasai. Tsuyaku wo yobimasu.* (Mot-tay kuu-dah-sie. T'sue-yah-kuu oh yoe-bee-mahss.)

Introduce *Shokai suru* (Show-kie sue-rue)
Please introduce (me/us). *Shokai shite kudasai.* (Show-kie ssh-tay kuu-dah-sie.) I want to/will introduce you to Mr. Suzuki. *Suzuki-San ni shokai shimasu.* (Sue-zoo-kee-Sahn nee show-kie she-mahss.) Allow me to introduce Mr. Smith. *Sumisu-San wo shokai shimasu.* (Sue-me-sue-Sahn oh show-kie she-mahss.) This is Mr. Smith. *Kochira wa Sumisu-San desu.* (Koe-chee-rah wah Sue-me-sue-Sahn dess.)

Invoice (statement of goods sent) *Okurijo* (Oh-kuu-ree-joe); also *Imboisu* (Em-boy-sue)
I need an invoice. *Okurijo ga irimasu.* (Oh-kuu-ree-joe gah ee-ree-mahss.) May I see the invoice, please? *Imboisu wo misete kudasai?* (Em-boy-sue oh me-say-tay kuu-dah-sie?)

Iron (press) *Airon kakeru* **(Aye-rone kah-kay-rue)**
Please press these trousers. *Kono zubon wo airon kakette kudasai.* (Koe-no zoo-bone oh aye-rone kah-kate-tay kuu-dah-sie.)

Island *Shima* **(She-mah)**
Japan is an island country. *Nihon wa shima Kuni desu.* (Nee-hone wah she-mah Kuu-nee dess.) Honshu is Japan's largest island. *Honshu wa Nihon no ichiban okii shima desu.* (Hone-shuu wah Nee-hone no ee-chee-bahn oh-kee she-mah dess.)

J

Jacket *Uwagi* **(Ou-wah-ghee);** also *Jaketto* (Jah-ket-toe)
Is this your jacket? *Kore wa anata-no jaketo desu ka?* (Koe-ray wah ah-nah-tah-no jah-ket-toe dess kah?) I forgot my jacket. *Jaketto wo wasurema-shita.* (Jah-ket-toe oh wah-sue-ray-masshta.)

Jam *Jamu* **(Jah-muu)**
Would you like some jam? *Jamu ikaga desu ka?* (Jah-muu ee-kah-gah dess kah?) May I have some more jam? *Jamu wo mo sukoshi kudasaimasen ka?* (Jah-muu oh moe sue-koe-she kuu-dah-sie-mah-sin kah?)

January *Ichigatsu* **(Ee-chee-got-sue)**
Today is January 2nd. *Kyo wa Ichigatsu no futsuka desu.* (K'yoe wah Ee-chee-got-sue no futes-kah dess.) Is Tokyo cold in January? *Ichigatsu ni Tokyo wa samui desu ka?* (Ee-chee-got-sue nee To-kyo wah sah-muu-e dess kah?)

Japan *Nihon* (Nee-hone)

Have you ever been to Japan? *Nihon e itta koto ga arimasu ka?* (Nee-hone eh eat-tah koe-toe gah ah-ree-mahss kah?) Are you from Japan? *Anata wa Nihon kara desu ka?* (Ah-nah-tah wah Nee-hone kah-rah dess kah?)

Japanese food *Nihon ryori* (Nee-hone rio-ree); also *Nihon shoku* (Nee-hone show-kuu)

Do you prefer Japanese food? *Nihon ryori no ho ga ii desu ka?* (Nee-hone rio-ree no hoe gah ee dess kah?) What kind of Japanese food do you have? *Donna Nihon ryori ga arimasu ka?* (Doan-nah Nee-hone rio-ree gah ah-ree-mahss kah?)

Japanese language *Nihongo* (Nee-hone-go)

I speak only a little Japanese. *Nihongo ga sukoshi dake hanasemasu.* (Nee-hone-go gah sue-koe-she dah-kay hah-nah-say-mahss.) I am studying Japanese. *Nihongo wo benkyoshite imasu.* (Nee-hone-go oh bane-k'yoe oh she-tay ee-mahss.) Please speak Japanese. *Nihongo de hanashite kudasai.* (Nee-hone-go day hah-nah-ssh-tay kuu-dah-sie.)

Japanese person *Nihonjin* (Nee-hone-jeen)

Are you Japanese? *Anata wa Nihonjin desu ka?* (Ah-nah-tah way Nee-hone-jeen dess kah?) Is he/she Japanese? *Anokata wa Nihonjin desu ka?* (Ah-no-kah-tah wah Nee-hone-jeen dess kah?) We have few Japanese guests. *Nihonjin no O'kyaku-San wa sukunai desu.* (Nee-hone-jeen no Oh-kyah-kuu-San wah sue-kuu-nie dess.)

Japanese style *Nihon-no sutairu* (Nee-hone-no sue-tie-rue)

I want to try a Japanese-style bath. *Nihon sutairu no ofuro ni haitte mitai desu.* (Nee-hone sue-tie-rue

no oh-fuu-roe nee hite-tay me-tie dess.) Is this
inn all Japanese style? *Kono ryokan wa zembu
Nihon no stairu desu ka?* (Koe-no rio-khan wah
zim-buu Nee-hone no sue-tie-rue dess kah?)

Japanese-style room *Nihon-ma (Nee-hone-mah)*
Do you have Japanese-style rooms? *Nihon-ma ga
arimasu ka?* (Nee-hone-mah gah ah-ree-mahss
kah?) May I see a Japanese-style room? *Nihon-
ma wo misete itadakemasen ka?* (Nee-hone-mah oh
me-say-tay e-tah-dah-kay-mah-sin kah?)

Japanese thing *Nihon-no mono* (Nee-hone-no
moe-no)
Is that Japanese? *Sore wa Nihon no mono desu ka?*
(Soe-ray wah Nee-hone-no moe-no dess kah?)

Japan Travel Bureau *Nihon Kotsu Kosha* (Nee-
hone Koe-t'sue Koe-shah)
In English the Japan Travel Bureau is usually
called JTB. *Eigo de Nihon Kotsu Kosha wa futsu JTB
to iimasu.* (A-e-go day Nee-hone Koe-t'sue Koe-
shah wah fute-sue JTB toe ee-mahss.) Are you
from JTB? *Anata wa JTB no kata desu ka?* (Ah-nah-
tah wah JTB no kah-tah dess kah?)

Jazz *Jazu* (Jah-zoo)
Is jazz popular in Japan? *Nihon de jazu wa ninki ga
arimasu ka?* (Nee-hone day jah-zoo wah neen-kee
gah ah-ree-mahss kah?) Do you like jazz? *Jazu
ga suki desu ka?* (Jah-zoo gah ski dess kah?)

Jeans *Jiinzu* (Jeen-zuu)
Will it be all right if I wear jeans? *Jiinzu wo haitte
mo yoroshii desho ka?* (Jeen-zuu oh hite-tay moe
yoe-roe-shee day-show kah?)

Jelly *Jeri* **(Jay-ree)**
Would you please put some jelly on this bread. *Kono pan ni jeri wo tsukete kudasai.* (Koe-no pahn nee jay-ree oh skate-tay kuu-dah-sie.) Would you like some jelly? *Jeri wa ikaga desu ka?* (Jay-ree wah e-kah-gah dess kah?)

Jet *Jetto* **(Jet-toe);** Jumbo jet *Janbo jetto* (Jahn-boe jet-toe)
Have you ever taken a Jumbo jet? *Janbo jetto ni notta koto ga arimasu ka?* (Jahn-bow jet-toe nee note-tah koe-toe gah ah-ree-mahss kah?)

Jet-lag *Jissa boke* **(Jees-sah bow-kay)**
Do you have jet-lag? *Jissa boke ga arimasu ka?* (Jees-sah boe-kay gah ah-ree-mahss kah?)

Jewelry *Hohseki* **(Hoeh-say-kee)**
Would you like to see some American Indian-made jewlery? *Amerika Indian sei no hohseki wo mitai desu ka?* (Ah-may-ree-kah Een-dee-ahn-say no hoe-say-kee oh me-tie dess kah?)

Jewelry store *Hohseki-ten* **(Hoeh-say-kee-tane)**
Is there a jewelry store near here? *Kono chikaku ni hohseki-ten ga arimasu ka?* (Koe-no chee-kah-kuu nee hoeh-say-kee-tane gah ah-ree-mahss kah?) I would like to buy some pearls. *Shinju wo kaitai desu.* (Sheen-juu oh kie-tie dess.)

Juice *Juusu* **(Juu-sue)**
Would you like some orange juice? *orenji juusu wa ikaga desu ka?* (Oh-rane-jee juu-sue wah e-kah-gah dess kah?)

July *Shichigatsu* **(She-chee-got-sue)**
I'm returning to Tokyo around the middle of July. *Shichigatsu no mannaka goro ni Tokyo e kaeri-*

masu. (She-chee-got-sue no mahn-nah-kah go-
roe nee Tokyo eh kie-ree-mahss.) I think we will
leave on July 1st. *Shichigatsu no tsuitachi ni tatsu
to omoimasu*. (She-chee-got-sue no t'sooey-tah-
chee nee tot-sue toe oh-moy-mahss.)

June *Rokugatsu* (Roe-kuu-got-sue)
In Tokyo summer begins in June. *Tokyo no natsu
wa Rokugatsu kara hajimarimasu*. (Tokyo no nah-
t'sue wah Roe-kuu-got-sue kah-rah hah-jee-mah-
ree-mahss.)

K

Key *Kagi* (Kah-ghee)
May I have two keys, please? *Futatsu no kagi wo
itadakemasen ka?* (Fuu-tot-sue no kah-ghee oh ee-
tah-dah-kay-mah-sin kah?) Don't forget your
key! *Kagi wo wasurenai de!* (Kah-ghee oh wah-sue-
ray-nie day!) This key does not fit. *Kono kagi wa
aimasen*. (Koe-no kah-ghee wah aye-mah-sin.)

Kidney *Jinzo* (Jeen-zoe)
My kidneys are in bad shape so I can't drink
much. *Jinzo ga warui no de, sake wo ammari nome-
masen*. (Jeen-zoe gah wah-rue-ee no day, sah-
kay oh ahm-mah-ree no-may-mah-sin.)

Kind (sort, class) *Shurui* (Shuu-rue-e); Gentle,
etc. *Shinsetsu* (Sheen-sate-sue)
Is this kind all right? *Kono shurui ga ii desu ka?*
(Koe-no shuu-rue-e gah ee dess kah?) Another
kind. *Hoka no shurui*. (Hoe-kah no shuu-rue-e.)
I'll take one of each kind. *Hito shurui zutsu wo
moraimasu*. (Ssh-toe shuu-rue-e zoot-sue oh

moe-rie-mahss.) He/she is very kind. *Anohito wa taihen shinsetsu desu.* (Ah-no-ssh-toe wah tie-hane sheen-sate-sue dess.)

Kitchen *Daidokoro* **(die-doe-koe-roe)**
Would you like to see the/my kitchen? *Daidokoro wo mitai desu ka?* (Die-doe-koe-roe oh me-tie dess ka?) Is your kitchen similar to this (one)? *Anata no daidokoro wa kore to daitai onaji desu ka?* (Ah-nah-tah no die-doe-koe-roe wah koe-ray toe die-tie oh-nah-jee dess kah?)

Kite *Tako* **(Tah-koe)**
Is kite-flying popular in Japan? *Nihon de tako-age wa ninki ga arimasu ka?* (Nee-hone day tah-koe-ah-gay wah neen-kee gah ah-ree-mahss kah?) Some kites are huge. *Aru tako wa taihen okii desu.* (Ah-rue tah-koe wah tie-hane oh-key dess.)

Knife *Naifu (nie-fuu);* Butcher/Chopping knife *Hocho* (hoe-choe)
Please bring me a knife. *Naifu wo motte kite kudasai.* (Nie-fuu oh moat-tay ke-tay kuu-dah-sie.) May I borrow a knife? *Naifu wo kashite kuremasu ka?* (Nai-fuu oh kahsh-tay kuu-ray-mahss kah?)

Knock (on a door) *Tatakimasu* **(Tah-tah-kee-mahss)**
Please knock before entering. *Hairu mae ni to wo tataite kudasai.* (Hie-rue my nee, toe oh tah-tie-tay kuu-dah-sie.)

Know *Shirimasu* **(She-ree-mahss)**
Do you know that person? *Anohito wo shitte imasu ka?* (Ah-no-ssh-toe oh ssh-tay ee-mahss kah?) Do you know? *Shitte imasu ka?* (Ssh-tay ee-mahss kah?) I don't know. *Shirimasen.* (She-ree-mah-sin.)

Korea *Taikan Koku* **(Tie-khan Koe-kuu);** *Kankoku*
(Khan-koe-kuu); Korean *Kankoku-jin* (Khan-
koe-kuu-jeen)
Korea is not far from Japan. *Kankoku wa Nihon
kara toku wa nai desu.* (Khan-koe-kuu wah Nee-
hone kah-rah toe-kuu wah nie dess.) Excuse me
but are you Korean or Japanese? *Shitsurei desu ga,
anata wa Kankoku-jin desu ka Nihon-jin desu ka?*
(Sheet-sue ray-e dess gah, ah-nah-tah wah Khan-
koe-kuu-jeen dess kah Nee-hone-jeen dess kah?)

Korean Airlines *Kankoku Kohku* **(Khan-koe-kuu
Koh-kuu)**
I have flown Korean Airlines many times. *Watakushi wa Kankoku Kohku ni nankai mo notta koto ga
arimasu.* (Wah-tock-she wah Khan-koe-kuu Koh-
kuu nee nahn-kie moe note-tah koe-toe gah ah-
ree-mahss.)

L

Lacquer *Urushi* **(Uuu-rue-she);** Lacquerware
Nurimono (New-ree moe-no)
Lacquerware is famous in Japan. *Nurimono wa
Nihon ni yumei desu.* (New-ree-moe-no wah Nee-
hone nee yuu-may-e dess.) Do department
stores sell lacquerware? *Depaato wa nurimono wo
utte imasu ka?* (Day-paah-toe wah new-ree-moe-
no oh ute-tay ee-mahss kah?)

Lady *Fujin* **(Fuu-jeen);** Young lady *Wakai fujin*
(Wah-kie fuu-jeen)
What is that young lady's name? *Ano wakai fujin
no namae wa nan desu ka?* (Ah-no wah-kie no fuu-

jeen no nah-my wah nahn dess kah?) Who is
that lady? *Ano fujin wa donata desu ka?* (Ah-no
fuu-jeen wah doe-nah-tah dess kah?)

Lake *Ike* **(Ee-kay);** also *Mizu-umi* (Me-zuu-uu-me)
Are there many lakes in Japan? *Nihon ni wa ike ga
takusan arimasu ka?* (Nee-hone nee wah ee-kay
gah tock-sahn ah-ree-mahss kah?) Yes, there
are. *Arimasu* (Ah-ree-mahss.) The largest one is
Lake Biwa. *Ichiban okii na no wa Biwa-ko desu.* (Ee-
chee-bahn oh-kee nah no wah Bee-wah-koe
dess.)

Lamb *Ko-hitsuji* **(Koe-he-t'sue-jee);** Lamb
chops *Ramu choppu* (Rah-muu choep-puu)
Lamb meat is imported into Japan from Austra-
lia. *Ko-hitsuji wa Osutorariya kara Nihon ni yunyu-
shite imasu.* (Koe-he-t'sue-jee wah Oh-sue-toe-
rah-ree-yah kah-rah Nee-hone nee yune-yuu-
ssh-tay ee-mahss.)

Lamp *Rampu* **(Rahm-puu)**
Shall I turn the lamp on? *Rampu wo tsukemasho
ka?* (Rahm-puu oh t'sue-kay-mah-show-kah?)
Yes, please. *Hai, tsukete kudasai.* (Hie, t'sue-tay
kuu-dah-sie.)

Landing field *Hikojo* **(He-koe-jo);** To make a
landing (by airplane) *Chakuriku suru* (Chah-kuu-
ree-kuu sue-rue); To land from a ship *Joriku
suru* (Joe-ree-kuu sue-rue)
Has the plane already landed? *Hikoki wa mo chakuriku shimashita ka?* (He-koe-kee wah moe chah-
kuu-ree-kuu she-mah-sshta kah?) It/we will
land in five minutes. *Ato gohun chakuriku shimasu.*
(Ah-toe go-hune chah-kuu-ree-kuu she-mahss.)

Japanese in Plain English

Landmark *Me-jirushi* **(May-jee-rue-she)**
Are there any landmarks in this area? *Kono hen ni me-jirushi ga arimasu ka?* (Koe-no hane nee may-jee-rue-she gah ah-ree-mahss kah?) Yes, there are more than a dozen. *Hai, ichi-dasu ijo arimasu.* (Hie, ee-chee dah-sue ee-joe ah-ree-mahss.) Will you take me to just one of them? *Hitotsu dake ni tsurete itte kuremasu ka?* (He-tote-sue dah-kay nee t'sue-ray-tay eet-tay kuu-ray-mahss kah?)

Late (tardy) *Osoi* **(Oh-soy)**
He/she/it is late. *Osoi desu.* (Oh-soy dess.) Is he (she, it) going to be late? *Osoku narimasu ka?* (Oh-soe-kuu nah-ree-mahss kah?) I'm sorry I'm late. *Osoku natte sumimasen.* (Oh-soe-kuu not-tay sue-me-mah-sin.)

Large *Okii* **(Oh-key)**
A large one, please. *Okii hoh kudasai.* (Oh-kee hoe kuu-dah-sie.) Which one is the largest? *Dochi no hoh ga okii desu ka?* (Doe-chee no hoe gah oh-kee dess kah?) That is too large. *Sore wa oki-sugimasu.* (Soe-ray wah oh-kee sue-ghee mahss.)

Laundry (place) *Sentaku-ya* **(Sane-tah-kuu-yah);**
Things to wash *Sentaku-mono* (Sane-tah-kuu moe-no)
Please take this to the laundry. *Kore wo sentaku-ya ni motte itte kudasai.* (Koe-ray oh sane-tah-kuu-yah nee mote-tay eet-tay kuu-dah-sie.) Is my laundry ready? *Watakushi no sentaku-mono wa deki-mashita ka?* (Wa-tock-she-no sane-tah-kuu-moe-no wah day-key-mah-sshta kah?)

Leave (depart) *Tachimasu* **(Tah-chee-mahss)**
I/we will be leaving soon. *Sugu tachimasu.* (Sue-guee tah-chee-mahss.) What time are

146

you/we/they leaving? *Nanji ni tachimasu ka?*
(Nahn-jee nee tah-chee-mahss kah?)

Left (direction) *Hidari* **(He-dah-ree);** Left turn
Sasetsu (Sah-sate-sue)
Turn left at the next corner. *Kono tsugi no kado de
hidari e mawatte kudasai.* (Koe-no t'sue-ghee no
kah-doe day he-dah-ree eh mah-wat-tay kuu-
dah-sie.) Can you make a left turn? *Sasetsu dekimasu ka?* (Sah-sate-sue day-kee-mahss kah?) It's
on the left. *Hidari gawa ni arimasu.* (Hee-dah-ree
gah-wah nee ah-ree-mahss.)

Leisure *Hima* **(He-mah);** also *Rejaa* (Ray-jaah)
When will you have (some) leisure time? *Itsu
hima ga arimasu ka?* (Eet-sue he-mah gah ah-ree-
mahss kah?) Are you free now? *Ima hima desu
ka?* (Ee-mah he-mah dess ka?)

Lemon *Remon* **(Ray-moan)**
May I have some lemon, please. *Remon wo kudasai.* (Ray-moan oh kuu-dah-sie.)

Let me see *Misete kudasai* **(Me-say-tay kuu-dah-
sie)**
Let me see that ring. *Sono yubi-wa wo misete kudasai.* (Soe-no yuu-bee-wah oh me-say-tay kuu-
dah-sie.)

Letter *Tegami* **(Tay-gah-me)**
Are there any letters for me? *Watakushi ni tegami
ga arimasu ka?* (Wah-tock-she nee tay-gah-me gah
ah-ree-mahss kah?) Please mail this letter. *Kono
tegami wo dashite kudasai.* (Koe-no tay-gah-me oh
dah-ssh-tay kuu-dah-sie.) I'll write to you. *Tegami wo kakimasu.* (Tay-gah-me oh kah-kee-
mahss.)

Japanese in Plain English

Lettuce *Retasu* (Ray-tah-sue)
Would you like a lettuce salad? *Retasu no sarada wa ikaga desu ka?* (Ray-tah-sue no sah-rah-dah wah e-kah-gah dess kah?)

Life jacket *Kyumei jaketto* (Que-may-e jah-ket-toe)
Your life jacket is under your seat. *Seki no shita ni kyumei jaketto ga arimasu.* (Say-kee no ssh-tah nee que-may-e jah-ket-toe gah ah-ree-mahss.)

Light (weight) *Karui* (Kah-rue-e); Light (Illumination) *Denki* (Dane-kee)
My bags are very light. *Watakushi no bagu wa taihen karui desu.* (Wah-tock-she no bah-guu wah tie-hane kah-rue-e dess.) Please turn on the light. *Denki wo tsukete kudasai.* (Dane-kee oh skate-tay kuu-dah-sie.)

Like (be fond of) *Suki* (Ski)
I like you. *Anata wo suki desu.* (Ah-nah-tah oh ski dess.) I like it. *Suki desu.* (Ski dess.) Do you like fruit? *Kudamono wo suki desu ka?* (Kuu-dah-moe-no oh ski dess kah?)

Like (same as) *Onaji* (Oh-nah-jee); Similar to *Onaji yo-na* (Oh-nah-jee yoe-nah)
Is it like this? *Kore to onaji desu ka?* (Koe-ray toe oh-nah-jee dess kah?) I want one like that. *Sore to onaji yo-na no wo hoshii desu.* (Soe-ray toe oh-nah-jee yoe-nah no oh hoe-she-e dess.)

Limousine *Rimujin* (Ree-muu-jeen); Limousine Service *Rimujin Sabisu* (Ree-muu-jeen Sah-bee-sue)
I would like to rent a limousine. *Rimujin wo kari-tai desu.* (Ree-muu-jeen oh kah-ree-tie dess.) Do

you have limousines for rent? *Kashi rimujin ga arimasu ka?* (Kah-she ree-muu-jeen gah ah-ree-mahss kah?)

List *Meibo* **(May-e-boe)** or *Risuto* (Rees-toe)
Please make a list of all your purchases. *Katta mono no risuto wo tsukutte kudasai.* (Kot-tah moe-no no rees-toe oh t'sue-coot-tay kuu-dah-sie.)

Little (size) *Chiisai* (Cheee-sie); Amount *Sukoshi* (Sue-koe-she)
It's small, isn't it? *Chiisai desu, ne?* (Cheee-sie dess, nay?) Give me just a little. *Sukoshi kudasai.* (Sue-koe-she kuu-dah-sie.)

Liver *Kanzoh* **(Khan-zoe)**
I have liver trouble. *Watakushi wa kanzoh ga warui desu.* (Wa-tock-she wah khan-zoe gah wah-rue-e dess.)

Lobby *Robi* **(Roe-bee)**
Please wait for me in the lobby. *Robi de matte kudasai.* (Roe-bee day mot-tay kuu-dah-sie.) I'll meet you in the lobby at 6 o'clock. *Rokuji ni robi de aimasho.* (Roe-kuu-jee nee roe-bee day aye-mah-show.)

Lobster *Oh-ebi* **(Oh-aa-bee)**
Do you like lobster? *Oh-ebi wo suki desu ka?* (Oh-aa-bee oh ski dess kah?) Shall we have (eat) lobster? *Oh-ebi wo tabemasho ka?* (Oh-aa-bee oh tah-bay-mah-show kah?)

Locker *Rokkaa* **(Roke-kah)**
Are there any lockers in this station? *Kono eki ni rokkaa ga arimasu ka?* (Koe-no a-kee nee roke-kah gah ah-ree-mahss kah?) Excuse me, where are

the lockers? *Sumimasen, rokkaa wa doko desu ka?*
(Sue-me-mah-sin, roke-kah wah doe-koe dess
kah?)

Look for *Sagasu* **(Sah-gah-sue)**
What are you looking for? *Nani wo sagashite imasu
ka?* (Nah-nee oh sah-gah-sshtay e-mahss kah?)
I'm looking for an envelope. *Futoh oh sagashite
imasu.* (Fuu-toh oh sah-gah-sshtay e-mahss.)

Look out! (Watch out!) *Abunai!* **(Ah-buu- nie!)**

Lose *Nakushimasu* **(Nah-kuu-she-mahss)**
Don't lose it (anything)! *Nakusanai-yo ni!* (Nah-
kuu-sah-nie-yoe nee!) I lost my wristwatch.
Ude-dokei wo nakushimashita. (Uu-day-doe-kay-e
oh nah-kuu-she-mah-sshtah.)

Lost & Found *Wasuremono Azukarijo* **(Wah-sue-
ray-moe-no Ah-zuu-kah-ree-joe)**
I'm looking for the Lost & Found. Can you
please help me? *Warsuremono Azukarijo wo sagashite imasu. Tetsudatte kuremasu ka?* (Wah-sue-ray-
moe-no Ah-zuu-kah-ree-joe oh sah-gah-sshtay
e-mahss. Tate-sue-dot-tay kuu-ray mahss kah?)

Lots (quantity) *Takusan* **(Tock-sahn);** Enough
Mo takusan (moe-tock-sahn)
There are lots of people in the lobby. *Robi ni takusan hitobito ga orimasu.* (Roe-bee nee tock-sahn
ssh-toe-bee-toe gah oh-ree-mahss.) That's
enough! *Moh takusan!* (Moh tock-sahn!)

Loud (flashy) *Hade-na* **(Hah-day-nah)**
This cloth is too loud. *Kono kiji wa ammari hade
desu.* (Koe-no kee-jee wah ahm-mah-ree hah-
day dess.)

Loud (sound) *Oki-na oto* **(Oh-kee-nah oh-toe)**;
Loud (voice) *Oh-goe* (Oh-go-eh)
Please speak a little louder. *Moh sukoshi oh-goe de hanashite kudasai.* (Moe sue-koe-shee oh-go-eh day hah-nah-sshtay kuu-dah-sie.)

Lunch *Chushoku* **(Chuu-sho-kuu)**; also *Ranchi* (Rahn-chee)
Where do you want to eat lunch? *Chushoku wo doko de tabetai desu ka?* (Chuu-sho-kuu oh doe-koe day tah-bay-tie dess kah?) What time is lunch? *Ranchi wa nanji desu ka?* (Rahn-chee wah nahn-jee dess kah?)

M

Magazine *Zasshi* **(Zah-she)**
Do you have any Japanese-language magazines? *Nihongo no zasshi ga arimasu ka?* (Nee-hone-go no zah-she gah ah-ree-mahss kah?) Do you carry English-language magazines? *Eigo no zasshi wo azukatte imasu ka?* (A-e-go no zah-she oh ah-zuu-kot-tay e-mahss kah?)

Maid *Jochu* **(Joe-chuu)**; also *Meido* (May-e-doe)
[Nowadays, inn, hotel, and house maids are generally called *meido* instead of the traditional *jochu*.] Please send a maid to my room. *Watakushi no heya ni meido wo yokoshite kudasai.* (Wah-tock-she no hay-yah nee may-e-doe oh yoe-koe-sshtay kuu-dah-sie.)

Mail *Yubin* **(Yuu-bean)**
Is there any mail for me? *Watakushi e yubin ga kite imasu ka?* (Wah-tock-she eh yuu-bean gah kee-tay e-mahss kah?) Has the mail come? *Yubin ga ki-*

mashita ka? (Yuu-bean gah kee-mah-sshta-kah?)
Where can I mail this letter? *Kono tegami wo doko de dasu koto ga dekimasu ka?* (Koe-no tay-gah-me oh doe-koe day dah-sue koe-toe gah day-kee-mahss kah?)

Mail a letter *Tegami wo dashimasu* (Tay-gah-me oh dah-she-mahss)

I would like to mail this letter. *Kono tegami wo dashitai desu.* (Koe-no tay-gah-me oh dah-she-tie dess.) Please mail this. *Kore wo dashite kudasai.* (Koe-ray oh dah-she-tay kuu-dah-sie.)

Mailbox *Yubin bako* (Yuu-bean bah-koe); also *Posuto* (Poe-sue-toe)

Where is the nearest mailbox? *Ichiban chikai yubin posuto wa doko desu ka?* (Ee-chee-bahn chee-kie yuu-bean poe-sue-toe wah doe-koe dess kah?)

Main entrance *Omote genkan* (Oh-moe-tay gane-khan)

I want to go to the main entrance. *Omote genkan ni ikitai desu.* (Oh-moe-tay gane-khan nee e-kee-tie dess.)

Man *Otoko-no-hito (Oh-toe-koe-no-ssh-toe)*

Who is that man? *Ano otoko-no-hito wa donata desu ka?* (Ah-no oh-toe-koe-no-ssh-toe wah doe-nah-tah dess kah?) Two men and one woman. *Otoko-no-hito futari, onna-no-hito hitori.* (Oh-toe-koe-no-ssh-toe fuu-tah-ree, own-nah-no-ssh-toe ssh-toe-ree.)

Manager *Shihainin* (She-hie-neen); also *Maneja* (Mah-nay-jah)

I would like to see the manager, please. *Maneja ni O'me ni kakaritai desu.* (Mah-nay-jah nee Oh-

may nee kah-kah-ree-tie dess.) Please call the
manager. *Shihainin wo yonde kudasai.* (She-hie-
neen oh yone-day kuu-dah-sie.)

Many (quantity) *Takusan* **(Tock-sahn)**
There are many temples in Kyoto. *Kyoto ni Otera
ga takusan arimasu.* (Kyoto nee Oh-tay-rah gah
tock-sahn ah-ree-mahss.) A lot. *Takusan.* (Tock-
sahn.)

Map *Chizu* (Chee-zuu)
Would you like a map of the U.S.? *Amerika no
chizu wa ikaga desu ka?* (Ah-may-ree-kah no chee-
zuu wah e-kah-gah dess kah?) I need a map of
Tokyo. *Tokyo no chizu ga irimasu.* (Tokyo chee-zuu
gah e-ree-mahss.)

March *Sangatsu* **(Sahn-got-sue)**
Is Tokyo still cold in March? *Sangatsu ni Tokyo wa
mada samui desu ka?* (Sahn-got-sue nee Tokyo wah
mah-dah sah-muu-e dess kah?) I will arrive on
March 15. *Sangatsu no jugo-nichi ni tsukimasu.*
(Sahn-got-sue no juu-go-nee-chee nee t'sue-kee-
mahss.)

Market *Ichiba* (Ee-chee-bah); also *Maketto* (Mah-
ket-toe)
I would like to see Tokyo's famous fish market.
Tokyo no yumei na uo-ichiba wo mitai desu. (Tokyo
no yuu-may-e nah uu-oh-ee-chee-bah oh me-tie
dess.) Is the market open today? *Kyo wa maketto
ga aite imasu ka?* (K'yoe wah mah-ket-toe gah
aye-tay e-mahss kah?)

Martini *Maatini* **(Mah-tee-nee)**
Do you know how to make a martini? *Maatini no
tsukuri-kata wo shitte imasu ka?* (Mah-tee-nee no

t'sue-kuu-ree-kah-tah oh ssh-tay e-mahss kah?)
Two martinis, please. *Maatini wo futatsu kudasai.*
(Mah-tee-nee oh fuu-tot-sue kuu-dah-sie.)

May *Gogatsu* **(Go-got-sue)**
In May the weather is very good. *Gogatsu ni tenki
ga totte mo ii desu.* (Go-got-sue nee tane-kee gah
tote-tay moh ee dess.) This is May 1st. *Kyo wa
Gogatsu no tsuitachi desu.* (K'yoe wah go-got-sue
no t'sue-e-tah-chee dess.)

Mayonnaise *Mayonezu* **(Mah-yoe-nay-zuu)**
Please pass the mayonnaise. *Mayonezu wo totte
kudasai.* (Mah-yoe-nay-zuu oh tote-tay kuu-dah-
sie.)

Me *Watakushi,* plus *ni, ga, wo* **(Wah-tock-she
nee, gah *or* oh)**
["Me" is the word for "I" plus *wa, ga* or *wo* to
make it grammatically correct (accusative or
nominative).] To me/for me. *Watakushi ni.* (Wah-
tock-shee nee.)

Meal *Shokuji* **(Show-kuu-jee);** also *Gohan* (Go-
hahn)
Are meals included? *Shokuji tsuki desu ka?* (Show-
kuu-jee t'sue-kee dess kah?) Have you eaten (a
meal)? *Shokuji wo shimashita ka?* (Show-kuu-jee oh
she-mah-sshta kah?) [Gohan means either
cooked rice or food (meal), depending on the
context.]

Measure *Sumpo wo toru* **(Sume-poe oh toe-rue)**
Please measure this. *Kore no sumpo wo totte kudasai.* (Koe-ray no sume-poe oh tote-tay kuu-dah-
sie.) What are the (its) measurements? *Sumpo
wa nan desu ka.* (Sume-poe wah nahn dess kah?)

Meat *Niku* **(Nee-kuu)**
What kind of meat is this? *Kore wa nanno niku desu ka?* (Koe-ray wah nahn-no nee-kuu dess kah?) I don't eat meat. *Niku wo tabemasen.* (Nee-kuu oh tah-bay-mah-sin.)

Mechanic *Shuurikoh* **(Shuu-ree-koh)**
My car has broken down. Please call a mechanic. *Kuruma ga kosho shite imasu. Shuurikoh wo yonde kudasai.* (Kuu-rue-mah gah koe-show sshtay e-mahss. Shuu-ree-koh oh yone-day kuu-dah-sie.)

Medicine *Kusuri* **(Kuu-sue-ree)**
Do you have any medicine for a cold? *Kaze no kusuri ga arimasu ka?* (Kah-zay no kuu-sue-ree gah-ah-ree-mahss kah?)

Medium (in cooking) *Futsu-yaki* **(Fute-sue-yah-kee);** also *Mediyamu* **(May-dee-yah-muu)**
Please make (cook) it medium. *Mediyamu ni yaite kudasai.* (May-dee-yah-muu nee yie-tay kuu-dah-sie.)

Medium-sized car *Chugata sha* **(Chuu-gah-tah shah)**
I'd like to rent a medium-sized car. *Chugata sha wo karitai desu.* (Chuu-gah-tah shah oh kah-ree-tie dess.) I'm sorry, we have no medium-sized cars now. *Sumimasen, ima chugata sha ga arimasen.* (Sue-me-mah-sin, e-mah chuu-gah-tah shah ga ah-ree-mah-sin.)

Meet *Aimasu* **(Aye-mahss)**
Pleae meet me here at 1:00 P.M. *Koko de ichi-ji ni atte kudasai.* (Koe-koe day e-chee-jee nee aht-tay kuu-dah-sie.) I will meet you again tomorrow.

Mata ashita aimasu. (Mah-tah ah-sshtah aye-mahss.) Can you meet me in ten minutes? *Ato jippun de au koto ga dekimasu ka?* (Ah-toe jeep-pune day ah-ou koe-toe gah day-kee-mahss kah?) I'm pleased to meet you. *Dozo yoroshiku.* (Doe-zoe yoe-roe-ssh-kuu.)

Men's wear *Otoko mono* (Oh-toe-koe moe-no)
What floor is men's wear on? *Otoko mono wa nan kai desu ka?* (Oh-toe-koe moe-no wah nahn kie dess kah?)

Menu *Menyu* (May-nyuu)
Menu, please. *Menyu kudasai.* (May-nyuu kuu-dah-sie.) Would you like to see a menu? *Menyu wo mitai desu ka?* (May-nyuu oh me-tie dess kah?)

Message *Kotozuke* (Koe-toe-zuu-kay); also *Messeji* (May-say-jee)
Are there any messages for me? *Watakushi ni nani ka kotozuke ga kite imasu ka?* (Wah-tock-she nee nah-nee kah koe-toe-zuu-kay gah kee-tay e-mahss kah?) Please take a message. *Messeji wo totte kudasai.* (May-say-jee oh tote-tay kuu-dah-sie.)

Messenger *Tsukai* (T'sue-kie); also *Messenja-boi* (May-sin-jah-boy)
Please have this delivered by messenger. *Kore wo messenja ni motasete yatte kudasai.* (Koe-ray oh may-sin-jah nee moh-tah-say-tay yacht-tay kuu-dah-sie.)

Meter (measurement) *Metoru* (May-toe-rue)
It is only 100 meters from here. *Koko kara tada hyaku metoru desu.* (Koe-koe kah-rah tah-dah h'yah-kuu may-toe-rue dess.)

Mezzanine *Chunikai* **(Chuu-nee-kie)**
The hotel offices are on the mezzanine floor. *Hoteru no ofisu wa chunikai ni arimasu.* (Hoe-toe-rue no oh-fee-su wah chuu-nee-kie nee ah-ree-mahss.)

Microcomputer *Mai kon* **(My kone)**
Do you have a microcomputer? *Anata wa mai kon ga arimasu ka.* (Ah-nah-tah wah my kone gah ah-ree-mahss kah?)

Mile *Mairu* **(My-rue)**
How many miles is it? *Nan mairu desu ka?* (Nahn my-rue dess kah?) Mt. Fuji is about 80 miles from Tokyo. *Fuji-San wa Tokyo kara daitai hachiju mairu desu.* (Fuu-jee-Sahn wah Tokyo kah-rah die-tie hah-chee-juu my-rue dess.)

Milk *Gyunyu* **(Gyune-yuu);** also *Miruku* (Me-rue-kuu)
May I have a glass of cold milk? *Tsumetai miruku wo itadakemasen ka?* (T'sue-may-tie me-rue-kuu oh e-tah-dah-kay-mah-sin kah?) Some milk, please. *Miruku wo kudasai.* (Me-rue-kuu oh kuu-dah-sie.)

Mine / My *Watakushi-no* **(Wah-tock-she-no);** also *Boku-no* (Boe-kuu-no)
That is mine. *Sore wa watakushi-no desu.* (Soe-ray wah wah-tock-shee-no dess.) Have you seen my ticket? *Watakushi-no kippu wo mita koto ga arimasu ka?* (Wah-tock-she-no keep-pu oh me-tah koe-toe gah ah-ree-mahss kah?)

Minimum charge *Saitei ryokin* **(Sie-tay rio-keen)**
What is the minimum charge? *Saitei ryokin wa ikura desu ka?* (Sie-tay rio-keen wah e-kuu-rah dess kah.) There is no minimum charge. *Saitei ryokin wa arimasen.* (Sie-tay rio-keen wa ah-ree-mah-sin.)

Minute *Fun/Pun/Hun* (Fune/Pune/Hune)

One minute—*Ippun* (Eep-pune); Two minutes—
Nihun (Nee-hune); Three minutes—*Sampun*
(Sahm-pune); Four minutes—*Yonpun* (Yone-
pune); Five minutes—*Gohun* (Go-hune); Six
minutes—*Roppun* (Rope-pune); Seven minutes—
Nanahun (Nah-nah-hune); eight minutes—*Hap-
pun* (Hop-pune); Nine minutes—*Kyuhun* (Que-
hune); Ten minutes—*Jippun* (Jeep-pune)

Mistake *Machigai* (Mah-chee-guy)

This is a mistake. *Kore wa machigai desu.* (Koe-ray
wah mah-chee-guy dess.) Pardon me, I made a
mistake. *Gomen nasai, machigai mashita.* (Go-mane
nah-sie, mah-chee-guy mah-sshta.) Haven't you
made a mistake? *Anata wa machigai wo shimasen
deshita ka?* (Ah-nah-tah wah mah-chee-guy oh
she-mah-sin desh-tah kah?)

Monday *Getsuyobi* (Gate-sue-yoe-bee)

We will leave Monday morning at 7:30. *Getsuyobi
no asa shichiji-han ni tachimasu.* (Gate-sue-yoe-bee
no ah-sah she-chee-jee-hahn nee tah-chee-
mahss.)

Money *Okane* (Oh-kah-nay)

I forgot my money! *Okane wo wasuremashita!* (Oh-
kah-nay oh wah-sue-ray-mah-sshtah.) Do you
have any money? *Okane wo motte imasu ka?* (Oh-
kah-nay oh mote-tay e-mahss kah?)

Month *Getsu* (Gate-sue); also *Tsuki* (T'ski)

This month—*Kon getsu* (Kone gate-sue); Next
month—*Rai getsu* (Rye gate-sue); Last month—
Sen getsu (Sane gate-sue); Month after next—*Sa
rai getsu* (Sah-rye-gate-sue); Beginning of the
month—*Tsuki no hajime* (T'ski no hah-jee-may)

Morning *Asa* **(Ah-sah)**
Tomorrow morning—*Ashita no asa* (Ah-sshtah no ah-sah); Yesterday morning—*Kino no asa* (Kee-no no ah-sah); This morning—*Kesa* (Kay-sah)

Mountain *Yama* **(Yah-mah)**
There are many high mountains in Japan. *Nihon ni wa takai yama ga takusan arimasu.* (Nee-hone nee wah tah-kie yah-mah gah tock-sahn ah-ree-mahss.) What is the name of that mountain? *Ano yama no namae wa nan desu ka?* (Ah-no yah-mah no nah-my wah nahn dess kah?) Mountain-climbing—*Tozan* (Toe-zahn).

Movie *Eiga* **(A-e-gah);** Japanese movie *Nihon-no eiga* (Nee-hone no a-e-gah); Western (cowboy) movie *Seibu geki* (Say-e-buu gay-kee); Samurai movie *Jidai geki* (Jee-die gay-kee)
Let's go see a movie. *Eiga wo mi ni ikimasho.* (A-e-gah oh me nee e-kee-mah-show.)

Movie theater *Eiga kan* **(A-e-gah khan)**
Is there a movie theater near here? *Kono chikaku ni eiga kan ga arimasu ka?* (Koe-no chee-kah-kuu nee a-e-gah khan gah ah-ree-mahss kah?)

Museum (fine arts) *Bijutsukan* **(Bee-jute-sue-khan)**
I want to go to a fine arts museum. *Bijutsukan ni ikitai desu.* (Bee-jute-sue-kahn nee e-kee-tie dess.)

Museum (historical) *Hakubutsukan* **(Hah-kuu-boot-sue-kahn)**
Where is Tokyo's largest historical museum? *Tokyo no ichiban okii hakubutsukan wa doko desu ka?* (Tokyo no e-chee-bahn oh-kee hah-kuu-boot-sue-kahn wah doe-koe dess kah?)

Music *Ongaku* **(Own-gah-kuu)**
What kind of music do you like? *Donna ongaku ga suki desu ka?* (Doan-nah own-gah-kuu gah ski dess ka?) Music is popular around the world. *Sekai ju ongaku wa ninki ga arimasu.* (Say-kie juu own-gah-kuu wah neen-kee gah ah-ree-mahss.)

Mustard *Karashi* **(Kah-rah-she);** also *Massutado* (Mahss-tah-doe)
Would you like some mustard? *Massutado wo hoshii desu ka?* (Mahss-tah-doe oh hoe-shee dess kah?)

Must go *Ikanakereba narimasen* **(E-kah-nah-kay-ray-bah nah-ree-mah-sin)**
I'm sorry, but I must go now. *Shitsurei desu ga, ima sugu ikanakereba narimasen.* (She-t'sue-ray-e dess gah, e-mah sue-guu e-kah-nah-kay-ray-bah nah-ree-mah-sin.)

Mutton *Hitsuji no niku* **(He-t'sue-jee no nee-kuu);** also *Maton choppu* (Mah-tone choe-puu)
Not many restaurants have mutton. *Maton choppu no aru resutoran wa sukunai desu.* (Mah-tone no ah-rue race-toe-rahn wah sue-kuu-nie dess.)

N

Name *Namae* **(Nah-my)**
What is your name? *O'namae wa nan desu ka?* (Oh-nah-my wah nahn dess kah?) My name is Smith. *Watakushi wa Sumisu desu.* (Wah-tock-she wah Sue-mee-sue dess.) Please sign your name here. *Onamae wo koko ni kaite kudasai.* (Oh-nah-

my oh koe-koe nee kie-tay kuu-dah-sie.) Is this
your last (family) name? *Kore wa anata no myoji
desu ka?* (Koe-ray wah ah-nah-tah no me-yoe-jee
dess ka?)

Name brand *Meika hin* (May-e-kah heen)
Which brand name are you looking for? *Dore no
meika hin wo sagashite imasu ka?* (Doe-ray no may-
e-kah heen oh sah-gah-ssh-tay e-mahss kah?)
This is the best name brand. *Kore wa ichiban ii
meika hin desu.* (Koe-ray wah e-chee-bahn ee
may-e-kah heen dess.)

Nap *Hiru-ne* (He-rue-nay)
I'm going to take a nap. *Hirune wo shimasu.* (He-
rue-nay oh she-mahss.) Please take a nap. *Hirune wo shite kudasai.* (He-rue-nay oh ssh-tay kuu-
dah-sie.) Did you have a good nap? *Ii hirune oh
shimashita ka?* (Ee he-rue-nay oh she-mah-sshtah
kah?)

Napkin *Napukin* (Nah-puu-keen)
One more napkin, please. *Napukin wo mo ichi-mai
kudasai.* (Nah-puu-keen oh moe e-chee-my kuu-
dah-sie.)

Near *Chikai* (Chee-kie)
Is it near? *Chikai desu ka?* (Chee-kie dess kah?)
Yes, it's very near. *Hai, taihen chikai desu.* (Hie,
tie-hane chee-kie dess.)

Necessary *Hitsuyo-na* (Heet-sue-yoe-nah)
Is this necessary? *Kore wa hitsuyo desu ka?* (Koe-
ray wah heet-sue yoe dess kah?) Yes, it is necessary. *Hai hitsuyo desu.* (Hie heet-sue yoe dess.) Is
it necessary to go there? *Asoko e iku hitsuyo ga arimasu ka?* (Ah-so-koe eh e-kuu heet-sue-yoe gah
ah-ree-mahss kah?)

Necklace *Kubikazari* **(Kuu-bee-kah-zah-ree);** also
Nekuresu (Nay-kuu-ray-sue)
I want to buy a pearl necklace. *Shinju no nekuresu
wo kaitai desu.* (Sheen-juu no nay-kuu-ray-sue oh
kie-tie dess.) How much is this necklace? *Kono
kubikazari wa ikura desu ka?* (Koe-no kuu-bee-kah-
zah-ree wah ee-kuu-rah dess kah?)

Necktie *Nekutai* **(Nay-kuu-tie)**
I'd like to buy a necktie. *Nekutai wo kaitai desu.*
(Nay-kuu-tie oh kie-tie dess.) This tie goes
good with your clothing. *Kono nekutai wa anato no
yofuku ni niaimasu.* (Koe-no nay-kuu-tie wah ah-
nah-tah no yoe-fuu-kuu nee nee-aye-mahss.)

Need *Iriyo* **(Ee-ree-yoe);** To need (want) *Irimasu*
(E-ree-mahss)
Do you need this? *Kore ga irimasu ka?* (Koe-ray
gah e-ree-mahss kah?) No, I don't need it. *Iri-
masen.* (E-ree-mah-sin.)

Needle *Hari* **(Hah-ree)**
Do you have a needle? *Hari ga arimasu ka?* (Hah-
ree gah ah-ree-mahss kah?) I need a needle.
Hari gah irimasu. (Hah-ree gah e-ree-mahss.)

Nervous *Shinkeishitsu* **(Sheen-kay-e-ssh-tsue);**
also *Ira-ira suru* (e-rah-e-rah sue-rue)
I am nervous. *Shinkeishitsu desu.* (Sheen-kay-e-
ssh-tsue dess.) Don't be so nervous! *Sonna ni
ira-ira shinai hoh ga ii desu!* (Soan-nah-nee e-rah-e-
rah she-nie hoh gah ee dess!)

News *Nyusu* **(Knew-sue)**
Have you heard today's news? *Kyo no nyusu wo
kikimashita?* (K'yoe no knew-sue oh kee-kee-
mah-sshtah- kah?) What is the latest news? *Ichiban saikin no nyusu wa nan desu ka?* (Ee-chee bahn
sie-keen no knew-sue wah nahn dess kah?)

Newspaper *Shimbun* **(Shimm-boon)**
I'd like to read today's newspaper. *Kyo no shimbun wo yomitai desu.* (K'yoe no shimm-boon oh
yoe-me-tie dess.) Where can I buy one? *Doko de
kau koto ga dekimasu ka?* (Doe-koe day kow koe-
toe gah day-kee-mahss kah?) Do you have English-language newspapers? *Eiji shimbun ga arimasu ka?* (A-e-jee shimm-boon gah ah-ree-mahss
kah?) How much? *Ikura?* (E-kuu-rah?)

New Year's Day *Ganjitsu* **(Gahn-jeet-sue);** New
Year's Eve *Omisoka* (Oh-me-soe-kah)
Are you going to a shrine on New Year's Day?
Ganjitsu ni Otera ni ikimasu ka? (Ghan-jeet-sue
nee Oh-tay-rah nee e-kee-mahss kah?) Happy
New Year! *Shinnen Omedeto Gozaimasu!* (Sheen-
nane Oh-may-day-toe Go-zie-mahss!)

Night *Yoru* **(Yoe-rue);** also *Ban* (Bahn); Tonight
Komban (Kome-bahn)
Do you work at night? *Yoru ni hatarakimasu ka?*
(Yoe-rue nee hah-tah-rah-kee-mahss kah?) I go
to bed early at night. *Watakushi wa yoru hayaku
nemasu* (Wah-tock-she wah yoe-rue hah-yah-kuu
nay-mahss.) Can you come tonight? *Komban
kuru koto ga dekimasu ka?* (Kome-bahn kuu-rue
koe-toe gah day-kee-mahss kah?)

Nightgown *Nemaki* **(Nay-mah-kee)**
I forgot my nightgown. *Nemaki wo wasuremashita.*
(Nay-mah-kee oh wah-sue-ray-mah-ssh-tah.)
Use this yukata. *Kono yukata wo tsukatte.* (Koe-no
yuu-kah-tah oh t'sue-kot-tay.)

Night life *Yoru-no asobi* **(Yoe-rue-no ah-so-bee)**
Is there much night life in this city? *Kono machi ni
yoru-no asobi ga takusan arimasu ka?* (Koe-no mah-
chee nee yoe-rue-no ah-so-bee gah tock-sahn ah-
ree-mahss kah?) Where is the best night life?

Ichiban ii yoru-no asobi wa doko desu ka? (Ee-chee bahn ee yoe-rue-no ah-so-bee wah doe-koe dess kah?)

Noise *Oto* **(Oh-toe)**
That noise is terrible. *Ano oto wa hidoi desu.* (Ah-no oh-toe wah he-doy dess.) Please don't make so much noise. *Sonna ni oto wo tatenai de kudasai!* (Soan-nah nee oh-toe oh tah-tay-nie day kuu-dah-sie!)

Noisy *Sozoshii* **(Soh-zoh-she-e)**
This (hotel) room is too noisy. *Kono heya wa amari sozoshii desu.* (Koe-no hay-yah wah ah-mah-ree soh-zoh-she-e dess.) Those drunks are too noisy. *Sono yopparai wa amari sozoshii desu.* (So-no yope-pah-rie wah ah-mah-ree soh-zoh-she-e dess.)

North *Kita* **(Hee-tah);** Northeast *Hokuto* (Hoe-kuu-toe); Northwest *Hokusei* (Hoe-kuu-say)
It snows a lot in northern Japan. *Kita Nihon ni yuki ga takusan furimasu* (Kee-tah Nee-hone nee yuu-kee gah tock-sahn fuu-ree-mahss.) The shop is on the north side of the street. *Mise wa michi no kita gawa ni arimasu.* (Me-say wah me-chee no kee-tah gah-wah nee ah-ree-mahss.) Which way is north? *Kita no ho wa dore desu ka?* (Kee-tah no hoh wah doe-ray dess kah?)

No Smoking (sign) *Kin-En* **(Keen-Inn)**
No smoking, please. *Tabako wa go-enryo kudasai.* (Toe-bah-koe wah go-inn-rio kuu-dah-sie.)

Notify (inform) *Tsuchi suru* **(T'sue-chee sue-rue);** Tell *Tsutaeru* (T'sue-tah-eh-rue)
Please tell Mr. Suzuki that I am waiting for him. *Suzuki-San ni watakushi ga matte iru to yu koto wo*

tsutaete kudasai. (Su-zu-kee-Sahn nee wah-tock-she gah mot-tay e-rue toe yuu koe-toe oh stite-tay kuu-dah-sie.)

Not included *Haitte imasen* **(Hite-tay e-mah-sin)**
This is not included in your bill. *Kore wa kanjo ni haitte imasen.* (Koe-ray wah kahn-joe nee hite-tay e-mah-sin.) Yes, it's included. *Hie, haitte imasu.* (Hie, hite-tay e-mahss.)

Not yet *Mada* **(Mah-dah)**
Isn't it ready yet? *Mada dekimasen ka?* (Mah-dah day-kee-mah-sin kah?) Hasn't he/she/it come yet? *Mada konai desu ka?* (Mah-dah koe-nie dess kah?) I'm not ready yet. *Mada yoi shite nai desu.* (Mah-dah yoe-e ssh-tay nie dess.)

November *Juichigatsu* **(Juu-e-chee-got-sue)**
Let's go in November. *Juichigatsu ni ikimasho.* (Juu-e-chee-got-sue nee e-kee-mah-sho.) Are there any festivals in November? *Juichigatsu ni matsuri ga arimasu ka?* (Ju-e-chee-got-sue nee mot-sue-ree gah ah-ree-mahss kah?)

Now *Ima* **(E-mah)**
Do you want it now? *Ima hoshii desu ka?* (E-mah hoe-she-e dess kah?) What time is it now? *Ima nanji desu ka?* (E-mah nahn-jee dess kah?) Let's go right now. *Ima sugu ikimasho.* (E-mah sue-guu e-kee-mah-sho.)

Number *Ban* **(Bahn)**
What number is it? *Nan ban desu ka?* (Nahn bahn dess kah?) My room number is 428. *Watakushi no heya no ban-go wa yon-hyaku ni-ju hachi desu.* (Wah-tock-she no hay-yah no bahn-go wah yone-h'yah-kuu nee-juu hah-chee dess.) What is your

telephone number? *Anata no denwa bango wa nan desu ka?* (Ah-nah-tah no dane-wah bahn-go wah nahn dess kah?)

Nurse *Kangofu* (Kahn-go-fuu)
Please call a nurse. *Kangofu wo yonde kudasai.* (Kahn-go-fuu oh yone-day kuu-dah-sie.)   Ask the nurse. *Kangofu ni kiite kudasai.* (Kahn-go-fuu nee kee-tay kuu-dah-sie.)

Nursery (for babies) *Junyu-shitsu* (June-yuu-sheet-sue); (for children) *Kodomo-beya* (Koe-doe-moe-bay-yah)
In Japan some department stores have nurseries. *Nihon de wa aru depaato wa junyu-shitsu ga arimasu.* (Nee-hone day wah ah-rue day-pah-toe wah june-yuu-sheet-sue gah ah-ree-mahss.)

O

Occasionally *Toki-doki* (Toe-kee-doe-kee)
I eat here sometimes. *Toki-doki koko de tabemasu.* (Toe-kee-doe-kee koe-koe day tah-bay-mahss.) Do you go to the movies? *Eiga wo mi ni ikimasu ka?* (A-e-gah oh me nee e-kee-mahss kah?)   I go sometimes. *Toki-doki ikimasu.* (Toe-kee-doe-kee e-kee-mahss.)

Ocean *Taiyo* (Tie-yoe); Atlantic Ocean *Taiseiyo* (Tie-say-e-yoe); Pacific Ocean *Taiheiyo* (Tie-hay-e-yoe); also *Umi* (Uu-mee)
Did you go to the ocean this summer? *Kotoshi no natsu ni umi e ikimashita ka?* (Koe-toe-she no not-sue nee uu-me eh e-kee-mah-sshtah kah?)

Ocean-side *Umi-gawa* **(Uu-me-gah-wah)**
His home is on the ocean-side. *Anohito no ie wa umi-gawa ni arimasu.* (Ah-no-ssh-toe no e-eh wah uu-me-gah-wah nee ah-ree-mahss.)

October *Jugatsu* **(Juu-got-sue)**
Let's wait until October. *Jugatsu made machimasho.* (Juu-got-sue mah-day mah-chee-mah-show.)
The weather is fine in October. *Jugatsu wa tenki ga ii desu.* (Juu-got-sue wah tane-kee gah ee dess.)

Octopus *Tako* **(Tah-koe)**
Octopus is a well-known food in Japan. *Nihon de wa tako ga yumei na tabemono desu.* (Nee-hone day wah tah-koe gah yuu-may-e nah tah-bay-moe-no dess.) Do you like octopus? *Tako ga suki desu ka?* (Tah-koe gah ski dess kah?) No. *Sukimasen.* (Ski-mah-sin.)

Odor (smell) *Nioi* **(Nee-oye)**
This food has a strange smell. *Kono tabemono wa henna na nioi shimasu.* (Koe-no tah-bay-moe-no wah hane-nah nee-oye she-mahss.) Does this smell bad (spoiled)? *Kore wa kusatta nioi ga shimasu ka?* (Koe-ray wah kuu-sot-tah nee-oye gah she-mahss kah?)

Off (get off of) *Orimasu* **(Oh-ree-mahss)**
We get off at the next station. *Kono tsugi no eki de orimasu.* (Koe-no t'sue-ghee no a-kee day oh-ree-mahss.) Where do we get off? *Doko de orimasu ka?* (Doe-koe day oh-ree-mahss kah?)

Office *Jimusho* **(Jeem-sho);** Head office *Honsha* (Hone-shah); Government office *Yakusho* (Yah-kuu-sho); Branch office *Shiten* (She-tane)
Please go to the office to get your tickets. *Kippu wo morau no ni jimusho e itte kudasai.* (Keep-puu

oh moe-rah-uu no nee jeem-sho eh eet-tay kuu-dah-sie.) Is that the office? *Are wa jimsho desu ka?* (Ah-ray wah jeem-show dess kah?)

Off-season *Kisetsu-hazure* **(Kee-sate-sue-hah-zuu-ray)**
Prices are cheaper during off-season. *Kisetsu-hazure ni wa nedan ga motto yasui desu.* (Kee-sate-sue-hah-zuu-ray nee wah nay-dahn gah mote-toe yah-sooey dess.) When is the off-season? *Kisetsu-hazure ga itsu kara itsu made desu ka?* (Kee-sate-sue-hah-zuu-ray gah eet-sue kah-rah eet-sue mah-day dess kah?)

Often *Tabi-tabi (Tah-bee-tah-bee);* also *Yoku* (Yoe-kuu)
She comes here often. *Kanojo wa yoku koko e kimasu.* (Kah-no-joe wah yoe-kuu koe-koe eh kee-mahss.) Do you go there often? *Asoko e tabi-tabi ikimasu ka?* (Ah-soe-koe eh tah-bee-tah-bee e-kee-mahss kah?)

Old (thing) *Furui* **(Fuu-rue-e);** Old person *Toshiyori* (Toe-she-yoe-ree)
This is an old building. *Kore wa furui biru desu.* (Koe-ray wah fuu-rue-e bee-rue dess.) Who is that old man/woman? *Sono O'toshiyori wa donata desu ka?* (Soe-no Oh-toe-she-yoe-ree wah doe-nah-tah dess kah?)

Omelet *Omuretsu* **(Oh-muu-rate-sue)**
I'll have an omelet. *Omuretsu ni shimasu.* (Oh-muu-rate-sue nee she-mahss.) What kind of omelets do you have? *Donna omuretsu ga arimasu ka?* (Doan-nah oh-muu-rate-sue gah ah-ree-mahss kah?) Would you like an omelet? *Omuretsu ga ikaga desu ka?* (Oh-muu-rate-sue gah e-kah-gah dess kah?)

Once *Ichido* **(E-chee-doe)**
Once a month. *Ikka-getsu ni ichido.* (Eek-kah-gate-sue nee e-chee-doe.) Once a week. *Isshukan ni ichido.* (Ees-shuu-kahn nee e-chee-doe.) I've been there once. *Asoko ni ichido itta koto ga arimasu.* (Ah-soe-koe nee e-chee-doe eet-tah koe-toe gah ah-ree-mahss.)

Once more *Moh ichido* **(Moe-e-chee-doe)**
One more time! *Mo ichido!* (Moe e-chee-doe!) I would like to go once more. *Mo ichido ikitai desu.* (Moe-e-chee-doe e-kee-tie dess.)

One *Hitotsu* **(He-tote-sue);** also *Ichi* (E-chee);
One hand *Kata-te* (Kah-tah-tay); One side *Kata-ho* (Kah-tah-hoe); One more *Moh hitotsu* (Moe he-tote-sue); One-by-one (people) *Hitori zutsu* (He-toe-ree zoot-sue); One after the other *Junjun ni* (June-june-nee)
We need one more cushion. *Mo hitotsu no zabuton ga irimasu.* (Moh he-tote-sue no zah-buu-tone gah e-ree-mahss.)

One way (street) *Ippo tsuko* **(Eep-poe t'sue-koe)**
This is a one-way street. *Kono michi ga ippo tsuko desu.* (Koe-no me-chee gah eep-poe t'sue-koe dess.) It is on a one-way street. *Ippo tsuko no michi ni arimasu.* (Eep-poe t'sue-koe no me-chee nee ah-ree-mahss.)

One-way ticket *Kata-michi Kippu* **(Kah-tah-me-chee keep-puu)**
Is this a one-way ticket? *Kore wa kata-michi no kippu desu ka?* (Koe-ray wah kah-tah me-chee no keep-puu dess kah?) One-way, please. *Kata-michi, Onegaishimasu.* (Kah-tah-me-chee, Oh-nay-guy-she-mahss.)

Onion *Tamanegi* **(Tah-mah-nay-ghee)**
Without onions. *Tamanegi nashi.* (Tah-mah-nay-ghee nah-she.) I don't like onions. *Tamanegi ga kirai desu.* (Tah-mah-nay-ghee gah kee-rye dess.) I love onions. *Tamanegi wa dai-suki desu.* (Tah-mah-nay-ghee wah die-ski dess.) Onions are good for your health. *Tamanegi ga kenko ni ii desu.* (Tah-mah-nay-ghee gah kane-koe nee ee dess.)

On the way *Tochu de* **(Toe-chuu-day)**
Let's stop on the way. *Tochu de tomarimasho.* (Toe-chuu day toe-mah-ree-mah-sho.) It's on the way. *Tochu ni arimasu.* (Toe-chuu nee ah-ree-mahss.)

Open *Akemasu* **(Ah-kay-mahss)**
Please open this. *Kore wo akete kudasai.* (Koe-ray oh ah-kay-tay kuu-dah-sie.) Please open your suitcase. *Sutsu kesu wo akete kudasai.* (Sue-t'su kay-sue oh ah-kay-tay kuu-dah-sie.) Must I open this box? *Kono hako wo akenakereba narimasen ka?* (Koe-no hah-koe oh ah-kay-nah-kay-ray-bah nah-ree-mah-sin kah?) Are the shops open? *Mise wa aite imasu ka?* (Me-say wah aye-tay e-mahss kah?) What time does it (do they) open? *Nanji ni akimasu ka?* (Nahn-jee nee ah-kee-mahss kah?) It's open. *Aite imasu.* (Aye-tay e-mahss.)

Operator (telephone) *Denwa kokanshu* **(Dane-wah koe-khan-shuu)**
Dial the international operator. *Kokusai denwa kokanshu ni kakete kudasai.* (Koke-sie dane-wah koe-kahn-shuu nee kah-kay-tay kuu-dah-sie.)

Optician *Megane-ya* **(May-gah-nay-yah)**
I broke my glasses. Is there an eye doctor nearby? *Megane wo kowashimashita. Kono chikaku ni me-*

gane-ya wa arimasu ka? (May-gah-nay oh koe-wah-she-mah-sshtah. Koe-no chee-kah-kuu nee may-gah-nay-yah wah ah-ree-mahss ka?)

Orange *Orenji* **(Oh-rane-jee);** Orange juice *Orenji jusu* (Oh-rane-jee juu-sue)
Does everyone want orange juice? *Minna-san orenji jusu wo hoshii desu ka?* (Meen-nah-sahn oh-rane-jee juu-sue oh hoe-she-e dess kah?) Is this orange juice fresh? *Kono orenji jusu wa fureshu desu ka?* (Koe-no oh-rane-jee juu-suu wah fuu-ray-shuu dess kah?)

Orchid *Ran* **(Rhan)**
Is this flower an orchid? *Kono hana wa ran desu ka?* (Koe-no hah-nah wa rahn dess kah?) There are many orchid varieties in Japan. *Nihon ni wa ran no shurui ga takusan arimasu.* (Nee-hone nee wah rahn no shuu-rue-e gah tock-sahn ah-ree-mahss.)

Order (food, etc.) *Chumon* **(Chuu-moan)**
Have you placed your order? *Chumon wo shimashita ka?* (Chuu-moan oh she-mah-sshtah kah?) This is not what I ordered. *Kore wa watakushi no chumon to chigaimasu.* (Koe-ray wah wah-tock-she no chuu-moan toe chee-guy-mahss.) I would like to order. *Chumon wo shitai desu.* (Chuu-moan oh she-tie dess.) Please cancel my order. *Watakushi no chumon wo torikeshite kudasai.* (Wah-tock-she no chuu-moan oh toe-ree-kay-ssh-tay kuu-dah-sie.)

Orient *Toyo* **(Toe-yoe);** Oriental *Toyo-no* (Toe-yoe-no)
This is my first time in the Orient. *Toyo ni kimashita no wa hajimete desu.* (Toe-yoe nee kee-mah-

171

sshtah-no wah hah-jee-may-tay dess.) I would like to buy an Oriental rug. *Toyo-no jutan wo kaitai desu.* (Toe-yoe-no juu-tahn oh kie-tie dess.)

Outside *Soto* **(Soe-toe);** *Omote* (Oh-moe-tay)
Please wait outside. *Soto de matte kudasai.* (Soe-toe day mot-tay kuu-dah-sie.) I'll meet you out-side. *Omote de aimasu.* (Oh-moe-tay day aye-mahss.) He/she is still outside. *Mada soto ni ori-masu.* (Mah-dah soe-toe nee oh-ree-mahss.)

Overcast (cloudy) *Ichimen ni kumotta* **(E-chee-mane nee kuu-mote-tah)**
Unfortunately, it is overcast today. *Ainiku, kyo wa ichimen ni kumotte imasu.* (Aye-nee-kuu, k'yoe wah e-chee-mane nee kuu-mote-tay e-mahss.)

Overcharge *Kakene* **(Kah-kay-nay)** or *Ohba chaji* (Oh-bah chah-jee)
I think I have been overcharged. *Ohba chaji to omoimasu.* (Oh-bah chah-jee toe oh-moy-mahss.) He/she overcharged you. *Anohito wa an-ata ni ohba chaji shimashita.* (Ah-no-ssh-toe wah ah-nah-tah nee oh-bah chah-jee she-mah-sshtah.)

Overcoat *Ohba* **(Oh-bah)**
Is this your overcoat? *Kore wa anata-no ohba desu ka?* (Koe-ray wah ah-nah-tah-no oh-bah dess ka?) Will I need an overcoat today? *Kyo wa ohba wo irimasu ka?* (K'yoe wah oh-bah oh e-ree-mahss kah?)

Overheat *Kanetsu* **(Kah-nay-t'sue)**
Be careful! Don't get overheated! *Ki wo tsukete! Kanetsu wo shinai yo ni!* (Kee oh skate-tay! Kah-nay-t'sue oh she-nie yoe nee!)

Overseas telephone *Kokusai denwa* **(Koke-sie dane-wah)**

You have an overseas (international) telephone call. *Kokusai denwa ga kakatte imasu.* (Koke-sie dane-wah gah kah-kot-tay e-mahss.) I want to make an overseas phone call. *Kokusai denwa wo kaketai desu.* (Koke-sie dane-wah oh kah-kay-tie dess.) How do I make an overseas phone call? *Kokusai denwa oh do yu fu ni kakemasu ka?* (Koke-sie dane-wah oh doe yuu fuu nee kah-kay mahss ka?)

Over there *Asoko* **(Ah-so-koe)**

Your baggage is over there. *Anata no nimotsu wa asoko ni arimasu.* (Ah-nah-tah no nee-mote-sue wah ah-so-koe nee ah-ree-mahss.)

Overweight *Juryo ohba* **(Juu-rio oh-bah)**

Your baggage is overweight. *Anata no nimotsu wa juryo-ohba desu.* (Ah-nah-tah no nee-mote-sue wah juu-rio oh-bah dess.)

Owe (debt) *Kari ga arimasu* **(Kah-ree gah ah-ree-mahss)**

Do I owe you anything? *Kari ga arimasu ka?* (Kah-ree gah ah-ree-mahss kah?) How much do I owe you? *Ikura kari ga arimasu ka?* (E-kuu-rah kah-ree gah ah-ree-mahss kah?) You don't owe me anything. *Kari wa arimasen.* (Kah-ree wah ah-ree-mah-sin.)

Oxygen *Sanso* **(Sahn-soe)**

Hurry! This person needs oxygen! *Hayaku! Kono-hito wa sanso ga irimasu!* (Hah-yah-kuu! Koe-no-ssh-toe wah sahn-soe gah e-ree-mahss!) Please bring some oxygen. *Sanso wo motte kite kudasai.* (Sahn-so oh moat-tay keet-tay kuu-dah-sie.)

Oyster *Kaki* **(Kah-kee);** Fried oysters *Kaki no furai* (kah-kee no fuu-rie.) Raw oysters *Nama no kaki* (Nah-mah no kah-kee)
I'll have fried oysters. *Kaki no furai ni shimasu.* (Kah-kee no fuu-rie nee she-mahss.)

P

Pacific Ocean *Taiheiyo* **(Tie-hey-e-yoe)**
The Pacific Ocean is especially beautiful from here. *Koko kara Taiheiyo wa toku ni utsukushi desu.* (Koe-koe kah-rah Tie-hey-e-yoe wah toe-kuu nee uu-t'sue-kuu-she dess.)

Pack (baggage) *Nizukuri suru* (Nee-zuu-kuu-ree sue-rue)
Have you packed? *Nizukuri shimashita ka?* (Nee-zuu-kuu-ree she-mah-sshta kah?) Yes, every-thing is packed. *Hai, zembu nizukuri shimashita.* (Hie, zim-buu nee-zuu-kuu-ree she-mah-sshta.)

Package (parcel) *Kozutsumi* (Koe-zuut-sue-me)
What is in this package? *Kono kozutsumi ni nani ga haitte imasu ka?* (Koe-no koe-zuut-sue-me nee nah-nee gah hite-tay e-mahss kah?) I want to send this package by airmail. *Kono kozutsumi wo kokubin de dashitai desu.* (Koe-no koe-zuut-sue-me oh koe-kuu-bean day dah-she-tie dess.)

Packing charge *Nizukuri ryo* **(Nee-zuu-kuu-ree rio);** Packing case/box *Nizukuri bako* (bah-koe); Packing paper *Tsutsumi gami* (T'sue-t'sue-me gah-me)

How much will the packing charge be for two boxes? *Futatsu-no hako no nizukuri ryo wa ikura ni narimasu ka?* (Fuu-tot-sue-no hah-koe no nee-zuu-kuu-ree rio wah e-kuu-rah nee nah-ree-mahss kah?)

Page (call) *Yobi-dashimasu* **(Yoe-bee-dah-she-mahss)**
Please page Mr. Brown. *Buraun-San wo yobi-da-shite kudasai.* (Buu-rah-unn-Sahn oh yoe-bee dah-ssh-tay kuu-dah-sie.)

Pain *Itami* **(E-tah-me);** *Itai* (E-tie)
Where does it hurt? *Doko ga itai desu ka?* (Doe-koe gah e-tie dess kah?) My stomach hurts. *On-aka ga itai desu.* (Oh-nah-kah gah itai dess.)

Pajamas *Pajama* (Pah-jah-mah)
I would like to buy some new pajamas. *Atarashii pajama wo kaitai desu.* (Ah-tah-rah-she-e pah-jah-mah oh kie-tie dess.) Are these your pajamas? *Kore wa anata no pajama desu ka?* (Koe-ray wah ah-nah-tah no pah-jah-mah dess kah?)

Palace *Kyuden* **(Que-den);** Where Japan's Emperor lives *Kyujo* (Que-joe)
Is it possible to enter the Palace? *Kyujo ni hairu koto ga dekimasu ka?* (Que-joe nee hie-rue koe-toe gah day-kee-mahss kah?) I want to see the Palace. *Kyujo wo mitai desu.* (Que-joe oh me-tie dess.)

Pancakes *Hotto keiki* **(Hot-toe kay-e-kee)**
Let's have pancakes for breakfast. *Choshoku ni hotto keiki wo tabemasho.* (Choe-show-kuu nee hot-toe kay-e-kee oh tah-bay-mah-sho.)

Pants (trousers) *Pantsu* **(Pahn-t'sue);** also *Zubon* (Zuu-bone)
I need a new pair of pants. *Atarashii zubon ga iri-masu.* (Ah-tah-rah-she-e zuu-bone gah e-ree-mahss.) Can I get these pants pressed? *Kono pantsu wo puresu shite moraemasu ka?* (Koe-no pahn-t'sue oh puu-ray-sue she-tay moe-rah-eh-mahss kah?)

Paper *Kami* **(Kah-me);** Newspaper *Shimbun* (Shimm-boon); Letter paper *Retapepa* (Ray-tah-pay-pah)
Do you have any thin letter paper? *Usui reta pepa ga arimasu ka?* (Uu-sue-e ray-tah-pay-pah gah ah-ree-mahss kah?)

Parcel (see Package)

Parents *Ryoshin* **(Rio-sheen)**
Are your parents still alive? *Anato no go-ryoshin wa mada ogenki de imasu ka?* (Ah-nah-tah no go-rio-sheen wah mah-dah oh-gain-key day e-mahss kah?) No, my parents have passed away. *Ie, ryoshin wa nakunarimashita.* (Ee-eh, rio-sheen wah nah-kuu-nah-ree-mah-sshtah.)

Park *Koen* **(Koe-inn)**
There are many famous parks in Tokyo. *Tokyo ni yumei-na koen ga takusan arimasu.* (Tokyo nee yuu-may-e-nah koe-inn gah tock-sahn ah-ree-mahss.) For example, Meiji Park. *Tatoeba, Meiji Koen.* (Tah-toe-eh-bah, May-e-jee Koe-inn.)

Park a car *Jidosha wo chusha suru* **(Jee-doe-shah oh chuu-shah sue-rue)**
Is it all right to park here? *Koko de chusha shite-mo ii desu ka?* (Koe-koe day chuu-shah ssh-tay-moe ee dess kah?)

Parking place (lot, etc.) *Chusha-jo* **(Chuu-shah-joe);** No Parking (sign) *Chusha Kinshi* (Chu-shah Keen-she)
Generally, shops and restaurants in Japan do not have parking lots. *Futsu Nihon no mise ya resutoran wa chusha-jo ga arimasen.* (Fute-sue Nee-hone no me-say yah race-toe-rahn wah chuu-shah-joe gah ah-ree-mah-sin.)

Party *Paati* **(Pahh-tee)**
Would you like to go to a party tonight? *Komban paati ni ikimasen ka?* (Kome-bahn pahh-tee nee e-kee-mah-sin kah?) Let's have a party! *Paati wo yarimasho!* (Pahh-tee oh yah-ree-mah-show!)

Passport *Pasupoto* **(Pah-sue-poe-toe);** also *Ryoken* (Rio-kin)
May I see your passport, please. *Pasupoto wo misete kudasai.* (Pah-sue-poe-toe oh me-say-tay kuu-dah-sie.) Do you have your passport now? *Ima pasupoto wo motte imasu ka?* (E-mah pah-sue-poe-toe oh mote-tay e-mahss kah?)

Passport Control *Shukkoku Tetsuzuki* **(Shuu-koe-kuu Tate-suu-zuu-kee)**
Please direct me to the passport control office. *Shukkoku tetsuzuki no jimusho wo oshiete kudasai.* (Shuu-koe-kuu tate-sue-zuu-kee no jim-sho oh oh-she-a-tay kuu-dah-sie.) Passport Control is on the 2nd floor. *Shukkoku Tetsuzuki wa nikai ni arimasu* (. . .Nee-kie nee ah-ree-mahss.)

Pattern (of cloth) *Gara* **(Gah-rah);** also *Moyo* (Moe-yoe)
Do you like this pattern? *Kono gara suki desu ka?* (Koe-no gah-rah ski dess kah?) Do you have a pattern book? *Gara mihon ga arimasu ka?* (Gah-rah me-hone gah ah-ree-mahss kah?)

Japanese in Plain English

Pay *Haraimasu* (Hah-rie-mahss)
Where do I pay? *Doko de haraimasu ka?* (Doe-koe day hah-rie-mahss kah?) When do I pay? *Itsu haraimasu ka?* (Eet-sue hah-rie-mahss kah?) Please pay at the counter. *Kaunta de haratte kudasai.* (Kah-un-tah day hah-rot-tay kuu-dah-sie.)

Peach *Momo* (Moe-moe)
Would you like a peach for dessert? *Dezato ni momo wa ikaga desu ka?* (Day-zah-toe nee moe-moe wah e-kah-gah dess kah?)

Pearl *Shinju* (Sheen-juu)
Do you know a good pearl shop? *Ii shinju no mise wo shitte imasu ka?* (Ee sheen-juu no me-say oh ssh-tay e-mahss kah?) I'd like to buy a pearl ring, earrings, and necklace. *Shinju no yubiwa to iya-ringu to nekuresu wo kaitai desu.* (Sheen-juu no yuu-bee-wah toe ee-yah-reen-guu toe nay-kuu-ray-sue oh kie-tie dess.)

Pedestrian crossing *Odan hodoh* (Oh-dahn hoe-doh)
When you cross a street always use a pedestrian crossing. *Michi wo wataru toki itsumo odan hodoh wo tsukatte kudasai.* (Me-chee oh wah-tah-rue toe-kee eet-sue-moe oh-dahn hoe-doh oh scot-tay kuu-dah-sie.)

Pen (writing) *Pen* (Pin)
Loan me your pen for a second. *Pen wo chotto kashite.* (Pen oh chote-toe kah-sshtay.)

Pepper *Kosho* (Koe-sho)
Pass the pepper, please. *Kosho wo totte kudasai.* (Koe-sho oh tote-tay kuu-dah-sie.) Want some pepper? *Kosho ikaga?* (Koe-sho e-kah-gah?)

Pepsi Cola *Pepushi Kora* **(Pep-she Koe-rah)**
Do you have chilled pepsi cola? *Tsumetai pepushi kora ga arimasu ka?* (T'sue-may-tie pep-she koe-rah gah ah-ree-mahss kah?)

Per day *Ichi nichi ni* (E-chee nee-chee nee)
How much is it per day. *Ichi nichi ni ikura desu ka?* (E-chee nee-chee nee e-kuu-rah dess kah?)

Perfume *Kosui* **(Koe-suu-e)**
Do you use perfume? *Kosui wo tsukaimasu ka?* (Koe-suu-e oh t'sue-kie-mahss kah?) May I see several kinds of perfume, please? *Kosui no ironna shurui wo misete kudasaimasen ka?* (Koe-suu-e no e-roan-nah shu-rue-e oh me-say-tay kuu-dah-sie-mah-sin kah?)

Person *Hito* **(Ssh-toe);** *Nin* (Neen)
Where is he/she from? *Doko no hito desu ka?* (Doe-koe no ssh-toe dess kah?) How many people (are here or are there)? *Nan nin orimasu ka?* (Nahn neen oh-ree-mahss kah?) Two people—*Futari* (Fuu-tah-ree); Three people—*San nin* (Sahn neen); Six people—*Roku nin (Roe-kuu neen.)*

Personal *Kojin* **(Koe-jeen);** One's own *Jibun no* (Jee-boon no)
Is this a personal (private) car? *Kore wa kojin no kuruma desu ka?* (Koe-ray wah koe-jeen no kuu-rue-mah dess kah?) It is my own (private) problem. *Jibun jishin no koto desu.* (Jee-boon jee-sheen no koe-toe dess.)

Personal computer *Paso kon* **(Pah-so kone)**
This next Saturday I'm going to buy a personal computer. *Kono tsugi no Doyobi ni paso kon wo kaimasu.* (Koe-no t'sue-ghee no Die-yoe-bee nee pah-so kone wo kie-mahss.)

Person-to-person *Shimei-tsu-wa* **(She-may-e t'sue wah)**

I would like to make a person-to-person (phone) call. *Shimei-tsu-wa no denwa wo kaketai desu.* (She-may-e t'sue wah no dane-wah oh kah-kay tie dess.)

Pharmacy *Kusuriya* **(Kuu-sue-ree-yah)**

Is there a pharmacy (drugstore) in the hotel? *Hoteru no naka ni kusuriya ga arimasu ka?* (Hoe-tay-rue no nah-kah nee kuu-sue-ree-yah gah ah-ree-mahss kah?) Where is the closest drugstore? *Ichiban chikai kusuriya wa doko desu ka?* (E-chee-bahn chee-kai kuu-sue-ree-yah wah doe-koe dess kah?)

Photograph *Shashin* **(Shah-sheen)**

May I take a photograph? *Shashin wo totte mo ii desu ka?* (Shah-seen oh tote-tay moe ee dess kah?) Would you please take (our) picture? *Shashin wo totte itadakemasen ka?* (Shah-sheen oh tote-tay e-tah-dah-kay-mah-sin kah?) Whose photo is this? *Kore wa donata no shashin desu ka?* (Koe-ray wah doe-nah-tah no shah-sheen dess kah?)

Pickles *O-shinko* **(Oh-sheen-koe);** also *Tsuke-mono* **(T'sue-kay-moe-no)**

["Pickles" in the Japanese context refers to bits of pickled cabbage, radishes, and other vegetables—not only cucumbers.] Would you like some pickled vegetables? *O-shinko ikaga desu ka?* (Oh-sheen-koe e-kah-gah dess kah?)

Pickpocket *Suri* **(Sue-ree)**

Beware of pickpockets. *Suri ni ki wo tsukenasai.* (Sue-ree nee kee oh ska-nah-sie.) Pickpockets are rare in Japan. *Nihon de wa suri ga sukunai desu.* (Nee-hone day wah sue-ree gah sue-kuu-nie dess.)

Pick-up (at airport) *Demukaeru* **(Day-muu-kie-rue)**
I will pick you up, so don't worry. *Demukae ni ikimasu kara, shimpai naku.* (Day-muu-kie nee e-kee-mahss kah-rah, sheem-pie nah-kuu.) Will somebody pick me up? *Dare ka demukae ni kite kuremasu ka?* (Dah-ray kah day-muu-kie nee kee-tay kuu-ray mahss kah?)

Picnic *Pikunikku* **(Pee-kuu-neek-kuu);** *Ensoku* (Inn-soe-kuu)
Let's go on a picnic. *Pikunikku ni ikimasho.* (Pee-kuu-neek-ku nee e-kee-mah-sho.)

Picture (photo) *Shashin* **(Shah-sheen);** Painting, Drawing *E* (Eh); Picture postcard *E hagaki* (Eh hah-gah-kee)
I'll take these six picture postcards. *Kono rokumai no e hagaki wo moraimasu.* (Koe-no roe-kuu-my no eh hah-gah-kee oh moe-rie-mahss.) Do you have pictures of the Festival of the Ages? *Jidai Matsuri no shashin ga arimasu ka?* (Jee-die Mot-sue-ree no shah-sheen gah ah-ree-mahss kah?)

Pilot (airline) *Sojushi* **(Soe-juu-she);** Airline captain *Kicho* (Kee-choe)
This is Captain Jones (speaking). *Jone-zuu Kicho desu.* (Kee-choe dess.) We are now passing over the Grand Canyon. *Gurando Kanyon no ue wo ima tonde imasu.* (Guu-rahn-doe Kahn-yone no way oh e-mah tone-day e-mahss.)

Platform (for train/subway) *Homu* **(Hoe-muu);** Arrival platform *Tochaku homu* (Toe-chah-kuu hoe-muu); Departure platform *Hassha homu* (Hah-shah hoe-muu)
Which is the platform for Kyoto? *Kyoto yuki no homu wa dochira desu ka?* (Kyoto yuu-kee no hoe-muu wah doe-chee-rah dess kah?)

Play (theatrical) *Shibai* **(She-by)**; Play (recreational) *Asobi* (Ah-so-bee)
Would you like to see a play tonight? *Komban shibai wo mitai desu ka?* (Kome-bahn she-by oh me-
tie dess kah?) Let's go out tonight and play
(have fun). *Komban asobi ni ikimasho.* (Kome-bahn
ah-so-bee nee e-kee-mah-sho.) Do you play tennis? *Tenisu wo yarimasu ka?* (Tay-nee-sue oh yah-
ree-mahss kah?)

Plenty (much) *Takusan* **(Tock-sahn)**; Plenty
(enough) *Jubun* (Juu-boon)
Give me a lot. *Takusan chodai.* (Tock-sahn choe-
die.) This is enough. *Kore wa jubun desu.* (Koe-
ray wah juu-boon dess.) I have (this is) enough.
Mo takusan desu. (Moh tock-sahn dess.)

Plug *Sashikomi* **(Sah-she-koe-me)**; also *Puragu*
(Puu-rah-guu)
Where is the nearest plug? *Ichiban chikai puragu
wa doko desu ka?* (E-chee-bahn chee-kie puu-rah-
guu wah doe-koe dess kah?)

Poetry *Shi* **(She)**
Do you write poetry. *Shi wo tsukurimasu ka?* (She
oh t'sue-kuu-ree-mahss kah?) Poetry is very
popular in Japan. *Nihon de shi wa taihen ninki ga
arimasu.* (Nee-hone day she wah tie-hane neen-
kee gah ah-ree-mahss.)

Poland *Porando* **(Poe-rahn-doe)**
Those people are from Poland. *Sonohito-tachi wa
Porando no hito desu.* (Soe-no-ssh-toe-tah-chee
wah Poe-rahn-doe no ssh-toe dess.) Where is
the Polish Embassy? *Porando no Taishikan wa doko
desu ka?* (Poe-rahn-doe no Tie-she-khan wah doe-
koe dess kah?)

Police *Keikan* **(Kay-e-khan);** Police station *Kei-satsu* (Kay-e-sot-sue); Police headquarters *Kei-satsusho* (Kay-e-sah-t'sue-sho)
Please take me to the nearest police station. *Ichi-ban chikai keisatsu ni tsurete itte kudasai.* (E-chee-bahn chee-kie kay-e-sot-sue nee t'sue-ray-tay eet-tay kuu-dah-sie.)

Police box *Koban* **(Koe-bahn)**
If you get lost, go to a police box. *Michi ni mayoi-mashitara koban ni ikinasai.* (Me-chee nee mah-yoe-e-mah-ssh-tah-rah, koe-bahn nee e-kee-nah-sie.)

Police officer *Keikan* **(Kay-e-khan);** also *Omawarisan* (Oh-mah-wah-ree-sahn)
Please call a policeman. *Omawarisan wo yonde ku-dasai.* (Oh-mah-wah-ree-sahn oh yone-day kuu-dah-sie.)

Popular *Taishuteki-na* **(Tie-shu-tay-kee-nah)**
Are there any popular amusement centers in this city? *Kono machi ni taishuteki-na asobi-ba ga arimasu ka?* (Koe-no mah-chee nee tie-shu-tay-kee-nah ah-so-bee-bah gah ah-ree-mahss kah?)

Pork *Buta-niku* **(Buu-tah-nee-kuu)**
Do you eat pork? *Buta-niku wo tabemasu ka?* (Buu-tah-nee-kuu oh tah-bay-mahss kah?) I don't like pork. *Buta wo kirai desu.* (Buu-tah oh kee-rie dess.)

Port *Minato* **(Me-nah-toe)**
Yokohama is a port city. *Yokohama wa minato ma-chi desu.* (Yokohama wah me-nah-toe mah-chee dess.) You should go to the port early. *Minato e hayaku iku ho ga ii desu.* (Me-nah-toe eh hah-yah-kuu e-kuu hoe gah ee dess.)

Japanese in Plain English

Porter (baggage carrier) *Pota* (Poe-tah)
I need a porter. *Pota ga irimasu.* (Poe-tah gah
e-ree-mahss.)

Postage *Yubindai* (Yuu-bean-die); *Yubinryo* (Yuu-bean-rio)
How much postage for this letter? *Kono tegami no
yubinryo wa ikura desu ka?* (Koe-no tay-gah-me no
yuu-bean-rio wah e-kuu-rah dess kah?) Is there
enough postage on this? *Kono yubindai de tari-
masu ka?* (Ko-no yuu-bean-die day tah-ree-mahss
kah?)

Postage stamp *Kitte* (Keet-tay)
Do you sell stamps here? *Koke de kitte wo urimasu
ka?* (Koe-koe day keet-tay oh uu-ree-mahss kah?)

Postcard *Hagaki* (Hah-gah-kee)
How much are these postcards? *Kono hagaki wa
ikura desu ka?* (Koe-no hah-gah-kee wah e-kuu-
rah dess kah?) Do you have any other postcards? *Hoka-no hagaki ga arimasu ka?* (Hoe-kah-no
hah-gah-kee gah ah-ree-mahss kah?)

Post office *Yubinkyoku* (Yuu-bean-k'yoe-kuu)
Is the post office open today? *Kyo yubinkyoku wa
aite imasu ka?* (K'yoe yuu-bean-k'yoe-kuu wah
aye-tay e-mahss kah?) Take me to the post office, please. *Yubinkyoku e tsurete itte kudasai.* (Yuu-
bean-k'yoe-kuu eh-t'sue-ray-tay eet-tay kuu-dah-
sie.)

Pound (weight) *Pondo* (Pone-doe)
How many pounds is this? *Kore wa nan pondo
desu ka?* (Koe-ray wah nahn pone-doe dess
kah?) One pound—*Ichi pondo* (E-chee pone-
doe); Two pounds—*Ni pondo* (Nee pone-doe).

Prefecture *Ken* **(Ken)**
There are 47 prefectures in Japan. *Nihon ni wa yon-ju-nana ken ga arimasu.* (Nee-hone nee wah yone-juu-nah-nah ken gah ah-ree-mahss.) Chiba Prefecture. *Chiba Ken* (Chee-bah Ken). Which prefecture do you live in? *Dono ken ni sunde imasu ka?* (Do-no ken nee soon-day e-mahss kah?)

Prepare (get ready) *Shitaku wo suru* **(She-tah-kuu oh sue-rue);** *Junbi wo suru* (June-bee oh sue-rue) Get ready, we're leaving soon. *Shitaku wo shite kudasai. Mo sugu demasu.* (She-tah-kuu oh ssh-tay kuu-dah-sie. Moe sue-guu day-mahss.)

Present (gift) *Omiyage* **(Oh-me-yah-gay);** Farewell present *Sembetsu* (Same-bate-sue); End of year present *Oseibo* (Oh-say-e-boe)
I want to give Mr. Kimura a present. *Kimura-San ni omiyage wo sashiagetai desu.* (Kimura-San nee oh-me-yah-gay oh sah-she-ah-gay-tie dess.) Please accept this gift. *Dozo, kono omiyage wo o-uke kudasai.* (Doe-zoe, koe-no oh-me-yah-gay oh oh-uu-kay kuu-dah-sie.)

President (of a company) *Shacho* **(Shah-choe)**
This is the president of the company. *Kono kata wa kaisha no shacho desu.* (Koe-no kah-tah wah kie-shah no shah-choe dess.) What is the president's name. *Shacho no namae wa nan desu ka?* (Shah-choe no nah-my wah nahn dess kah?)

President (of a country) *Daitoryo* **(Die-toe- rio)**
President Reagan was very popular in Japan. *Nihon de Regon Daitoryo wa taihen ninki ga arimashita.* (Nee-hone day Regon Die-toe-rio wah tie-hane neen-kee gah ah-ree-mah-sshtah.)

Pretty *Kirei* **(Kee-ray-e)**
She is pretty. *Kanojo wa kirei desu.* (Kah-no-joe wah kee-ray-e dess.) That is really pretty. *Sore wa honto ni kirei desu.* (Soe-ray wah hone-toe nee kee-ray-e dess.)

Printed matter *Insatsu butsu* **(Inn-sot-sue boot-sue)**
Please send this as printed matter. *Kore wo insatsu butsu de dashite kudasai.* (Koe-ray oh inn-sot-sue boot-sue day dah-sshtay kuu-dah-sie.)

Private (personal) *Kojin* **(koe-jeen);** Private bath *Kojin buro* (Koe-jeen buu-roe); Private room *Koshitsu* (Koe-sheet-sue); Private expense *Kojin no hiyo* (Koe-jeen no he-yoe)
Do you want a private room? *Koshitsu hoshii desu ka?* (Koe-sheet-sue hoe-she-e dess kah?) Do you have a private bath? *Kojin buro ga arimasu ka?* (Koe-jeen buu-roe gah ah-ree-mahss kah?) Please call a private taxi. *Kojin takushi wo yonde kudasai.* (Koe-jeen tah-kuu-she oh yone-day kuu-dah-sie.)

Problem *Mondai* **(Moan-die)**
What is the problem? *Do yu mondai desu ka?* (Doe-yu moan-die dess kah?)

Program (entertainment) *Puroguramu* **(Puu-roe-guu-rah-muu)**
Would you like to buy a program? *Puroguramu wo kaitai desu ka?* (Puu-roe-guu-rah-muu oh kie-tie dess kah?)

Public (open to all) *Kokai no* **(Koe-kie no);** Public bath *Sento* (Sin-toe); Public hall *Kokai do* (Koe-kie-doe)
When I go to Japan I would like to try a public

bath. *Nihon ni ittara toki sento ni haitte mitai desu.*
(Nee-hone nee eat-tah-rah toe-kee sin-toe nee
hite-tay me-tie dess.)

Punctual *Seikaku* **(Say-kah-kuu)**
Please be punctual. *Seikaku ni shite kudasai.* (Say-
kah-kuu nee ssh-tay kuu-dah-sie.) Japanese
trains are very punctual. *Nihon no ressha wa taihen
seikaku desu.* (Ne-hone no ray-shah wah tie-hane
say-e-kah-kuu dess.)

Puppet show *Ningyo shibai* (Neen-g'yoe she-
by); *Bunraku* (Boon-rah-kuu)
Can I see a puppet show in Tokyo? *Tokyo de ningyo shibai wo miru koto ga dekimasu ka?* (Tokyo day
neen-g'yoe she-by oh me-rue koe-toe gah day-
kee-mahss kah?) Yes, but the bunraku in Osaka
is the best. *Dekimasu kedo, Osaka no bunraku wa
ichiban ii desu.* (Day-kee-mahss kay-doe, Oh-sah-
kah no boon-rah-kuu wah e-chee-bahn ee dess.)

Purple *Murasaki* **(Muu-rah-sah-kee)**
I'm looking for a purple shirt. *Murasaki no shatsu
wo sagashite imasu.* (Muu-rah-sah-kee no shaht-
t'sue oh sah-gah-ssh-tay e-mahss.)

Purse *Saifu* **(Sie-fuu)**
Whose purse is this? *Kore wa donata no saifu desu
ka?* (Koe-ray wah doe-nah-tah no sie-fuu dess
kah?) Have you seen my purse. *Watakushi no
saifu wo mita koto ga arimasu ka?* (Wah-tock-she no
sie-fuu oh me-tah koe-toe gah ah-ree-mahss
kah?)

Purser (ship) *Jimucho* **(Jee-muu-choe);** *Paasaa*
(Pah-sah)
I'd like to speak to the purser. *Jimucho ni hanashi-
tai desu.* (Jee-muu-choe nee hah-nah-she-tie
dess.)

Q

Quality (products) *Hinshitsu* (Heen-sheet-sue);
Good quality *Ryoshitsu* (Rio-sheet-sue); High
grade *Kokyu* (koe-que); Good quality (prod-
uct) *Ii shina* (Ee she-nah)
Let me see your best products. *Ichiban ii shina wo
misete kudasai.* (E-chee-bahn ee she-nah oh me-
say-tay kuu-dah-sie.)

Quantity (amount) *Bunryo* (Boon-rio); Number
Suryo (Sue-rio); Large amount *Takusan* (Tock-
sahn); Small amount *Sukoshi no bunryo* (Sue-koe-
she no boon-rio)
Give me a large amount. *Takusan chodai.* (Tock-
sahn choe-dai.) Just give me a little. *Hono sukoshi chodai.* (Hone-no sue-koe-she choe-die.)

Quarantine *Ken-eki* (Ken-a-kee)
Your cat must be quarantined. *Anato no neko wa
ken-eki wo shinakereba narimasen.* (Ah-nah-tah no
nay-koe wah ken-a-kee oh she-nah-kay-ray-bah
nah-ree-mah-sin.)

Queer (strange) *Hen-na* (Hane-nah)
This meat has a strange smell. *Kono niku wa hen-
na nioi shite imasu.* (Koe-no nee-kuu wah hane-
nah nee-oh-e ssh-tay e-mahss.) He is strange.
Anohito wa hen desu. (Ah-no-ssh-toe wah hane
dess.)

Question *Shitsumon* (Sheet-sue-moan); Matter of
concern *Mondai* (Moan-die); *Koto* (Koe-toe)
May I ask a question? *Shitsumon shite mo ii desu
ka?* (Sheet-sue-moan ssh-tay moe ee dess kah?)
That is another (question) matter. *Sore wa hoka no*

mondai desu. (Soe-ray wah hoe-kah no moan-die dess.)

Questionnaire *Ankeito* **(An-kay-e-toe)**
Please fill out this questionnaire. *Kono ankeito ni kaite kudasai.* (Koe-no ahn-kay-e-toe nee kie-tay kuu-dah-sie.)

Quick *Hayai* **(Hah-yie);** Quickly *Hayaku* (Hah-yah-kuu)
Be as quick as possible! *Dekiru dake hayaku!* (Day-kee-rue dah-kay hah-yah-kuu!) Hurry! *Hayaku!* (Hah-yah-kuu!) She is really fast, isn't she! *Kanojo wa taihen hayai desu, ne!* (Kah-no-joe wah tie-hane hah-yie dess, nay!)

Quiet (not noisy) *Shizuka-na* **(She-zuu-kah-nah);**
Quiet character *Otonashii* (Oh-toe-nah-she-e)
I want the quietest room. *Ichiban shizuka-na heya wo hoshii desu.* (E-chee-bahn she-zuu-kah-nah hay-yah oh hoe-she-e dess.) My life is very quiet. *Watakushi no seikatsu wa taihen shizuka desu.* (Wah-tock-she no say-e-kot-sue wah tie-hane she-zuu-kah dess.) Be quiet! *Shizuka ni shinasai!* (She-zuu-kah nee she-nah-sie!) He is a quiet person. *Anohito wa otonashii hito desu.* (Ah-no-ssh-toe wah oh-toe-nah-shee ssh-toe dess.)

R

Radio *Rajio* **(Rah-jee-oh)**
Is there a radio in the room? *Heya ni rajio ga arimasu ka?* (Hay-yah nee rah-jee-oh gah ah-ree-mahss kah?) I'd like to buy a radio for my car. *Kuruma no tame ni rajio wo kaitai desu.* (Kuu-rue-mah no tah-may nee rah-jee-oh oh kie-tie dess.)

Radish (giant Japanese variety) *Daikon* **(Die-kone);** Common radish *Hatsuka daikon* (Hot-sue-kah die-kone)
Please put some radish in my salad. *Sarada ni hatsuka daikon wo irete kudasai.* (Sah-rah-dah nee hot-sue-kah die-kone oh e-ray-tay kuu-dah-sie.)

Railroad / Railway *Tetsudo* **(Tate-sue-doe);** Railroad crossing *Tetsudo fumikiri* (Tate-sue-doe fuu-me-kee-ree); Railway station *Eki* (Eh-kee)
Take me to Tokyo Station, please. *Tokyo Eki ni tsurete itte kudasai.* (Tokyo A-kee nee t'sue-ray-tay eet-tay kuu-dah-sie.)

Railway ticket *Josha-ken* **(Joe-shah-ken);** *Kippu* (Keep-puu)
May I see your ticket, please. *Joshaken wo haiken itashimasu.* (Joe-shah-ken oh hie-kane e-tah-she-mahss.) Where is the ticket office? *Kippu no uriba wa doko desu ka?* (Keep-pu no uu-ree-bah wah doe-koe dess kah?) How much is a one-way ticket to Nagoya? *Nagoya katamichi ichi-mai wa ikura desu ka?* (Nah-go-yah kah-tah-me-chee e-chee-my wah e-kuu-rah dess kah?)

Rain *Ame* **(Ah-may);** Heavy rain *O-ame* (Oh-ah-may); Light rain *Ko-ame* (Koe-ah-may)
It is raining. *Ame ga futte imasu.* (Ah-may gah fute-tay e-mahss.) It may rain tomorrow. *Ashita ame ga furu kamo shiremasen.* (Ah-ssh-tah ah-may gah fuu-rue kah-moe she-ray-mah-sin.) It will soon stop raining. *Ame wa sugu yamimasu.* (Ah-may wah sue-guu yah-me-mahss.)

Raincoat *Renkoto* **(Rane-koe-toe)**
Don't forget a/your raincoat. *Renkoto wo wasurenai de.* (Rane-koe-toe oh wah-sue-ray-nie day.) You should take a raincoat. *Renkoto wo motte iku hoh*

ga ii desu. (Rane-koe-toe oh mote-tay e-kuu hoh gah ee dess.)

Rainy season *Nyubai* **(Knew-by);** *Tsuyu* (T'sue-yuu)
When is Japan's rainy season? *Nihon no nyubai wa itsu desu ka?* (Nee-hone no knew-by wah eet-sue dess kah?) Usually it is in June. *Taitei Rokugatsu desu.* (Tie-tay-e Roe-kuu-got-sue dess.)

Rare (in cooking) *Nama-yaki* **(Nah-mah yah-kee)**
Cook my steak rare, please. *Watakushi no suteki wo nama-yaki ni shite kudasai.* (Wah-tock-she no sue-tay-kee oh nah-mah-yah-kee nee ssh-tay kuu-dah-sie.)

Rare (in number) *Sukunai* **(Sue-kuu-nie)**
Horses are rare in Tokyo. *Tokyo ni wa uma ga sukunai desu.* (Tokyo nee wah uu-mah gah sue-kuu-nie dess.)

Rate (of exchange) *Kawase soba* **(Kah-wah-say so-bah)**
What is today's rate of exchange? *Kyo no kawase soba wa nan desu ka?* (K'yoe no kah-wah-say so-bah wah nahn dess kah?)

Raw *Nama* **(Nah-mah)**
This meat is too raw. *Kono niku wa amari nama desu.* (Koe-no nee-kuu wah ah-mah-ree nah-mah dess.) I prefer it raw. *Nama no ho ga ii desu.* (Nah-mah no hoe gah ee dess.)

Razor *Kamisori* **(Kah-me-so-ree);** Razor blade *Kamisori no ha* (Kah-me-so-ree no hah)
I forgot my razor. *Kamisori wo wasuremashita.* (Kah-me-so-ree oh wah-sue-ray-mah-ssh-tah.)

Ready (to go, etc.) *Yoi suru* **(Yo-e sue-rue);** *Shitaku* (She-tah-kuu); *Jumbi* (Jume-bee); *Dekimashita* (Day-kee-mah-ssh-tah)
Is it ready? *Dekimashita ka?* (Day-kee-mah-ssh-tah kah?) Are you ready? *Shitaku shimashita ka?* (She-tah-kuu-she-mah-ssh-tah kah?)

Real (genuine) *Hommono* **(Home-moe-no)**
Are these pearls genuine? *Kono shinju wa hommono desu ka?* (Koe-no sheen-juu wah home-moe-no dess kah?)

Receipt *Ryoshusho* **(Rio-shuu-sho);** *Reshiito* (Ray-sheet-toe)
A receipt, please. *Ryoshusho, kudasai.* (Rio-shuu-sho, kuu-dah-sie.)

Receive *Uketorimasu* **(Uu-kay-toe-ree-mahss)**
Did you receive my message? *Watakusho no meseji wo uketorimashita ka?* (Wah-tock-she no may-say-jee oh uu-kay-toe-ree-mah-ssht-tah kah?)

Refrigerator *Reizoko* **(Ray-e-zoe-koe)**
(In a hotel) I would like a room with a refrigerator. *Reizoko no aru heya ga hoshii desu.* (Ray-e-zoe-ko no ah-rue hay-yah gah hoe-she-e dess.)

Refund *Haraimodoshi* **(Hah-rie-moe-doe-she)**
When will you make the refund? *Itsu haraimodoshimasu ka?* (Eet-sue hah-rie-moe-doe-she-mahss kah?)

Register (at hotel) *Namae wo kakimasu* **(Nah-my oh kah-kee-mahss)**
Please register. *Namae wo kaite kudasai.* (Nah-my oh kie-tay kuu-dah-sie.) Have you already registered? *Mo namae wo kakimashita ka?* (Moe nah-my oh kah-kee-mah-ssh-tah kah?)

Register (a letter) *Kakitome ni suru* **(Kah-kee-toe-may nee sue-rue)**; Registered mail *Kakitome* (Kah-kee-toe-may)
Please register this letter. *Kono tegami wo kakitome ni shite kudasai.* (Koe-no tay-gah-me oh kah-kee-toe-may nee ssh-tay kuu-dah-sie.)

Religion *Shukyo* **(Shuu-k'yoe)**; Buddhist religion *Bukkyo* (Buke-yoe); Shinto religion *Shinto* (Sheen-toe); Christian religion *Kirisutokyo* (Kee-ree-sue-toe-k'yoe)
Are the Japanese very religious? *Nihonjin wa shin-jimbukai desu ka?* (Nee-hone-jeen wah sheen-jeem-buu-kie dess kah?)

Rent *Kariru* **(Kah-ree-rue)**
I would like to rent a car. *Jidosha wo karitai desu.* (Jee-doe-shah oh kah-ree-tie dess.) Is this for rent? *Kore wa kashidashi-yo desu ka?* (Koe-ray wah kah-she-dah-she-yoe dess kah?)

Rent-A-Car *Renta-Ka* **(Rane-tah-Kah)**
Is there a rent-a-car office in the hotel? *Hoteru ni renta-ka no jimusho ga arimasu ka?* (Hoe-tay-rue nee rane-tah-kah no jeem-sho gah ah-ree-mahss kah?)

Repair *Naosu* **(Nah-oh-sue)**
Can you fix this? *Kore wo naosemasu ka?* (Koe-ray oh nah-oh-say-mahss kah?) Please repair this. *Kore wo naoshite kudasai.* (Koe-ray oh nah-oh-ssh-tay kuu-dah-sie.)

Reservations *Yoyaku* **(Yoe-yah-kuu)**
I would like to reserve a single room. *Shinguru no heya no yoyaku wo toritai desu.* (Sheen-guu-rue no hay-yah no yoe-yah-kuu oh toe-ree-tie dess.) I have reservations. *Yoyaku shite arimasu.* (Yoe-yah-kuu ssh-tay ah-ree-mahss.)

Reserved seat *Shitei seki* **(She-tay-e say-kee)**
These seats are reserved. *Kono seki wa shitei seki desu.* (Koe-no say-kee wah she-tay-e say-kee dess.) Do you have a reserved-seat ticket? *Shitei seki no kippu wo motte imasu ka?* (She-tay-e say-kee no keep-pu oh mote-tay e-mahss kah?) Is this seat reserved? *Kono seki wa yoyaku zumi desu ka?* (Koe-no say-kee wah yoe-yah-kuu zuu-me dess kah?) Free seat (not reserved). *Jiyu seki* (Jee-yuu say-kee.)

Residence *Sumai* **(Sue-my)**
Where is your residence? *O-sumai wa doko desu ka?* (Oh-sue-my wah doe-koe dess kah?)

Resort (health) *Hoyochi* **(Hoe-yoe-chee);** Summer resort *Hishochi* (He-sho-chee); Winter resort *Hikanchi* (He-kahn-chee); Recreational resort *Korakuchi* (Koe-rah-kuu-chee)
There are many famous resorts near Tokyo. *Tokyo no chikaku ni takusan yumei-na korakuchi ga arimasu.* (Tokyo no chee-kah-kuu nee tock-sahn yuu-may-e-nah koe-rah-kuu-chee gah ah-ree-mahss.)

Rest *Yasumi* **(Yah-sue-me);** Rest-break *Kyukei* (Que-kay-e)
Let's take a little rest. *Shibaraku yasumimasho.* (She-bah-rah-kuu yah-sue-me-mah-sho.) He/she is taking a rest. *Yasunde imasu.* (Yah-soon-day e-mahss.) It's break time. *Kyukei no jikan desu.* (Que-kay-e no jee-kahn dess.)

Restaurant (Japanese) *Ryoriya* **(Rio-ree-yah);**
Restaurant (European) *Resutoran* (Race-toe-rahn); also *Shokudo* (Show-kuu-doe)
Are there any good restaurants in this area? *Kono hen ni ii resutoran ga arimasu ka? (Koe-no hane nee ee race-toe-rahn gah ah-ree-mahss kah?)*

Return *Kaerimasu* **(Kie-ree-mahss)**
When will you return? *Itsu kaerimasu ka?* (Eet-sue kie-ree-mahss kah?) We will return at 6:00 o'clock. *Roku-ji ni kaerimasu.* (Roe-kuu-jee nee kie-ree-mahss.)

Rice (uncooked) *Kome* **(Koe-may);** Rice (cooked) *Gohan* (Go-hahn); also *raisu* (rie-sue) Would you like rice (with your meal)? *Gohan ikaga desu ka?* (Go-hahn e-kah-gah dess kah?)

Right (side/direction) *Migi* **(Mee-ghee)**
It's on the right side. *Migi gawa ni arimasu.* (Me-ghee gah-wah nee ah-ree-mahss.) Turn right, please. *Migi e mawatte kudasai.* (Me-ghee eh mah-wot-tay kuu-dah-sie.)

River *Kawa* **(Kah-wah);** also *Gawa* (Gah-wah)
Are there any rivers near Tokyo? *Tokyo no chikaku ni kawa ga arimasu ka?* (Tokyo no chee-kah-kuu nee kah-wah gah ah-ree-mahss kah?) Yes, several rivers run through Tokyo. *Hai, ikutsu-ka kawa ga Tokyo no naka wo totte nagaremasu.* (Hie, ee-kute-sue-kah kah-wah gah Tokyo no nah-kah oh tote-tay nah-gah-ray-mahss.)

Roast beef *Rosuto biifu* **(Roe-sue-toe bee-fuu)**
The roast beef here is very good. *Kono resutoran no rosuto biifu wa taihen oishii desu.* (Koe-no race-toe-rahn no roe-sue-toe bee-fuu wah tie-hane oh-e-she-e dess.)

Room (Western style) *Heya* **(Hay-yah);** Room (Japanese style) *Zashiki* (Zah-she-kee); also *shitsu* (sheet-sue) and *ma* (mah) in compounds This room will be fine. *Kono heya wa kekko desu.* (Koe-no hay-yah wa keck-koe dess.) I want a room with bath. *Ofuro tsuki no heya ga hoshii desu.*

(Oh-fuu-roe t'sue-ski no hay-yah gah hoe-she-e dess.) Do you have a larger room? *Motto okii heya ga arimasu ka?* (Mote-toe oh-kee hay-yah gah ah-ree-mahss kah?)

Room charge *Heya dai* **(Hay-yah die)**
How much is the room charge? *Heya dai wa ikura desu ka?* (Hay-yah die wah e-kuu-rah dess kah?)

Room number *Heya-no bango* **(Hay-yah-no bahn-go)**
What is your room number? *Anata-no heya-no bango wa nan desu ka?* (Ah-nah-tah-no hay-yah-no bahn-go wah nahn dess kah?) My room number is 307. *San-zero-nana desu.* (Sahn-zay-roe-nah-nah dess.)

Room service *Ruumu sabisu* **(Rue-muu sah-bee-sue)**
Room service is available from 6:00 A.M. until 12:00 P.M. *Ruumu sabisu wa asa no roku-ji kara yoru no ju-ni-ji made desu.* (Rue-muu sah-bee-sue wa ah-sah no roe-kuu-jee kah-rah yoe-rue no juu-nee-jee mah-day dess.)

Round trip *O-fuku* **(Oh-fuu-kuu);** Round-trip ticket *O-fuku kippu* (Oh-fuu-kuu keep-puu)
Round trip, please. *O-fuku, dozo.* (Oh-fuu-kuu, doe-zoe). Two round-trip tickets to Osaka. *Osaka e o-fuku kippu wo ni-mai kudasai.* (Oh-sah-kah eh oh-fuu-kuu keep-puu oh nee-my kuu-dah-sie.)

Rush hour *Raashu Awaa* **(Rah-shu ah-wah)**
It is better not to go downtown during the rush hour. *Raashu awaa no aida ni wa machi no chushin ni ikanai ho ga ii desu.* (Rah-shu ah-wah no aye-dah nee wah mah-chee no chuu-sheen nee e-kah-nie hoe gah ee dess.)

S

Sake (rice wine) *Sake* **(Sah-kay);** also *Nihonshu* (Nee-hone-shuu)
Do you drink sake? *Sake wo nomimasu ka?* (Sah-kay oh no-me-mahss kah?) Please warm it up. *Atatamete kudasai.* (Ah-tah-tah-may-tay kuu-dah-sie.)

Salad *Sarada* **(Sah-rah-dah)**
Please bring the salad now. *Ima sugu sarada wo motte kite kudasai.* (E-mah sue-guu sah-rah-dah oh mote-tay kee-tay kuu-dah-sie.)

Salmon *Shake* **(Shah-kay);** Smoked salmon *Shake no kunsei* (Shah-kay no koon-say-e)
We have salmon today. Would you like that? *Kyo wa shake ga arimasu. Sore wo ikaga desu ka?* (K'yoe wah shah-kay gah ah-ree-mahss. Soe-ray oh e-kah-gah dess kah?)

Salt *Shio* **(She-oh)**
May I have some salt, please. *Shio wo itadakemasen ka?* (She-oh oh e-tah-dah-kay-mah-sin kah?) This fish is too salty. *Kono sakana wa amari shio-karai desu.* (Koe-no sah-kan-nah wah ah-mah-ree she-oh-kah-rie dess.)

Same *Onaji* **(Oh-nah-jee)**
Is this the same as that? *Kore wa sore to onaji desu ka?* (Koe-ray wah soe-ray toe oh-nah-jee dess kah?) I'll have the same. *Onaji mono ni shimasu.* (Oh-nah-jee moe-no nee she mahss.)

Sandwich *Sando* **(Sahn-doe);** also *Sando-wi-chi* (Sahn-doe-we-chee); Ham sandwich *Hamu sando* (Hah-muu); Roast beef sandwich *Rosuto bifu sando* (Roe-sue-toe bee-fuu)

Just a sandwich will be fine. *Sando dake de ii desu.* (Sahn-doe dah-kay day ee dess.) What kind of sandwiches do you have? *Donna sando ga arimasu ka?* (Doan-nah sahn-doe gah ah-re-mahss kah?)

Sanitary napkin *Seiriyo* (Say-ee-ree-yoh nah-puu-keen)
What brand of sanitary napkins do you have? *Seiriyo no napukin wa dore no burando ga arimasu ka?* (Say-ee-ree-yoh no nah-puu-keen wah doe-ray no buu-rahn-doe gah ah-ree-mahss kah?)

Saturday *Doyobi* (Doe-yoe-bee)
Are department stores open on Saturday? *Depaato wa Doyobi ni aite imasu ka?* (Day-pahh-toe wah Doe-yoe-bee nee aye-tay e-mahss kah?) I'm leaving on Saturday. *Doyobi ni demasu.* (Doe-yoe-bee nee day-mahss.)

Sauna bath *Mushi buro* (Muu-she buu-roe)
We also have a sauna bath. *Mushi buro mo arimasu.* (Muu-she buu-roe moe ah-ree-mahss.)

Sausage *Soseji* (Soe-say-jee)
Would you like sausage with your eggs? *Tamago to issho ni soseji wa ikaga desu ka?* (Tah-mah-go to e-sshow nee soe-say-jee wah e-kah-gah dess kah?)

Scenery *Keishiki* (Kay-she-kee)
In Arizona the scenery is especially beautiful. *Arizona wa keshiki ga toku ni kirei desu.* (Ah-ree-zoe-nah wah kay-she-kee gah toe-kuu nee kee-ray-e dess.) A beautiful sight. *Ii keshiki desu.* (Ee kay-she-kee dess.)

Schedule (time table) *Jikanhyo* (Jee-kahn-h'yoe); *Yotei* (Yoe-tay-e)
What is your schedule from here? *Koko kara anata no yotei wa nan desu ka?* (Koe-koe kah-rah ah-nah-

tah no yoe-tay wah nahn dess kah?)   According
to my schedule I leave tomorrow morning. *Yotei
de wa ashita no asa ni demasu.* (Yoe-tay day-wah
ah-she-tah no ah-sah nee day-mahss.)

School *Gakko* **(Gahk-koe);** Elementary school
Sho gakko (Show gahk-koe); Junior high school
Chu gakko (Chu gahk-koe); High school *Koto
gakko* (Koe-toe gahk-koe)
It is always interesting to visit schools. *Gakko wo
homon suru no wa itsumo omoshiroi desu.* (Gahk-
koe oh hoe-moan sue-rue no wah eet-sue-moe
oh-moe-she-roy dess.)

Scotch & water *Sukocchi no mizuwari* **(Sue-koe-
chee no mee-zuu-wah-ree)**
Two Scotch and waters, please. *Sukocchi no
mizuwari wo futatsu kudasai.* (Sue-koe-chee no
mee-zuu-wah-ree ho fu-tot-sue kuu-dah-sie.)

Scroll (hanging) *Makimono* **(Mah-kee-moe-no);**
Kakeji-ku (Kah-kay-jee-kuu)
I would like to buy several scrolls. Can you rec-
ommend a good shop? *Kakejiku wo ni-san kaitai
desu. Ii mise wo oshieru koto ga dekimasu ka?* (Kah-
kay-jee-kuu oh nee-sahn kie-tie dess. Ee me-say
oh oh-she-eh-rue koe-toe gah day-kee-mah-sue
kah?)

Sea *Umi* **(Uu-me);** Seaside *Kaigan* (Kie-gahn);
Seacoast *Engan* (Inn-gahn)
I would like to rent a house near the ocean. *Umi
no soba ni ie wo karitai desu.* (Uu-me no soe-bah
nee e-eh oh kah-ree-tai dess.)

Sea mail *Funa-bin* **(Fuu-nah-bean)**
Please send this by sea mail. *Kore wo funa-bin de
dashite kudasai.* (Koe-ray oh fuu-nah-bean day
dahsh-tay kuu-dah-sie.)

Seasick *Funayoi* **(Fuu-nah-yoe-e)**
I do not get seasick. *Watakushi wa fune ni yoima-
sen.* (Wah-tock-she wah fuu-nay nee yoe-e-mah-
sin.) I'm seasick. *Funayoi shitemasu.* (Fuu-nah
yoe-e she-tay mahss.)

Season *Kisetsu* **(Kee-sate-sue);** Rainy season
Nyubai (Knew-by); Season ticket *Teikiken* (Tay-
e-kee-ken); In season (food) *Shun* (Shune);
Out of season (food) *Kisetsu hazure* (Ke-sate-sue
hah-zuu-ray)
Are oysters in season? *Kaki wa ima shun desu ka?*
(Kah-kee wah e-mah shune dess kah?)

Seat (chair) *Isu* **(E-sue);** Place where one sits
Seki (Say-kee)
Is this seat free (untaken)? *Kono seki wa aite imasu
ka?* (Koe-no say-kee way aye-tay e-mahss kah?)
Please keep this seat for me. *Kono seki wo totte
oite kudasai.* (Koe-no say-kee oh tote-tay oh-e-tay
kuu-dah-sie.) Please reserve two seats. *Seki wo
futatsu yoyaku shite kudasai.* (Say-kee oh fuu-tot-
sue yoe-yah-kuu ssh-tay kuu-dah-sie.)

Seat belt *Za-seki beruto* **(Zah-say-kee-bay-rue-
toe)**
Please fasten your seatbelts. *Za-seki beruto oh shimete kudasai.* (Zah-say-kee bay-rue-toe oh she-
may-tay kuu-dah-sie.)

Security guard *Keibi-in* **(Kay-e-bee-inn)**
There are security guards in the hotel, so it is
safe. *Hoteru ni keibi-in ga orimasu kara anzen desu.*
(Hoe-tay-rue nee kay-e-bee-inn gah oh-ree-
mahss kah-rah ahn-zen dess.)

See *Mimasu* **(Me-mahss)**
Let me see. *Misete.* (Me-say-tay.) Let me see
that. *Sore wo misete.* (Soe-ray oh me-say-tay.)

Have you seen it/him/her? *Mimashita ka?* (Me-mah-ssh-tah kah?) Look! *Mite goran!* (Me-tay go-rahn!) Let's go see it. *Mi ni ikimasho.* (Me nee e-kee-mah-sho.) See you later. *Mata ato de.* (Mah-tah ah-toe day.)

Self-service *Serufu saabisu* (Say-rue-fuu saah-bee-sue)
The salad bar is self-service. *Sarada baa wa serufu sabisu desu.* (Sah-rah-dah baah wah say-rue-fuu saah-bee-sue dess.)

Send *Okurimasu* (Oh-kuu-ree-mahss); Deliver (nearby) *Todokemasu* (Toe-doe-kay-mahss); Send (by mail) *Dashimasu* (Dah-she-mahss)
I want to send this package to America. *Kono kozutsumi wo Amerika ni okuritai desu.* (Koe-no koe-zuut-sue-me oh Ah-may-ree-kah nee oh-kuu-ree-tie dess.)

Separate (checks) *Betsu-betsu ni* (Bate-sue-bate-sue nee)
Separate checks, please. *Kanjo wa betsu-betsu ni shite kudasai.* (Kahn-joe wah bate-sue-bate-sue nee ssh-tay kuu-dah-sie.) Separate rooms. *Betsu-betsu no heya.* (Bate-sue-bate-sue no hay-yah.)

September *Kugatsu* (Kuu-got-sue)
It will get cool in September. *Kugatsu ni wa suzu-shiku narimasu.* (Kuu-got-sue nee wah sue-zuu-she-kuu nah-ree-mahss.) Wait until September. *Kugatsu made matte kudasai.* (Kuu-got-sue mah-day mot-tay kuu-dah-sie.)

Service charge *Sabisu ryo* (Sah-bee-sue rio)
Is the service charge included in the bill? *Kanjo ni sabisu ryo haitte imasu ka?* (Kahn-jo nee sah-bee-sue rio hite-tay e-mahss kah?) How much is

your service charge? *Anato no sabisu ryo wa ikura desu ka?* (Ah-nah-tah no sah-bee-sue rio wah e-kuu-rah dess kah?)

Seven-Up *Sebun-Appu* **(Say-bune Ahp-puu)**
Do you have Seven-Up? *Sebun-Appu arimasu ka?* (Say-bune-Ahp-puu ah-ree-mahss kah?) Two, please. *Ni-hon kudasai.* (Nee-hone kuu-dah-sie.)

Shake hands *Akushu shimasu* **(Ah-kuu-shuu she-mahss)**
We shook hands. *Akushu shimashita.* (Ah-kuu-shuu she-mah-ssh-tah.) All over the world people shake hands. *Sekai ju de hitobito wa akushu shimasu.* (Say-kie juu day ssh-toe-bee-toe wah ah-kuu-shuu she-mahss.)

Shinto shrine *Jinja* **(Jeen-jah)**
There are over 100,000 Shinto shrines in Japan. *Nihon ni wa jinja ga ju-man ijo arimasu.* (Nee-hone nee wah jeen-jah gah juu-mahn e-joe ah-ree-mahss.) Large shrines have torii in front of them. *Okii jinja no mae ni torii ga arimasu.* (Oh-kee jeen-jan no mah-eh nee toe-ree-e gah ah-ree-mahss.)

Ship *Fune* **(Fuu-nay);** Merchant ship *Shosen* (Sho-sin); Warship *Gunkan* (Goon-kahn)
What time will the ship arrive. *Fune wa nanji ni tochaku shimasu ka?* (Fuu-nay wah nahn-jee nee toe-chah-kuu she-mahss kah?) I love traveling by ship. *Fune no ryoko ga dai-suki desu.* (Fuu-nay no rio-koe gah die-ski dess.)

Shirt *Shatsu* **(Shot-sue);** Long-sleeved shirt *Naga-sode shatsu* (Nah-gah-soe-day shot-sue); Short-sleeved shirt *Han-sode shatsu* (Hahn-soe-day shot-sue)
Please wash these shirts. *Kono shatsu wo sentaku*

shite kudasai. (Koe-no shot-sue oh sane-tah-kuu
ssh-tay kuu-dah-sie.) Do you have this same
style of shirt in red? *Onaji sutairu no akai shatsu ga
arimasu ka?* (Oh-nah-jee sue-tie-rue no ah-kie
shot-sue gah ah-ree-mahss kah?)

Shoes *Kutsu* **(Koot-sue);** *Shuuzu* (Shuu-zuu);
Tennis shoes *Tenisu no kutsu* (Tay-nee-sue no
koot-sue)
These shoes are too tight. *Kono kutsu wa kitsui
desu.* (Koe-no koot-sue wa keet-sue-e dess.) Do
you have wider ones? *Haba no motto hiroi no wa
arimasu ka?* (Hah-bah no mote-toe he-roy no wah
ah-ree-mahs kah?)

Shop *Mise* **(Me-say);** *Ya* (yah)
What kind of shop do you want to go to? *Donna
mise ni ikitai desu ka?* (Doan-nah me-say nee e-
kee-tie dess kah?) That is a bread shop. *Sore wa
pan-ya desu.* (Soe-ray wah pahn-yah dess.) How
late are the shops open? *Mise wa nanji made desu
ka?* (Me-say wah nahn-jee mah-day dess ka?)

Shopping *Kaimono* **(Kie-moe-no)**
Do you want to go shopping now? *Ima kaimono
ni ikitai desu ka?* (E-mah kie-moe-no nee e-kee-tie
dess kah?) Let's go shopping. *Kaimono ni ikimasho.* (Kie-moe-no nee e-kee-mah-sho.)

Shopping arcade *Aakeido* **(Ah-kay-e-doe);** *Shotengai* (Sho-tane-guy)
Do large hotels in Japan have shopping arcades?
Nihon no okii hoteru wa aakeido ga arimasu ka?
(Nee-hone no oh-kee hoe-tay-rue wah ah-kay-e-
doe gah ah-ree-mahss kah?) Yes, they have.
There are also many covered-street shopping arcades. *Hai, arimasu. Hokanimo takusan shotengai ga
arimasu.* (Hie, ah-ree-mahss. Hoe-kah-nee-moe
tock-sahn sho-tane-guy gah ah-ree-mahss.)

Shopping center *Shoppingu senta* (Shope-peen-guu sane-tah)
Is there a shopping center in the area? *Kono hen ni shoppingu senta ga arimasu ka?* (Koe-no hane nee shope-peen-gu sane-tah gah ah-ree-mahss kah?)

Show (let see) *Misemasu* (Mee-say-mahss); Point out *Oshiemasu* (Oh-she-eh-mahss)
Show me a sample. *Sampuru wo misete kudasai.* (Sahm-puu-rue oh me-say-tay kuu-dah-sie.) Show me the way. *Michi wo oshiete kudasai.* (Me-chee-oh oh-she-eh-tay kuu-dah-sie.)

Shower *Shawa* (Shah-wah)
I'm going to take a shower. *Shawa wo abimasu.* (Shah-wah oh ah-bee-mahss.) Have you already had a shower? *Shawa mo abimashita ka?* (Shah-wah moe ah-bee-mah-ssh-tah kah?)

Shrimp *Ebi* (A-bee); Fried shrimp *Ebi furai* (A-bee fuu-rie); Shrimp cocktail *Ebi no kakuteru* (A-bee no kah-kuu-tay-rue)
This shop (restaurant) specializes in shrimp. *Kono mise no tokushoku wa ebi desu.* (Koe-no me-say no toe-kuu-sho-kuu wah a-bee dess.) Shall we order shrimp? *Ebi wo chumon shimasho ka?* (A-bee oh chuu-moan she-mah-sho kah?)

Sick *Byoki* (B'yoe-kee); Feel bad *Kibun ga warui* (Kee-boon gah wah-rue-e)
I'm sick. Please call a doctor. *Watakushi wa byoki desu. Oisha wo yonde kudasai.* (Wah-tock-she wah b'yoe-kee dess. Oh-e-shah oh yone-day kuu-dah-sie.) Do you feel bad? *Kibun ga warui desu ka?* (Kee-boon gah wah-rue-e dess kah?)

Side *Gawa* (Gah-wah); *Kawa* (Kah-wah)
Which side? *Dochira gawa?* (Doe-chee-rah gah-wah?) This side. *Kochira gawa.* (Koe-chee-rah

gah-wah.) That side. *Achira gawa.* (Ah-chee-rah gah-wah.)

Sidewalk *Hodo* (Hoe-doe)
Be careful. Many streets do not have sidewalks. *Ki wo tsukete. Hodo no nai tori ga oi desu.* (Hoe-doe no nie toe-ree gah oh-ee dess.)

Sightsee *Kenbutsu* (Kane-boot-sue)
Would you like to go sightseeing? *Kenbutsu ni ikitai desu ka?* (Kane-boot-sue nee e-kee-tie dess kah?) There are many sightseeing places near here. *Kono chikaku ni takusan kenbutsu suru tokoro ga arimasu.* (Koe-no chee-kah-kuu nee tock-sahn kane-boot-sue sue-rue toe-koe-roe gah ah-ree-mahss.)

Sightseeing bus *Kanko basu* (Kahn-koe bah-sue)
The sightseeing bus will be here soon. *Kanko basu ga mo sugu kimasu.* (Kahn-koe basu gah moe-sue-guu kee-mahss.) Please get on the bus. *Basu ni notte kudasai.* (Bah-sue nee note-tay kuu-dah-sie.)

Sign (signboard) *Kamban* (Kahm-bahn)
The shop has a large sign. *Sono mise wa okii na kamban ga arimasu.* (Soe-no me-say wah oh-ke-nah kahm-bahn gah ah-ree-mahss.)

Signature *Shomei* (Sho-may)
Please sign here. *Koko ni shomei wo shite kudasai.* (Koe-koe nee sho-may oh ssh-tay kuu-dah-sie.) May I use my stamp (name-chop)? *Hanko wo tsukatte mo ii desu ka?* (Hahn-koe oh scot-tay moe ee dess kah?)

Silk *Kinu* (Kee-nuu); Artificial silk *Jinken* (Jeen-kane); Natural silk *Honginu* (Hone-ghee-nuu); Raw silk *Kiito* (Kee-toe); *Shiruku* (She-rue-kuu)

Japanese in Plain English

Do you have any silk material? *Kinu no kiji ga arimasu ka?* (Kee-nuu no kee-jee gah ah-ree-mahss kah?) What kind of silk is this? *Kore wa do-yu kinu desu ka?* (Koe-ray wah doe-yuu kee-nuu dess kah?)

Silver *Gin* **(Geen);** also *Shiruba* (She-rue-bah); Silver plated *Gimmekki* (Geem-make-kee); Silverware *Gin-seihin* (Geen-say-e-heen)
Is this genuine silver? *Kore wa hommono no gin desu ka?* (Koe-ray wah home-moe-no no geen dess kah?)

Single (room) *Shinguru* **(Sheen-guu-rue);** Not married *Hitori-mono* (Ssh-toe-ree-moe-no) or *Dokushin* (Doe-kuu-sheen)
How much is a single? *Shinguru wa ikura desu ka?* (Sheen-guu-rue wah e-kuu-rah dess kah?) Are you single? *Anata wa hitori mono desu ka?* (Ah-nah-tah wah ssh-toe-ree-moe-no dess kah?) I'd like to reserve a single, please. *Shinguru no yoyaku wo toritai desu.* (Sheen-guu-rue no yoe-yah-kuu oh toe-ree-tie dess.)

Sirloin steak *Saroin suteiki* **(Sah-roe-en sue-tay-kee)**
A well-done sirloin steak, please. *Yoku yaita saroin suteiki wo kudasai.* (Yoe-kuu yie-tah sah-roe-en sue-tay-kee oh kuu-dah-sie.)

Sister *Onna-no-kyodai* **(Own-nah-no-k'yoe-die);** Older sister *O-nei-san* (Oh-nay-sahn); Younger sister *Imoto* (E-moe-toe)
Do you have any sisters? *Onna-no-kyodai ga orimasu ka?* (Own-nah-no-k'yoe-die gah oh-ree-mahss kah?) I have one older sister and two younger sisters. *O-nei-san hitori to imoto futari ori-*

206

masu. (Oh-nay-sahn ssh-toe-ree to e-moe-toe fuu-tah-ree oh-ree-mahss.)

Size *Okisa* **(Oh-kee-sah);** *Saizu* (Sie-zuu)
What is your shoe size? *Kutsu no okisa wa nan desu ka?* (Koot-sue no oh-kee-sah wah nahn dess kah?) Will this size be all right? *Kono saizu ga yoroshii desu ka?* (Koe-no sie-zuu gah yoe-roe-she-e dess kah?)

Sky *Sora* **(Soe-rah)**
The sky is blue today. *Kyo wa sora ga aoi desu.* (K'yoe wah soe-rah gah ah-oh-e dess.) The sky is beautiful, isn't it? *Sora ga kirei desu, ne?* (Soe-rah gah kee-ray-e dess, nay?)

Sleep *Nemurimasu* **(Nay-muu-ree-mahss)**
I did not sleep well last night. *Yube yoku nemure-masen deshita.* (Yuu-bay yoe-kuu nay-muu-ray-mah-sin desh-tah.) Are you sleepy? *Nemui desu ka?* (Nay-muu-e dess kah?) Let's go to sleep early tonight. *Komban hayaku nemasho.* (Kome-bahn hah-yah-kuu nay-mah-sho.)

Sleeping car/coach (train) *Shindai sha* **(Sheen-die shah)**
What number is the sleeping coach? *Shindai sha no bango wa nan ban desu ka?* (Sheen-die shah no bahn-go wah nahn bahn dess kah?)

Slow *Osoi* **(Oh-soy);** Behind time *Okuremasu* (Oh-kuu-ray-mahss)
He is really slow. *Anohito wa honto ni osoi desu.* (Ah-no-ssh-toe wah hone-toe nee oh-soy dess.) The train is late. *Kisha wa osoi desu.* (Kee-shah wah oh-soy dess.) My watch is slow. *Tokei wa okurete imasu.* (Toe-kay-e wah oh-kuu-ray-tay e-mahss.)

Slowly *Yukkuri* **(Yuke-kuu-ree)**
Go a little more slowly, please. *Mo sukoshi yukkuri itte kudasai.* (Moe sue-koe-she yuke-kuu-ree eet-tay kuu-dah-sie.)

Small *Chiisai* **(Cheee-sie);** Small car *Kogata sha* (Koe-gah-tah shah)
This is too small. *Kore wa chiisa sugimasu.* (Koe-ray wah cheee-sah suu-ghee-mahss.) I want a small car. *Kogata sha ga hoshii desu.* (Koe-gah-tah shah gah hoe-she-e dess.) It's too small. *Chiisai desu.* (Cheee-sie dess.)

Smart (stylish) *Sumaato* **(Sue-mahh-toe)**
That is a very stylish coat. *Sono koto wa taihen sumaato desu.* (Soe-no koe-toe wah tie-hane sue-mahh-toe dess.)

Smile *Niko-niko shimasu* **(Nee-koe-nee-koe she-mahss)**
Smile! *Niko-niko shite!* (Nee-koe-nee-koe sshtay!) Why are you smiling? *Doshite niko-niko shite imasu ka?* (Doe-ssh-tay nee-koe-nee-koe ssh-tay e-mahss kah?)

Snack *Keishoku* **(Kay-e-sho-kuu);** *Sunakku* (Sue-nah-kuu) or *Oyatsu* (Oh-yaht-sue)
Let's have a snack. *Sanakku ni shimasho.* (Sue-nah-kuu nee she-mah-sho.) Snack time! *Oyatsu desu yo!* (Oh-yaht-sue dess yoe!)

Snow *Yuki* **(Yuu-kee);** Snowstorm *Fubuki* (Fuu-buu-kee)
Does it snow in Tokyo? *Tokyo de wa yuki ga furimasu ka?* (Tokyo day wah yuu-kee gah fuu-ree-mahss kah?) In northern Japan it snows a lot. *Kita Nihon de wa yuki ga takusan furimasu.* (Kee-tah Nee-hone day wah yuu-kee gah tock-sahn fuu-ree-mahss.)

Soap *Sekken* **(Sake-kane)**
Please bring me some soap. *Sekken wo motte kite kudasai.* (Sake-kane oh mote-tay kee-tay kuu-dah-sie.) Where is the soap? *Sekken wa doko desu ka?* (Sake-kane wah doe-koe dess kah?)

Socks *Kutsushita* **(Koot-sue-ssh-tah)**
I lost my red socks! *Akai kutsushita wo nakushimashita!* (Ah-kah-ee koot-sue-she-tah oh nah-kuu-she-mah-she-tah!)

Sold out *Urikiremashita* **(Uu-ree-kee-ray-mahssh-tah)**
I'm sorry, we're (that's) sold out. *Sumimasen, urikiremashita.* (Sue-me-mah-sin, uu-ree-kee-ray-mahssh-tah.)

Son *Musuko* **(Muu-sue-koe)**
Do you have any sons? *Musuko-san ga imasu ka?* (Muu-sue-koe-sahn gah ee-mahss kah?) Yes, I have one son. *Hai, hitori imasu.* (Hie, ssh-toe-ree ee-mahss.)

Soon *Sugu* **(Suu-guu)**
He/she/it will be here soon. *Sugu kimasu.* (Sue-guu kee-mahss.) I/you/he/she must go soon. *Sugu ikanakereba narimasen.* (Sue-guu ee-kah-nah-kay-ray-bah nah-ree-mah-sin.)

Soup *Suupu* **(Sue-puu)**
Would you like soup? *Suupu ikaga desu ka?* (Sue-puu e-kah-gah dess kah?) What kind of soup do you have? *Donna suupu ga arimasu ka?* (Doan-nah sue-puu gah ah-ree-mahss kah?)

Souvenir (gift) *Omiyage* **(Oh-me-yah-gay)**
Have you already bought gifts? *Omiyage wo mo kaimashita ka?* (Oh-me-yah-gay oh moe kie-mah-ssh-tah kah?) I want to buy two more gifts. *Ato*

futatsu no omiyage wo kaitai desu. (Ah-toe fuu-tot-sue no oh-me-yah-gay oh kie-tie dess.)

Speak *Hanashimasu* (Hah-nah-she-mahss)

Can you speak English? *Eigo wo hanasemasu ka?* (A-e-go oh hah-nah-say-mahss kah?) Please speak slowly. *Yukkuri hanashite kudasai.* (Yuke-kuu-ree hah-nah-ssh-tay kuu-dah-sie.) I cannot speak Japanese. *Nihongo ga hanasemasen.* (Nee-hone-go gah hah-nah-say-mah-sin.)

Special charge *Tokubetsu ryokin* (Toe-kuu-bate-sue rio-keen)

There is a special charge for this train. *Kono kisha ni wa tokubetsu ryokin ga arimasu.* (Koe-no kee-shah nee wah toe-kuu-bate-sue rio-keen gah ah-ree-mahss.)

Special delivery *Soku tatsu* (Soe-kuu tot-sue)

I want to send this special delivery. *Kore wo soku tatsu de dashitai desu.* (Koe-ray oh soe-kuu tot-sue day dah-ssh-tie dess.)

Speed *Supido* (Sue-pee-doe); Speed limit *Supido seigen* (Sue-pee-doe Say-e-gane)

Don't go so fast! *Supido wo konnani dasanai de!* (Sue-pee-doe oh kone-nah-nee dah-sah-nie day!)

Spoon *Saji* (Sah-jee); *Supun* (Sue-pune)

May I have a soup spoon. *Suupu no saji wo itadakemasen ka?* (Sue-puu no sah-jee oh e-tah-dah-kay-mah-sin kah?)

Spring *Haru* (Hah-rue)

Is spring a good time to go to Japan? *Nihon ni iku no ni haru wa ii jiki desu ka?* (Nee-hone nee e-kuu no nee hah-rue wah ee jee-kee dess kah?)

Stamp (postage) *Kiite* **(Kee-tay);** Stamp machine *Kiite hanbaiki* (Kee-tay hahn-by-kee)
If you want stamps there is a stamp machine next to the bookshop. *Kiite wo hoshikereba honya no tonari ni kiite hanbaiki ga arimasu.* (Kee-tay oh hoe-she-kay-ray-bah hone-yah no toe-nah-ree nee kee-tay hahn-by-kee gah ah-ree-mahss.)

Start (begin) *Hajimemasu* **(Hah-jee-may-mahss);** *Demasu* (Day-mahss); *Shuppatsu shimasu* (Shupe-pot-sue she-mahss)
When does it start? *Itsu hajimarimasu ka?* (Eet-sue hah-jee-mah-ree-mahss kah?) What time does the train leave? *Kisha wa nanji ni demasu ka?* (Kee-shah wah nahn-jee nee day-mahss kah?) The train is leaving now! *Kisha ga ima shuppatsu shimasu!* (Kee-shah gah e-mah shupe-pot-sue she-mahss!)

Station (bus/train) *Eki* **(A-kee)**
How far is the station? *Eki made dono gurai desu ka?* (A-kee mah-day doe-no guu-rie dess kah?) The station is 10 minutes from here. *Eki wa koko kara jippun desu.* (A-kee wah koe-koe kah-rah jeep-pune dess.)

Stay (stop over) *Tomarimasu* **(Toe-mah-ree-mahss)**
Where are you staying? *Doko de tomarimasu ka?* (Doe-koe day toe-mah-ree-mahss kah?) I will stay at the Imperial Hotel for one night. *Hitoban Teikoku Hoteru ni tomarimasu.* (Ssh-toe-bahn Tay-e-koe-kuu Hoe-tay-rue nee toe-mah-ree-mahss.)

Steak *Suteki* **(Sue-tay-kee);** Filet mignon *Hire* (He-ray); Sirloin *Saroin* (Sah-roe-en)
I have heard that Japanese steaks are especially delicious. Is that true? *Nihon no suteki ga sugoku oishii to yu koto wo kikimashita. Sore wa honto desu*

ka? (Nee-hone no sue-tay-kee gah sue-go-kuu oh-e-shee toe yuu koe-toe oh kee-kee-mah-ssh-tah. Soe-ray wah hone-toe dess kah?)

Steward *S'chuwado* **(S'chuu-wah-doe);** Steward-ess *S'chuwadesu* (S'chuu-wah-day-suu)

Stomach *Onaka* **(Oh-nah-kah);** Stomachache *Onaka ga itai* (Oh-nah-kah gah e-tie) My stomach hurts because I am not used to the food here. *Koko no shokuji ni narete nai no de onaka ga itai desu.* (Koe-koe no sho-ku-jee nee nah-ray-tay nie no day oh-nah-kah gah e-tie dess.)

Stoplight *Shingo* **(Sheen-go)** Turn right at the next stoplight. *Kono tsugi no shingo de migi e magatte kudasai.* (Koe-no t'sue-ghee no sheen-go day me-ghee eh mah-got-tay kuu-dah-sie.)

Straight *Massugu* **(Mahs-sue-guu)** Please go straight. *Massugu ni itte kudasai.* (Mahs-sue-guu nee eet-tay kuu-dah-sie.)

Street *Tori* **(Toe-ree);** *Dori* (Doe-ree) What is the name of this street? *Kono tori no namae wa nan desu ka?* (Koe-no toe-ree no nah-my wah nahn dess kah?) Central Avenue. *Chuo Dori.* (Chuu-oh Doe-ree.) Aoyama Avenue. *Aoyama Dori.* (Ah-oh-yah-mah Doe-ree.)

Streetcar *Romen densha* **(Roe-mane dane-shah)** The streetcars of San Francisco are famous. *San Furanshisuko no romen densha wa yumei desu.* (Sahn Fuu-rahn-she-sue-koe no roe-mane dane-shah wah yuu-may-e dess.)

Strike (baseball/labor) *Sutoraiki* **(Sue-toe-rie-kee)** A strike is going on. *Sutoraiki wo shite imasu.* (Sue-toe-rie-kee oh ssh-tay e-mahss.)

String *Himo* (He-moe)
Do you have a short piece of string (I can have)? *Mijikai himo ga arimasu ka?* (Me-jee-kie he-moe gah ah-ree-mahss kah?)

Stroll *Sanpo* (Sahn-poe)
Would you like to take a stroll? *Sanpo ni ikimasen ka?* (Sahn-poe nee e-kee-mah-sin kah?) Let's take a stroll. *Sanpo shimasho.* (Sahn-poe she-mah-sho.)

Student *Gakusei* (Gock-say-e); Student I.D.
Gaku-sei Sho (Gock-say-e Show)
Are you still a student? *Mada gakusei desu ka?* (Mah-dah gock-say-e dess kah?) Please show me your student I.D. *Gakusei Sho wo misete kudasai.* (Gock-say-e Show oh me-say-tay kuu-dah-sie.)

Subway *Chikatetsu* (Chee-kah-tate-sue)
Let's go by subway. *Chikatetsu de ikimasho.* (Chee-kah-tate-sue day e-kee-mah-sho.) Where is the nearest subway entrance? *Ichiban chikai chikatetsu no iri-guchi wa doko desu ka?* (E-chee-bahn chee-kie chee-kah-tate-sue no ee-ree-guu-chee wah doe-koe dess kah?)

Sugar *Sato* (Sah-toe)
Do you put sugar in your coffee? *Kohi ni sato wo iremasu ka?* (Koe-hee nee sah-toe oh e-ray-mahss kah?) Sugar, please. *Sato, chodai.* (Sah-toe choe-die.)

Suit *Suutsu* (Suu-t'sue)
Please iron this suit. *Kono suutsu ni airon kakete kudasai.* (Koe-no suu-t'sue nee aye-rone kah-kay-tay kuu-dah-sie.) I want to have a suit made. *Suutsu wo tsukutte hoshii desu.* (Suu-t'sue oh scoot-tay hoe-she-e dess.)

Suitcase *Suutsukeisu* **(Suu-t'sue-kay-e-suu)**
Is this your suitcase? *Kore wa anato no suutsukeisu desu ka?* (Koe-ray wah ah-nah-tah no suu-t'sue-kay-e-suu dess kah?) Mine is brown. *Watakushi no wa chairo desu.* (Wah-tock-she no wah chah-e-roe dess.)

Summer *Natsu* **(Not-sue)**
In summer it is good to travel to the mountains. *Natsu ni yama e ryoko suru no wa ii desu.* (Not-sue nee yah-mah eh rio-kuu sue-rue no wah ee dess.) It is hot and humid in summer. *Natsu ni mushi-atsui desu.* (Not-sue nee muu-shee-aht-suu-ee dess.)

Sun *Hi* **(He);** Rising sun *Asahi* (Ah-sah-he); Setting sun *Yuhi* (Yuu-he); Sunbath *Nikkoyoku* (Neek-koe-yoe-kuu); Sunset *Nichibotsu* (Nee-chee-boat-sue)
The sun is shining today. *Kyo wa hi ga kagayaite imasu.* (K'yo wah he gah kah-gah-yite-tay e-mahss.)

Sunburn *Hiyake* **(He-yah-kay)**
Don't get sunburned. *Hi ni yakenai yo ni.* (He nee yah-kay-nie yoe nee.) I'm sunburned. *Hi ni yakemashita.* (He nee yah-kay-mah-ssh-tah.)

Sunday *Nichiyobi* **(Nee-chee-yoe-bee)**
Are the stores open on Sunday? *Nichiyobi ni mise ga aite imasu ka?* (Nee-chee-yoe-bee nee me-say gah aye-tay e-mahss kah?) Let's go swimming next Sunday. *Kono tsugi no Nichiyobi ni oyogi ni ikimasho.* (Koe-no t'sue-ghee no Nee-chee-yoe-bee nee oh-yoe-ghee nee e-kee-mah-show.)

Sunglasses *Iro-megane* **(E-roe-may-gah-nay);** also *Sangurasu* (Sahn guu-rah-sue)
Did I leave my sunglasses here? *Koko ni sangur-*

asu wo okimashita ka? (Koe-koe nee sahn-guu-rah-suu oh oh-kee-mah-ssh-tah kah?)

Sunnyside up (eggs) *Medama yaki* **(May-dah-mah yah-kee)**
Two eggs sunnyside up. *Tamago futatsu medama yaki.* (Tah-mah-go fuu-tot-sue may-dah-mah yah-kee.)

Supermarket *Suupaamaaketto* **(Sue-pah-mah-kate-toe);** *Suupaa* (Sue-pah)
I'd like to see a Japanese supermarket. *Nihon no suupaa wo mitai desu.* (Nee-hone no sue-pah oh me-tie dess.)

Surfing *Saafin* **(Sah-feen)**
Have you ever been surfing? *Saafin ni itta koto ga arimasu ka?* (Sah-feen nee eet-tah koe-toe gah ah-ree-mahss kah?) Can you go surfing here? *Koko de saafin dekimasu ka?* (Koe-koe day sah-feen day-kee-mahss kah?)

Sweater *Setaa* **(Say-tah)**
You should bring a sweater. *Seta wo motte iku ho ga ii desu.* (Say-tah oh mote-tay e-kuu hoe gah ee dess.)

Sweet (sugary) *Amai* **(Ah-my)**
Is it too sweet? *Amasugimasu ka?* (Ah-mah-sue-ghee-mahss kah?) I like it sweet. *Amai ho ga suki desu.* (Ah-my hoe gah ski dess.)

Swim *Oyogimasu* **(Oh-yoe-ghee-mahss)**
Would you like to go swimming? *Oyogi ni ikimasu ka?* (Oh-yoe-ghee nee e-kee-mahss kah?)

Swimming pool *Puru* **(Puu-rue)**
Do you have a swimming pool? *Puru ga arimasu ka?* (Puu-rue gah ah-ree-mahss kah?)

Sword *Katana* (Kah-tah-nah)

In Japan's feudal era, swords were often referred to as the soul of the samurai. *Nihon no hoken jidai ni, katana wa samurai no tamashii to yoku iimashita.* (Nee-hone no hoh-kane jee-die nee kah-tah-nah wah sah-muu-rie no tah-mah-she-e toe yoe-kuu ee-mahssh-tah.)

T

Table *Teburu* (Tay-buu-rue)

Is this table all right? *Kono teburu wa yoroshii desu ka?* (Koe-no tay-buu-rue wah yoe-rue-she-e dess kah?) Is that table open? *Sono teburu wa aite imasu ka?* (Soe-no tay-buu-rue wah aye-tay e-mahss kah?)

Tailor *Yofuku-ya* (Yoe-fuu-kuu-yah); *Teiraa* (Tay-e-rah)

Please call this tailor and see if my suit is finished. *Kono teiraa ni denwa wo shite watakushi no suutsu ga dekiagarimashita ka do ka kiite kudasai.* (Koe-no tay-e-rah nee dane-wah wo ssh-tay wah-tock-she no suut-sue gah day-kee-ah-gah-ree-mah-ssh-tah kah doe kah keet-tay kuu-dah-sie.)

Take-off (in plane) *Ri-riku* (Ree-ree-kuu)

We are taking-off momentarily. *Mamonaku ri-riku shimasu.* (Mah-moe-nah-kuu ree-ree-kuu she-mahss.)

Take pictures *Shashin wo torimasu* (Shah-sheen oh toe-ree-mahss)

I want to take some pictures. *Shashin wo toritai desu.* (Shah-sheen oh toe-ree-tie dess.) May I take your picture? *Anato no shashin wo totte yoro-*

shii desu ka? (Ah-nah-tah no shah-sheen oh tote-tay yoe-roe-she-e dess kah?)

Tariff (tax rate) *Zeiritsu* **(Zay-reet-sue)**
The tax rate on this is 15 percent. *Kore ni zeiritsu wa jugo pasento desu.* (Koe-ray nee zay-reet-sue wah juu-go pah-sin-toe dess.)

Taste *Aji* **(Ah-jee)**
This really tastes good. *Kore wa honto ni ii aji shite imasu.* (Koe-ray wah hone-toe nee ee ah-jee ssh-tay e-mahss.) How is the taste? *Aji wa do desu ka?* (Ah-jee wah doe dess kah?) Do you like the taste? *Aji wa suki desu ka?* (Ah-jee wah ski dess kah?)

Tax *Zeikin* **(Zay-e-keen)**
Do I have to pay tax on this? *Kore ni zeikin wo harau no desu ka?* (Koe-ray nee zay-e-keen oh hah-rah-uu no dess kah?) No, that is tax-free. *Iie, sore wa mu-zei desu.* (E-eh, soe-ray wah muu-zay-e dess.) How much is the tax? *Zeikin wa ikura desu ka?* (Zay-e-keen wah e-kuu-rah dess kah?)

Taxi *Takushi* **(Tah-kuu-she);** Taxi driver *Takushi no untenshu* (Tah-kuu-she no uun-tane-shuu); Taxi fare *Takushi dai* (Tah-kuu-she die); Taxi stand *Takushi noriba* (Tah-kuu-shee no-ree-bah) Please call a taxi. *Takushi wo yonde kudasai.* (Tah-kuu-she oh yone-day kuu-dah-sie.) Where is a taxi-stand? *Takushi-noriba wa doko desu ka?* (Tah-kuu-she-no-ree-bah wah doe-koe dess kah?) Wait here, I'll call you a taxi. *Koko de matte, takushi wo yobimasu.* (Koe-koe day mot-tay, tah-kuu-she oh yoe-bee-mahss.)

Tea *Ocha* **(oh-chah);** Black/brown tea *Kocha* (Koe-chah); Green (Japanese) tea *Nihon-cha*

(Nee-hone-chah); Lemon tea *Remon ti* (Ray-moan tee)

Tea, please. *Ocha kudasai.* (Oh-chah kuu-dah-sie.) Make it lemon tea. *Remon ti ni shite.* (Ray-moan tee nee ssh-tay.) Do you like green tea? *Nihon-cha suki desu ka?* (Nee-hone-chah ski dess kah?)

Teach *Oshiemasu* **(Oh-she-eh-mahss)**
Please teach me a little Japanese. *Nihongo wo sukoshi oshiete kudasai.* (Nee-hone-go oh suu-koe-she oh-she-a-tay kuu-dah-sie.) I'll teach you. *Oshiemasu.* (Ohs-she-a-mahss.)

Telegram *Dempoh* **(Dame-poe);** Telegraph office *Dempo kyoku* (Dame-poe k'yo-kuu)
Where is the telegram office? I want to send a telegram. *Dempo kyoku wa doko desu ka? Dempo wo uchitai desu.* (Dame-poe k'yo-kuu wah doe-koe dess kah? Dame-poe oh uu-chee-tie dess.) Please send this telegram. *Kono dempo wo utte kudasai.* (Koe-no dame-poe oh uut-tay kuu-dah-sie.)

Telephone *Denwa* **(Dane-wah);** Telephone directory *Denwa cho* (Dane-wah choe); Telephone extension *Naisen* (Nie-sin); Telephone number *Denwa bango* (Dane-wah bahn-go); Public telephone *Koshu denwa* (Koe-shuu dane-wah); Telephone booth *Denwa shitsu* (dane-wah sheet-sue); Telephone operator *Denwa kokanshu* (Koe-kahn-shuu); Long-distance telephone *Chokyori denwa* (Choe-k'yoe-ree dane-wah); International telephone *Kokusai denwa* (Koke-sie dane-wah) I will call you. *Denwa wo kakemasu.* (Dane-wah oh kah-kay-mahss.) Please call me. *Denwa wo kakete kudasai.* (Dane-wah oh kah-kay-tay kuu-dah-sie.) Please answer the phone. *Denwa ni dete ku-*

dasai. (Dane-wah nee day-tay kuu-dah-sie.)
Please call this number for me. *Kono denwa bango ni kakete kudasai.* (Koe-no dane-wah bahn-go nee kah-kay-tay kuu-dah-sie.)

Television *Terebi* **(Tay-ray-bee);** Color television *Kara terebi* (Kah-rah tay-ray-bee)
Does the room have a TV set? *Heya ni terebi ga arimasu ka?* (Hay-yah nee tay-ray-bee gah ah-ree-mahss kah?)

Telex *Terekkusu* **(Tay-ray-kuu-suu)**
I want to send a telex. *Terekkusu wo uchitai desu.* (Tay-ray-kuu-suu oh uu-chee-tie dess.)

Temperature (air) *Ondo* **(Own-doe);** Temperature (body) *Taion* (Tie-own)
Today's temperature is going to be very low. *Kyo no ondo wa taihen hikuku narimasu.* (K'yoe no own-doe wah tie-hane he-kuu-kuu nah-ree-mahss.)
You have a high temperature. *Anata no taion wa takai desu.* (Ah-nah-tah no tie-own wah tah-kie dess.)

Tennis *Tenisu* **(Tay-nee-sue);** Tennis club *Tenisu kurabu* (Kuu-rah-buu); Tennis court *Koto* (Koe-toe); Tennis match *Tenisu shiai* (she-aye); Tennis racquet *raketto* (rah-kate-toe); Tennis balls *boru* (boe-rue)
Do you play tennis? *Tenisu wo shimasu ka?* (Tay-nee-sue oh she-mahss kah?) Are there any tennis matches going on today? *Kyo wa tenisu shiai ga arimasu ka?* (K'yoe wah tay-nee-sue she-aye gah ah-ree-mahss kah?)

Thailand *Tai* **(Tie);** *Tiekoku* (Tie-koe-kuu)
Do many Japanese go to Thailand? *Takusan Nihonjin ga Tai e ikimasu ka?* (Tock-sahn Nee-hone-jeen gah Tie eh e-kee-mahss kah?)

Japanese in Plain English

Thanksgiving *Kanshasai* **(Kahn-shah-sie)**

Theater (stage) *Gekijo* **(Gay-kee-joe);** *Shibai* (She-by)
I'd like to go to the theater Saturday night.
Doyobi no ban ni shibai e ikitai desu. (Doe-yoe-bee no bahn nee she-by eh e-kee-tie dess.)

Thermometer (weather) *Kandankei* **(Kahn-dahn-kay-e);** (for body temperature) *Taionkei* (Tie-own-kay-e)

Thief *Dorobo* **(Doe-roe-boe)**
Please be careful of thieves. *Dorobo ni chui shite kudasai.* (Doe-roe-boe nee chuu-e sshtay kuu-dah-sie.)

Thirsty *Nodo ga kawakimasu* (No-doe gah kah-wah-kee-mahss)
I'm thirsty. *Nodo ga kawakimashita.* (No-doe gah kah-wah-kee-mah-ssh-tah.)

Thursday *Mokuyobi* **(Moe-kuu-yoe-bee)**
Today is Thursday. *Kyo wa Mokuyobi desu.* (K'yoe wah moe-kuu-yoe-bee dess.)

Ticket *Kippu* **(Keep-puu);** Ticket window *Kippu uriba* (Keep-puu uu-ree-bah)
[Note: Tickets for Japan's famous "Bullet Trains" are sold at special windows called *Midori-no Madoguchi* (Me-doe-ree-no Mah-doe-guu-chee), or "Green Windows."] Have you already bought your ticket? *Kippu wo mo kattan desu ka?* (Keep-puu oh moe kot-tahn dess kah?)

Tidbits *Tsumami* **(T'sue-mah-me)**
[These are peanuts, dried peas, dried octopus, sembei, etc., eaten while drinking.] Some tidbits, please. *O'tsumami chodai.* (Oh-t'sue-mah-me choe-die.)

220

Time *Jikan* **(Jee-kahn);** Wake-up time *Okiru jikan* (Oh-kee-rue jee-kahn); Time to go *Iku jikan* (E-kuu jee-kahn)
Do you have time now? *Ima jikan arimasu ka?* (E-mah jee-kahn ah-ree-mahss kah?) What time is it now? *Ima nanji desu ka?* (E-mah nahn-jee dess kah?)

Tip (gratuity) *Chippu* **(Cheep-puu)**
Shall I leave a tip? *Chippu wo yarimasho ka?* (Cheep-puu oh yah-ree-mah-sho kah?) [Note: Individual tipping at restaurants, bars, in hotels, and to taxi drivers is not done in Japan.]

Tired *Tsukaremashita* **(T'sue-kah-ray-mah-ssh-tah)**
I'm beat! *Tsukareta!* (T'sue-kah-ray-tah!) Are you tired? *Tsukaremashita ka?* (T'sue-kah-ray-mah-she-tah-kah?)

Tissue paper (kleenex) *Tisshu pepa* **(Tish-yuu pay-pah)**
We are out of tissue paper. *Tisshu pepa ga nakunarimashita.* (Tish-yuu pay-pah gah nah-kuu-nah-ree-mahssh-tah.)

Toilet paper *Toireto pepa* **(Toe-e-ray-toe pay-pah)**
Don't forget. Take some toilet paper with you. *Wasure nai de. Toireto pepa wo motte ikinasai.* (Wah-sue-ray nie day. Toe-e-ray-toe pay-pah oh mote-tay e-kee-nah-sie.)

Toast *Tosuto* **(Tos-toe)**
Just toast and coffee. *Tosuto to kohi de ii desu.* (Tos-toe toe koe-he day ee dess.)

Today *Kyo* **(K'yoe)**
What time will you/she/he/they arrive today. *Kyo nanji ni tsukimasu ka?* (K'yoe nahn-jee nee ski-

mahss kah?) I'm going out today. *Kyo dekake-masu.* (K'yoe day-kah-kay-mahss.)

Toilet (washroom) *Otearai* **(Oh-tay-ah-rie)**
Where is the washroom? *Otearai wa doko desu ka?* (Oh-tay-ah-rie wah doe-koe dess kah?)

Tomorrow *Ashita* **(Ah-ssh-tah)**
Is it going to rain tomorrow? *Ashita ame ga furimasu ka?* (Ah-ssh-tah ah-may gah fuu-ree-mahss kah?) We're (I'm) going tomorrow. *Ashita ikimasu.* (Ah-ssh-tah e-kee-mahss.)

Too big *Okiisugimasu* **(Oh-keee-sue-ghee-mahss);** Too much *Osugimasu* (Oh-sue-ghee-mahss); Too little *Chiisasugimasu* (Cheee-sah-sue-ghee-mahss); Too long *Nagasugimasu;* Too short *Mijikasugimasu;* Too heavy *Omosugimasu*

Toothache *Ha-itami* **(Hah-e-tah-me)**
I have a toothache. *Ha ga itai desu.* (Hah gah e-tie dess.) I must go to a dentist. *Haisha ni ikanakereba narimasen.* (Hie-shah nee e-kah-nah-kay-ray-bah nah-ree-mah-sin.)

Toothpaste *Hamigaki* **(Hah-me-gah-kee)**
I need some toothpaste. *Hamigaki ga irimasu.* (Hah-me-gah-kee gah e-ree-mahss.)

Town *Machi* **(Mah-chee)**
What is the name of this town? *Kono machi no namae wa nan desu ka?* (Koe-no mah-chee no nah-mah-eh wah nahn dess kah?)

Tour *Tsuaa* **(T'sue-ahh);** also *Kanko* (Kahn-koe); Tour desk *Tsuaa desuku* (T'sue-ah des-kuu); also *Kanko annaijo* (Kahn-koe ahn-nie-joe); Tour group *Tsuaa;* also *Kanko dan-in* (Kahn-koe dahn-een); Tour bus *Kanko basu* (Kahn-koe bah-sue)

Tour guide *Tsuaa gaido* **(T'sue-ah guy-doe)**
I am your tour guide. *Watakushi wa anata no tsuaa gaido desu.* (Wah-tock-she wah ah-nah-tah no t'sue-ah guy-doe dess.)

Tourist *Ryokosha* **(Rio-koe-shah);** *Kankokyaku* (Kahn-koe-k'yah-kuu); *Tsurisuto* (T-sue-reese-toe) They are all tourists. *Sonohito-tachi wa minna ryokosha desu.* (Soe-no-ssh-toe-tah-chee wah meen-na rio-koe-shah dess.)

Tourist hotel *Kanko hoteru* **(Kahn-koe hoe-tay-rue)**
Is that a tourist hotel? *Sore wa kanko hoteru desu ka?* (Soe-ray wah kahn-koe hoe-tay-rue dess kah?)

Tour member *Tsuaa membaa* **(T'sue-ah mame-bah)**
Are you a tour member? *Anata wa tsuaa membaa desu ka?* (Ah-nah-tah wah t'sue-ah mame-bah dess kah?)

Towel *Taoru* **(Tah-oh-rue);** Hand towel *Tenugui* (Tay-nuu-guu-e)
Would you like more towels? *Taoru wo motto irimasu ka?* (Tah-oh-ue oh mote-toe e-ree-mahss kah?)

Toy *Omocha* **(Oh-moe-chah)**
I'd like to buy some toys for my grandchildren. *Mago ni Omocha wo kaitai desu.* (Mah-go nee O'moe-chah oh kie-tie dess.)

Train *Kisha* **(Kee-shah);** also *Ressha* (Ray-shah) or *Densha* (Dane-shah); Express train *Kyuko ressha* (Que-koe ray-shah); Ordinary train *Futsu ressha* (Fute-sue ray-shah); Super express *Tokkyu* (Toke-que); Super Express train ticket *Tokkyu ken* (Toke-que ken)

223

What time is the last train for Tokyo? *Tokyo yuki no shu ressha wa nanji desu ka?* (Tokyo yuu-kee no shuu ray-shah wah nahn-jee dess kah?)

Transfer *Norikaemasu* **(No-ree-kie-mahss)**
Where do we transfer? *Doko de norikaemasu ka?* (Doe-koe day no-ree-kie-mahss kah?)

Travel *Ryoko* **(Rio-koe)**
Are you traveling for pleasure? *Kanko ryoko shite imasu ka?* (Kahn-koe rio-koe ssh-tay e-mahss kah?)

Traveler's check *Ryokosha kogitte* **(Rio-koe-shah koe-geet-tay)**
May I pay with a traveler's check? *Ryokosha kogitte de haratte mo ii desu ka?* (Rio-koe-shah koe-geet-tay day hah-rot-tay moe ee dess kah?)

Truck *Torakku* **(Toe-rock-kuu)**
Be careful of trucks. *Torakku ni chui shite kudasai.* (Toe-rah-kuu nee chuu-e-ssh-tay kuu-dah-sie.)

Try on (clothing) *Kite mimasu* **(Kee-tay me-mahss)**
Please try it on. *Kite mite kudasai.* (Kee-tay-me-tay kuu-dah-sie.) May I try it on? *Kite mite mo ii desu ka?* (Kee-tay-me-tay moe ee dess kah?)

T-shirt *Tii shatsu* **(Tee-shot-sue)**
Many tourists buy T-shirts in Honolulu. *Honoruru de takusan no ryokosha wa T-shatsu wo kaimasu.* (Hoe-no-rue-rue de tock-sahn no rio-koe-shah wah Tii-shot-sue oh kie-mahss.)

Tuesday *Kayobi* **(Kah-yoe-bee)**
It will be ready by Tuesday. *Kayobi made ni dekimasu* (Kah-yoe-bee mah-day nee day-kee-mahss.)

Turkish bath *Toruko* **(Toe-rue-koe)**

[Note: Massage parlor/bathhouses are no longer called "Turkish baths." They are now known as "Soaplands"—in deference to Turkey.]

Turn (direction) *Magarimasu* **(Mah-gah-ree-mahss)**

Turn there. *Asoko de magatte.* (Ah-soe-koe day mah-got-tay.) Turn left. *Hidari e magatte.* (He-dah-ree eh mah-got-tay.) Turn right. *Migi e magatte.* (Me-ghee eh mah-got-tay.) Turn here. *Koko de magatte.* (Koe-koe day mah-got-tay.) Go straight. *Massugu itte kudasai.* (Mahs-sue-guu eet-tay kuu-dah-sie.)

U

Umbrella *Kasa* **(Kah-sah)**

Should I take an umbrella? *Kasa wo motte itta ho ga ii desu ka?* (Kah-sah oh mote-tay eet-tah hoe gah ee dess kah?) Don't forget your umbrella. *Kasa wo wasurenai de* (Kah-sah oh wah-sue-ray-nie day.)

Uncle *Ohji* **(Ohh-jee)**

Is he your uncle? *Anokata wa anato no ohji-san desu ka?* (Ah-no-kah-tah wa ah-nah-tah no oh-jee-sahn dess kah?)

Understand *Wakarimasu* **(Wah-kah-ree-mahss)**

Do you understand? *Wakarimasu ka?* I don't understand. *Wakarimasen* (Wah-kah-ree-mah-sin.)

Underwear *Shita-gi* **(Sstah-ghee)**

Unique *Yuitsuno* **(Yuu-eet-sue-no);** also *Hitotsu kiri no* (He-tote-sue kee-ree no) or *Yuniku* (Yuu-nee-kuu)
This pattern is unique. *Kono moyo wa yuniku desu.* (Koe-no moe-yoe wah yuu-nee-kuu dess.)

United States *Gasshu Koku* **(Gosh-yuu Koe-kuu);** United States of America *Amerika Gasshu Koku* (Ah-may-ree-kah Gosh-yuu Koe-kuu)

University *Daigaku* **(Die-gah-kuu)**
Tokyo is a university town. *Tokyo wa daigaku no machi desu.* (Tokyo wah die-gah-kuu no mah-chee dess.) Have you already graduated from university? *Mo daigaku wo sotsugyo shimashita ka?* (Moe die-gah-kuu oh sote-sue-g'yoe-she-mah-ssh-tah kah?)

Use *Tsukaimasu* **(T'sky-mahss)**
How do you use this? *Kore wo do yu hu ni tsukaimasu ka?* (Koe-ray oh doe-yuu huu nee t'sky-mahss kah?) May I use that? *Sore wo tsukatte mo ii desu ka?* (Soe-ray oh scot-tay moe ee dess kah?)

U-turn *Yu-tan* **(Yuu-tahn)**
Can you make a U-turn? *U-tan dekimasu ka?* (Yuu-tahn day-kee-mahss kah?)

V

Vacant room *Aite iru heya (Aye-tay e-rue hay-yah);* Vacant seat *Aite iru seki* (Aye-tay e-rue say-kee)
Is that seat vacant? *Sono seki wa aite imasu ka?* (Soe-no say-kee wah aye-tay e-mahss kah?)

Vacation *Bakeshon* **(Bah-kay-shone);** also *Yasumi* (Yah-sue-me); Summer vacation *Natsu yasumi* (Not-sue yah-sue-me)
Are you on vacation now? *Ima yasumi desu ka?* (E-mah yah-sue-mah dess kah?) When does your vacation start? *Yasumi wa itsu kara desu ka?* (Yah-sue-me wah eet-sue kah-rah dess kah?)

Vaccination *Yobo-chusha* **(Yoh-boh-chuu-shah)**
Have you had all of your shots? *Yobo-chusha wo zembu moraimashita ka?* (Yoh-boh-chuu-shah oh zim-buu moe-rie-mah-ssh-tah kah?)

Valuable (money value) *Neuchi no aru* **(Nay-uu-chee no ah-rue)**
This is a valuable ring. *Kore wa neuchi no aru yubiwa desu.* (Koe-ray wah nay-uu-chee no ah-rue yuu-bee-wah dess.)

Valuables *Kokana-mono* **(Koe-kah-nah moe-no)** or *Kichohin* (Kee-choe-heen)
Put your valuables in the hotel safe, please. *Kichohin wa hoteru no kinko ni irete kudasai.* (Kee-choe-heen wah hoe-tay-rue no keen-koe nee e-ray-tay kuu-dah-sie.)

Van (vehicle) *Vaan* **(Bahn)**

Various kinds *Chigau shurui* **(Chee-gow shuu-rue-e);** *Iro-iro* (E-roe-e-roe)
We have various kinds. *Iro-iro no shurui ga arimasu.* (E-roe-e-roe no shuu-rue-e gah ah-ree-mahss.)

Vegetables *Yasai* **(Yah-sie);** Vegetable soup *Yasai supu* (Yah-sie sue-puu)
What kind of vegetable(s) would you like? *Donna yasai ga ii desu ka?* (Doan-nah yah-sie gah ee-dess kah?)

227

Vegetarian *Saishoku-shugisha* **(Sai-sho-kuu-shu-ghee-shah)**
I am a vegetarian. *Watakushi wa saishoku-shugisha desu.* (Wah-tock-she wah sie-sho-kuu-shuu-ghee-shah dess.)

Via (by way of) *Keiyu* **(Kay-e-yuu);** passing through . . . *wo totte (oh tote-tay)*
Are you going via Honolulu? *Honoruru keiyu de ikimasu ka?* (Hoe-no-rue-rue kay-e-yuu day e-kee-mahss kah.) I will pass through Nagoya. *Nogoya wo totte ikimasu.* (Nah-go-yah oh tote-tay e-kee-mahss.)

Video recorder *Bideo* **(Bee-day-oh)**

View (scenery) *Keshiki* **(Kay-she-kee)**
There is a beautiful view from the hotel. *Hoteru kara totemo ii keshiki ga miemasu.* (Hoe-tay-rue kah-rah toe-tay-moe ee kay-she-kee gah me-eh-mahss.)

Villa *Besso* **(Base-soh)**
He has his own villa in Hakone. *Anohito wa Hakone ni jibun no besso ga arimasu.* (Ah-no-ssh-toe wah Hah-koe-nay nee jee-boon no base-soh gah ah-ree-mahss.)

Village *Mura* **(Muu-rah)**
What is the name of this village? *Kono mura no namae wa nan desu ka?* (Koe-no muu-rah no nah-mah-eh wah nahn dess kah?)

Vinegar *Su* **(Sue)**

VIP Lounge *Tokubetsu Machiai Shitsu* **(Toe-kuu-bate-sue Mah-chee-aye Sheet-sue);** *BIP Raunji* (Rah-un-jee)
Where is your VIP Lounge? *Anata no BIP Raunji*

wa doko desu ka? (Ah-nah-tah no Bee-Aye-Pee
Rah-uhn-jee wah doe-koe dess kah?)

Visa *Bisa* **(Bee-sah);** *Sasho* (Sah-sho)
Do I need a visa? *Bisa ga irimasu ka?* (Bee-sah gah
e-ree-mahss kah?)   Yes, a tourist visa is necessary. *Hai, tsuurisuto no bisa ga hitsuyo desu.* (Hie,
tsuu-reese-toe no bee-sah gah heet-sue-yoe
dess.)

Visitor *Homonsha* **(Hoe-moan-shah);** also *O'kyaku-
san* (Oh-kyack-sahn)
We have visitors. *O'kyaku-san ga kite orimasu.*
(Oh-kyack-sahn gah kee-tay oh-ree-mahss.)

Vitamins *Bitamin* **(Bee-tah-meen);** Vitamin pills
Bitamin zai (Bee-tah-meen zie)
Do you take vitamin C every day? *Mainichi bitamin shi wo torimasu ka?* (My-nee-chee bee-tah-
meen she oh toe-ree-mahss kah?)

Volcano *Kazan* **(Kah-zahn);** Active volcano *Kakkazan* (Kah-kah-zahn); Dormant volcano *Kyuka-
zan* (Que-kah-zahn)
Are there many active volcanoes in Japan? *Nihon
ni takusan kakkazan ga arimasu ka?* (Nee-hone nee
tock-sahn kah-kah-zahn gah ah-ree-mahss kah?)

W

Wait *Machimasu* **(Mah-chee-mahss)**
Please wait. *Matte kudasai.* (Mot-tay kuu-dah-
sie.) Just a moment, please. *Chotto matte kudasai.*
(Chote-toe mot-tay kuu-dah-sie.) Please wait
here. *Koko de matte kudasai.* (Koe-koe day mot-tay
kuu-dah-sie.)

Japanese in Plain English

Waiter *Uetaa* **(Way-tah);** Waitress *Uetoresu* (Way-toe-ray-sue)

Waiting list *Machi meibo* **(Mah-chee may-boe)** or *Uetingu risuto* (Oo-ate-in-guu ree-sue-toe) I am on the waiting list. *Machi meibo ni notte imasu.* (Mah-chee may-boe nee note-tay e-mahss.)

Wake *Okoshimasu* **(Oh-koe-she-mahss);** To wake up *Me ga samemasu* (May gah sah-may-mahss) Please wake me at six o'clock. *Rokuji ni okoshite kudasai.* (Roe-kuu-jee nee oh-koe-ssh-tay kuu-dah-sie.) I woke up at 4:00 this morning. *Kesa yoji ni me ga samemashita.* (Kay-sah yoe-jee nee may gah sah-may-mah-ssh- tah.)

Wake-up call *Moningu koru* **(Moe-neen-guu koe-rue);** Wake-up phone call *Mezamashi no denwa* (May-zah-mah-she no dane-wah)

Walk *Arukimasu* **(Ah-rue-kee-mahss)** Stroll *Sampo* (Sahm-poe) Let's walk. *Arukimasho.* (Ah-rue-kee-mah-sho.) Can we/I walk there? *Soko made arukemasu ka?* (Soe-koe mah-day ah-rue-kay-mahss kah?)

Ward (district in Japanese cities) *Ku* **(Kuu);** Ward Office *Ku Yakusho* (Kuu Yah-kuu-sho) What ward is this? *Koko wa nani ku desu ka?* (Koe-koe wah nah-nee kuu dess kah?)

Warm *Atatakai* **(Ah-tah-tah-kie)** It's warm tonight. *Komban atatakai desu.* (Kome-bahn ah-tah-tah-kie dess.) The wind is warm. *Kaze ga atatakai desu.* (Kah-zay gah ah-tah-tah-kie dess.)

Wash *Araimasu* **(Ah-rie-mahss)**
Please wash this. *Kore wo aratte kudasai.* (Koe-ray oh ah-rot-tay kuu-dah-sie.) I want to wash my hands. *Te wo araitai desu.* (Tay oh ah-rie-tie dess.)

Watch your step! *Ashimoto ni go chui kudasai!* **(Ah-she-moe-toe nee go chuu-e kuu-dah-sie!)**

Water *Mizu* **(Me-zuu);** Drinking water *Nomi mizu* (No-me me-zuu); Chilled drinking water *O'hiya* (Oh-he-yah); Hot water *Oyu* (Oh-yuu); Ice water *Aisu wota* (Ice wah-tah); Mineral water *Kosen* (Koe-sen) or *Mineraru wota* (Mee-nay-rah-rue wah-tah)
Water, please. *Mizu kudasai.* (Me-zoo kuu-dah-sie.)

Waterfall *Taki* **(Tah-kee)**

Water fountain *Hunsui* **(Hune-sue-e)**

Watermelon *Suika* **(Sue-e-kah)**
Do you have watermelon? *Suika ga arimasu ka?* (Sue-e-kah gah ah-ree-mahss kah?)

Weather *Tenki* **(Tane-kee);** Weather forecast *Tenki yoho* (Tane-kee yoe-hoe)
It's beautiful weather, isn't it? *Ii o'tenki desu, ne?* (Ee oh-tane-kee dess, nay?) The weather is bad today. *Kyo wa tenki ga warui desu.* (K'yoe wah tane-kee gah wah-rue-e dess.)

Wedding ceremony *Kekkon shiki* **(Keck-kone she-kee)**
That bride is going to a wedding. *Sono Oyome-san ga kekkon shiki ni iku tokoro desu.* (Soe-no Oh-yoe-may-sahn gah keck-kone ssh-kee nee e-kuu toe-koe-roe dess.)

Wednesday *Suiyobi* **(Sue-e-yoe-bee)**
I leave next week on Wednesday. *Raishu no Suiyobi ni demasu.* (Rie-shuu no Sue-e-yoe-bee nee day-mahss.)

Week *Shu* **(Shuu);** Week (of time) *Shukan* (Shuu-kahn); Two weeks *Ni shukan* (Nee shuu-kahn); Three weeks *San shukan* (Sahn shuu-kahn); This week *Kon shu* (Kone shuu); Next week *Raishu* (Rie-shuu); Last week *Sen shu* (Sane shuu)

Weigh *Hakarimasu* **(Hah-kah-ree-mahss);**
Weight *Mekata* (May-kah-tah)
Please weigh this. *Kore wo hakatte kudasai.* (Koe-ray oh hah-kot-tay kuu-dah-sie.) How much does it weigh? *Mekata wa dono kurai desu ka?* (May-kah-tah wah doe-no kuu-rie dess kah?)

Welcome (noun) *Kangei* **(Kahn-gay-e);** Welcome! *Yoku irasshaimashita!* (Yoe-kuu e-rah-shy-mah-ssh-tah!); You are welcome (for favor) *Do itashimashite* (Doe e-tah-she-mah-ssh-tay.)

Well (feeling) *Genki* **(Gane-kee)**
How are you? *Genki desu ka?* (Gane-kee dess kah?) I'm fine. *Genki desu.* (Gane-kee dess.)

Well done (accomplishment) *Yoku dekimashita!* **(Yoe-kuu day-kee-mah-ssh-tah!)**

West (direction) *Nishi* **(Nee-she)**
Which way is west? *Dochi no ho ga nishi desu ka?* (Doe-chee no hoh gah nee-shee dess kah?)

Western food *Yo shoku* **(Yoe sho-kuu)**
Would you like to eat Western food tonight? *Komban yo shoku wo tabetai desu ka?* (Kome-bahn yoe-show-kuu oh tah-bay-tie desu kah?)

Western-style room *Yo shitsu* **(Yoe sheet-sue)**
I want a Western-style room. *Yo shitsu wo hoshii desu.* (Yoe sheet-sue oh hoe-she-e dess.)

What *Nani* **(Nah-nee)**
What do you want? *Nani wo hoshii desu ka?* (Nah-nee oh hoe-she-e dess kah?) What are you doing? *Nani wo shite imasu ka?* (Nah-nee oh she-tay e-mahss kah?) What time is it? *Nanji desu ka?* (Nahn-jee dess kah?)

When *Itsu* **(Eet-sue)**
When are you going? *Itsu ikimasu ka?* (Eet-sue e-kee-mahss kah?)

Where *Doko* **(Doe-koe)**
Where do you live? *O'sumai wa doko desu ka?* (Oh-sue-my wah doe-koe dess kah?) Where are you going? *Dochira e?* (Doe-chee-rah eh?)

Which (of several) *Dore* **(Doe-ray);** (of two) *Dochi* (Doe-chee)
Which one do you like best? *Dore ga ichiban suki desu ka?* (Doe-ray gah e-chee-bahn ski dess kah?)

Whiskey *Uisuki* **(We-sue-kee)**

White *Shiroi* **(She-roy)**
Do you have a white one? *Shiroi no wa arimasu ka?* (She-roy no wah ah-ree-mahss kah?)

Who *Donata* **(Doe-nah-tah)**
Who is it? *Donata desu ka?* (Doe-nah-tah dess kah?) Whose coat is this? *Kono koto wa donata no desu ka?* (Koe-no koe-toe wah doe-nah-tah no dess kah?)

Wholesaler *Tonya* **(Tone-yah)**
Let's go to a wholesaler. *Tonya ni ikimasho.* (Tone-yah nee ee-key-mah-show.)

Why *Dohshite* **(Doh-ssh-tay);** *Naze* (Nah-zay)
Why are you not eating? *Doshite tabete inai no?*
(Doh-ssh-tay tah-bay-tay e-nie-no?)

Wide *Hiroi* **(He-roy)**
That is too wide. *Sore wa hiro-sugimasu.* (Soe-ray
wah he-roy sue-ghee mahss.)

Wife (one's own) *Kanai* **(Kah-nie);** (other person's) *Oku-san* (Oak-sahn)
This is my wife. *Kono hito wa watakushi no kanai
desu.* (Koe-no ssh-toe wah wah-tock-she no kah-nie dess.) Is your wife also coming? *Oku-san mo
kimasu ka?* (Oak-sahn moe kee-mahss kah?)

Wind *Kaze* **(Kah-zay)**
The wind is blowing today. *Kyo wa kaze ga fuite
imasu.* (K'yoe wah kah-zay gah fuu-ee-tay e-mahss.) The wind is strong. *Kaze ga tsuyoi desu.*
(Kah-zay gah t'sue yoe-e dess.)

Window *Mado* **(Mah-doe)**
Please open the window. *Mado wo akete kudasai.*
(Mah-doe oh ah-kay-tay kuu-dah-sie.) Please
close the window. *Mado wo shimete kudasai.* (Mah-doe oh she-may-tay kuu-dah-sie.)

Winter *Fuyu* **(Fuu-yuu)**
How long does winter last? *Fuyu wa itsu made
desu ka?* (Fuu-yuu wah eet-sue mah-day dess
kah?) Does it get cold in winter? *Fuyu ni samuku
narimasu ka?* (Fuu-yuu nee sah-muu-kuu nah-ree-mahss kah?)

With (together) *To* **(Toe);** *Issho ni* (E-sshow nee);
by means of *De* (Day)
Please come with me. *Watakushi to issho ni kite
kudasai.* (Wah-tock-she toe e-sshow nee kee-tay
kuu-dah-sie.) Open it with this. *Kore de akete.*
(Koe-ray day ah-kay-tay.)

Woman (women) *Onna no hito* **(Own-nah no ssh-toe)**
Who is that woman? *Sono onna no hito wa donata desu ka?* (Soe-no own-nah no ssh-toe wah doe-nah-tah dess kah?)

Work *Shigoto* **(She-go-toe)**
I still have a lot of work. *Mada takusan shigoto ga arimasu.* (Mah-dah tock-sahn she-go-toe gah ah-ree-mahss.) How late do you work? *Nanji made shigoto wo shimasu ka?* (Nahn-jee mah-day she-go-toe oh she-mahss kah?)

Worry *Shimpai shimasu* **(Sheem-pie she-mahss)**
I'm worried. *Shimpai shite imasu.* (Sheem-pie she-tay e-mahss.) Don't worry! *Shimpai shi nai de!* (Sheem-pie she nie day!)

Wrap *Tsutsumimasu* **(T'sue-t'sue-me-mahss)**
Please wrap this. *Kore wo tsutsunde kudasai.* (Koe-ray wo t'sue-t'soon-day kuu-dah-sie.)

Write *Kakimasu* **(Kah-kee-mahss)**
Please write it down. *Kaite kudasai.* (Kie-tay kuu-dah-sie.) Please write me a letter. *Tegami wo kaite kudasai.* (Tay-gah-me oh . . .)

X

X-ray *Ekisu sen* **(A-kee-sue sin)**

X-ray examination *Rentogen kensa* **(Rane-toe-gane kane-sah)**
Do you take X-rays? *Rentogen kensa wo yarimasu ka?* (Rane-toe gane kane-sah oh yah-ree-mahss kah?)

Y

Year *Toshi* **(Toe-she);** also *Nen* (Nane); This
year *Kotoshi* (Koe-toe-she); Last year *Kyo nen*
(K'yoe nane); Every year *Mai nen* (My nane);
All year around *Ichi nen ju* (E-chee nane juu);
During this year *Kotoshi ju* (Koe-toe-she juu)
I would like to go to Japan next year. *Rainen Nihon e ikitai desu.* (Rie-nane Nee-hone eh e-kee-tie
dess.)

Year model (car) *Nen gata* **(Nane gah-tah)**
What year is your car? *Anato no jidosha wa nan
nen gata desu ka?* (Ah-nah-tah no jee-doe-shah
wah nahn nane gah-tah dess kah?)

Yellow *Kiiro* **(Kee-ee-roe)**
Let me see the yellow one. *Kiiro no wo misete kudasai.* (Kee-ee-roe no oh me-say-tay kuu-dah-sie.)

Yes *Hai* **(Hie)**

Yesterday *Kino* **(Kee-no)**
We arrived yesterday. *Kino tsukimashita.* (Kee-no
t'sue-kee-mah-ssh-tah.) It snowed yesterday.
Kino yuki ga furimashita. (Kee-no yuu-kee gah
fuu-ree-mah-ssh-tah.)

You *Anata* **(Ah-nah-tah);** You (plural) *Anata-tachi* (Ah-nah-tah-tah-chee)
[Note: In Japanese the "you" is often understood
(not expressed).] Are you going? *Ikimasu ka?* (Ee-key-mahss kah?)

Young *Wakai* **(Wah-kie)**
My son is still young. *Watakushi no musuko wa
mada wakai desu.* (Wah-tock-she no muu-sue-koe
wah mah-dah wah-kie dess.)

Your *Anata no* **(Ah-nah-tah no)**
Is this yours? *Kore wa anata no desu ka?* (Kore wah ah-nah-tah no dess kah?)

Z

Zebra *Shima-uma* **(She-mah-uu-mah)**

Zero *Zero* **(Zay-roe)**; *Rei* (Ray-e)

Zip code *Yubin bango* **(Yuu-bean bahn-go)**
What is the zip code? *Yubin bango wa nan ban desu ka?* (Yuu-bean bahn-go wah nahn bahn dess kah?)

Zoo *Dobutsu-en* **(Doe-boot-sue-en)**
San Diego has a famous zoo. *San Diego ni wa yumei-na dobutsuen ga arimasu.* (Sahn Dee-a-go nee wah yuu-may-e-nah doe-boot-sue-inn gah ah-ree-mahss.)

LANGUAGE AND TRAVEL BOOKS

Multilingual
The Insult Dictionary:
  How to Give 'Em Hell in 5 Nasty Languages
The Lover's Dictionary:
  How to be Amorous in 5 Delectable Languages
Multilingual Phrase Book
Let's Drive Europe Phrasebook
CD-ROM "Languages of the World"
  Multilingual Dictionary Database

Spanish
Vox Spanish and English Dictionaries
The Spanish Businessmate
Nice 'n Easy Spanish Grammar
Spanish Verbs and Essentials of Grammar
Getting Started in Spanish
Guide to Spanish Idioms
Guide to Correspondence in Spanish

French
NTC's New College French and English Dictionary
French Verbs and Essentials of Grammar
Getting Started in French
Guide to French Idioms
Guide to Correspondence in French
The French Businessmate
Nice 'n Easy French Grammar
NTC's Dictionary of Faux Amis

German
New Schöffler-Weis German and English Dictionary
Klett German and English Dictionaries
Getting Started in German
German Verbs and Essentials of Grammar
Guide to German Idioms
The German Businessmate
Nice 'n Easy German Grammar

Italian
Zanichelli New College Italian and English
  Dictionary
Getting Started in Italian
Italian Verbs and Essentials of Grammar

Greek
NTC's New College Greek and English Dictionary

Latin
Essentials of Latin Grammar

Russian
Essentials of Russian Grammar
Business Russian

Japanese
Japanese in Plain English
Everyday Japanese
Japanese Cultural Encounters

"Just Enough" Phrase Books
Dutch, French, German, Greek, Italian, Japanese,
  Portuguese, Scandinavian, Serbo-Croat, Spanish

Audio and Video Language Programs
Just Listen 'n Learn Spanish, French,
  German, Italian and Greek
Just Listen 'n Learn PLUS: in Spanish,
  French, German
Practice & Improve Your...Spanish, French
  and German
Practice & Improve Your...Spanish, French and
  German PLUS
VideoPassport French
VideoPassport Spanish

Travel Guides and References
International Herald Tribune Guides to Business
  Travel: Asia, Europe
World at Its Best Travel Series: Britain, France,
  Germany, Italy, Spain, Switzerland, Holland,
  Hawaii, London, Paris, New York
Mystery Reader's Walking Guides: London, England
Business Capitals of the World
European Atlas
Health Guide for International Travelers
Everything Japanese
Passport's Travel Paks: Spain, Germany, France, Italy,
  Britain
Japan at Night
Japan Today
Japan Made Easy
British/American Language Dictionary
Bon Voyage!
Hiking and Walking Guide to Europe
Passport's Regional Guides of France
Exploring Rural Europe Series
Passport's Regional Guides of Indonesia

PASSPORT BOOKS
a division of *NTC Publishing Group*
4255 West Touhy Avenue
Lincolnwood, Illinois 60646-1975